C. S. LEWIS: A BIOGRAPHY

C. S. Lewis
A Biography

ROGER
LANCELYN
GREEN
&
WALTER
HOOPER

A Harvest Book

Harcourt Brace Jovanovich
New York and London

Printed in the United States of America

Library of Congress Cataloging in Publication Data

Green, Roger Lancelyn.
C. S. Lewis.

(A Harvest book ; HB 331)
Includes index.
1. Lewis, Clive Staples, 1898-1963.
I. Hooper, Walter, joint author. II. Title.
[BX5199.L53G73   1974c]   828'.9'1209 [B]   75-29425
ISBN 0-15-623205-7

First Harvest edition 1976

A B C D E F G H I J

CONTENTS

FRATRIBUS UNANIMIS
CLIVE STAPLES ET WARREN HAMILTON LEWIS
HUNC LIBRUM DEDICANT
SCRIPTORES AMANTISSIMI

PREFACE

To write the biography of a man of genius as many-sided as C. S. Lewis is a daunting task, and it has not been undertaken lightly. His ideal biographer would have to be at once a Classical and English scholar, a theologian, a philosopher, an expert on fantasy, science fiction and children's books – and no one but Lewis himself possessed all these qualifications in sufficient degree.

The two of us who have collaborated in the present volume fall far short of his learning, even in our own subjects: the Reverend Walter Hooper is a theologian who has read English; Roger Lancelyn Green is an English scholar who has written fantasy and children's books – both of us know and love the classical lands and have studied their literature; neither of us is a philosopher.

Why, then, are we undertaking this book? As early as May 1953 Lewis suggested to Roger Lancelyn Green that he should one day undertake his biography: when asked by his publisher Jocelyn Gibb of Geoffrey Bles Ltd to write a more formal autobiography than *Surprised by Joy*, Lewis replied: 'Oh, no, but when I'm dead I suppose Roger will write my biography and Jock will publish it.' And during the last six months of his life he was apologizing to Roger for giving Walter (who was acting as his secretary for much of this time, and was then engaged on a critical study of his works) material which he might have thought was his special perquisite as chosen biographer.

Under these circumstances when we were approached by several of Lewis's closest friends, including Jock Gibb, and supported by Warren Lewis, it seemed our duty, as it was our pleasure, to accept the honour, however frightening.

Our particular qualifications were fairly evenly balanced. Green had attended Lewis's lectures, been his pupil for a B.Litt. course, and later became his friend at the time when the Narnian books were being written – a friendship that grew closer with time and with shared interests and experiences, culminating in the visit to Greece in 1960; he had also written the Bodley Head Monograph on Lewis which its subject had read in manuscript and approved, though usually averse to books about himself or other living authors.

Walter Hooper's personal acquaintance with Lewis was shorter – fewer months indeed than Green's years – but much more intimate during that brief period. He had already studied Lewis's works preparatory to writing the critical volume which did not materialize, and since Lewis's death had given much of his time to collecting and editing his miscellaneous and unpublished works, making collections of his letters or copies of them, and generally soaking himself in everything written by or about Lewis until he had become the leading authority on his life and works.

The material for any authorized biography of C. S. Lewis is immense, though singularly uneven. When the family home on the outskirts of Belfast was broken up after his father's death in September 1929, Lewis found a gigantic mass of old letters, diaries and papers: his father seemed to have kept everything and destroyed nothing. He transported most of this to Oxford, and during the next few years his brother, Major Warren Lewis, selected and typed the larger portion, making a history of the family to the end of 1930. The *Lewis Papers* takes up eleven volumes of single-spaced typing averaging 300 pages to a volume. When the typescript was completed all the original manuscripts were destroyed.

This colossal monument of paper contains many hundreds of letters from C. S. Lewis to his father, his brother, his close friend Arthur Greeves, and a few other family connections; it also includes diaries, sometimes kept with great minuteness, covering many years. After 1929 Lewis wrote no more diaries.

Thus the basic material for the first chapters of the present book was so vast that it took many months to read and sift – and many more to convert into a balanced narrative, and then cut and prune so as not to overweight this biography. Doubtless in time to come other books on C. S. Lewis will be written which will incorporate much of what we were forced to leave out: for we would like to stress that the present work is only *a* biography of C. S. Lewis; it was never intended to be *the* biography – a book which, if ever written, must still be well in the future when Lewis will have found his true level among writers and theologians.

Also, the material contained in the *Lewis Papers* covers the period about which Lewis had written most fully in *Surprised by Joy: The shape of my early life* (1955) and many of the letters, with numerous extracts from the diaries, had been included by Warren Lewis in his volume of *Letters of C. S. Lewis* (1966), from neither of which did we wish to quote more than was necessary, or overlap except to present a rounded picture of our subject and the story of his life. The diaries and letters in the *Lewis Papers*, though of considerable interest, deal mainly with the simple, everyday facts of his life, and tell at great length of his adventures among books – of his vast reading and of his own early literary attempts – but surprisingly little of his inner life, his more personal experiences, or even of his spiritual pilgrimage: for almost all that we are likely to know of these we must turn to his published works, notably *The Pilgrim's Regress* and *Surprised by Joy*.

After 1930 the material available consists mainly of letters, and recollections of Lewis's many friends and acquaintances. Since he died at the relatively early age of 64, most of these friends survived him and have supplied an almost embarrassing largesse of recollections. Indeed, only Arthur Greeves and Charles Williams, two of Lewis's closest friends, were no longer available for consultation – and Greeves had preserved a remarkable series of letters from Lewis, mainly from the earlier part of his life, which has enriched the present volume considerably.

But Lewis had many other friends who by their age or position knew him far better than either of his present biographers could ever have done – and to these we, and our readers, owe a deep debt of gratitude. Foremost among these is Lewis's brother, Major Warren Hamilton Lewis, who gave us full access to the *Lewis Papers*, many extracts from his own diary, and the benefit of his own personal recollections: and there can seldom have been two brothers so devoted to each other. It is a matter of the deepest grief and regret that Major Lewis died before this book was published, though he had read and approved all but the last chapter in manuscript.

Among the close friends of longest standing we would like in particular to thank Owen Barfield, Nevill Coghill, J. R. R. Tolkien, Colin Hardie, Gervase Mathew, Jocelyn Gibb, Lady Dunbar of Hempriggs, the late Austin and Kay Farrer, George Sayer, John Lawlor, Richard Ladborough, Adam Fox, Clifford Morris, and many less intimate acquaintances at University College and Magdalen College, Oxford, at Magdalene College, Cambridge, together with all those numerous correspondents who have placed their treasured letters from Lewis at our disposal, and have told us of their contacts with him as friends, colleagues, pupils or pen-friends. Among these we would particularly like to thank Cyril Hartmann, Laurence Whistler, Sir Donald Hardman, Miss Kaye Webb, Miss Pauline Baynes, John Wain, Derek Brewer, Arthur C. Clarke, Chad Walsh, Warfield M. Firor, and Charles Gilmore. Also the Literary Executors of the late Charles Williams, Dorothy Sayers, T. S. Eliot, E. R. Eddison.

Many books and articles have already appeared about C. S. Lewis as writer or religious teacher, and many more will doubtless be written. We have not attempted in this book either to criticize Lewis's works or to assess his place in literature. Accepting that there are very many readers both young and old who consider that place to be high, and who take a natural interest in the man himself, we have sought to tell his story as best we could, to lay before them as clear a picture as we could capture of his everyday life, of his friendships and interests, and of how he came to write the books which are still claiming a wide and appreciative public in many parts of the world and particularly in Great Britain, the British Commonwealth and the United States.

Works of scholarship are superseded sooner or later, though some of Lewis's critical and appreciative writings are likely to survive and be read with enjoyment for many years to come; new generations demand fresh approaches to the Word of God, though *Mere Christianity* and *The Screwtape Letters* do not seem likely to lose any of the vitality and directness of their message. As tastes in literature come and go, fade and return, the Ransom trilogy and *Till We Have Faces* will probably fall out of fashion, be condemned by critics and readers of a different tradition – and may well be rediscovered and reinstated, perhaps even higher than anyone expects, in some future shake-up of the kaleidoscope of literature. At present the seven *Chronicles of Narnia*, that unexpected creation of his middle age, which are selling over a million copies a year, seem to be Lewis's greatest claim to immortality, setting him high in that particular branch of literature in which few attain more than a transitory or an esoteric fame – somewhere on the same shelf as Lewis Carroll and E. Nesbit and George Mac-Donald, as Kipling and Kenneth Grahame and Andrew Lang: a branch of literature in which there are relatively few great classics but in which, as he himself said, 'the good ones last'.

And so we offer our humble tribute to a great man, an important and interesting writer, an inspiring teacher – and above all such a friend as we are not likely to find again.

ROGER LANCELYN GREEN
WALTER HOOPER

PROLOGUE — ANCESTRY

'Live in Hope and die in Caergwrle' says the pun still current in these two North Wales villages between Hawarden and Wrexham in Flintshire. C. S. Lewis's great-great-grandfather fulfilled at least the second part of this dictum, though he was probably also born in Caergwrle, about the year 1775, and was certainly a farmer there for most of his life. He had one daughter and six sons, the fourth of whom, Joseph – a farmer like his father – moved some miles north-east and settled at Saltney, then still a little village just south of Chester.

The family were members of the Church of England until Joseph, thinking he was not given the prominence which was his due in the parish, seceded and became a Methodist minister. Farming must have been merely the necessary means of supplementing the scanty tribute of his congregation, for it is as a Methodist minister that he is remembered, and in this capacity he enjoyed a considerable local reputation. Though the handwriting and letters of Joseph Lewis are not those of an educated man, it is recorded that he was an impressive speaker of an emotional type.

Of Joseph's eight children, it is his fourth son, Richard, born in 1832, who first emigrated to Ireland, where he found work in the Cork Steamship Company as a master boiler maker. Richard was one of the working-class intelligentsia in the fore of that artisan renaissance of which the chief symptoms in the 1860s were the birth of the Trades Union and the Co-operative movements. In his concern for the elevation of the working classes, he set about improving his education, and writing essays for the edification of fellow members of the Workmen's Reading Room in the Steamship Company. Most of his essays were theological and are remarkably eloquent for a man who had had so little education.

Though he had returned to the Anglican Church, his essays were sufficiently evangelical for his Methodist father.

In 1853 Richard married Martha Gee of Liverpool. Their six children, Martha, Sarah Jane, Joseph, William, Richard and Albert James,were all born in Cork. Albert, who was the father of C. S. Lewis, was born in 1863, and in 1864 his father proceeded to Dublin to take up a better job. His new position was something like an 'outside manager' in the shipbuilding firm of Messrs Walpole, Webb and Bewly.

In 1868 Richard moved with his family to Belfast, where he and John H. MacIlwaine entered into partnership under the firm-name of 'MacIlwaine and Lewis: Boiler Makers, Engineers, and Iron Ship Builders'. The business was a success, for a time anyway, and in 1870 the Lewises moved from the area of Mount Pottinger to the more fashionable one of Lower Sydenham.

Whether it was because of his early precocity or because of the rising fortunes of the family, his father was induced to give Albert a more elaborate education than had been bestowed on his three brothers. After leaving the District Model National School he went in 1877, when he was fourteen, to Lurgan College in Co. Armagh. This was a fortunate choice and was to have wide-reaching effects, for the headmaster of Lurgan College at this time was W. T. Kirkpatrick – the 'Great Knock' who was to play an important part in C. S. Lewis's life, and of whom we shall hear more in the course of this narrative. Kirkpatrick was 31 at the time and a brilliant teacher. He seems to have taken Albert under his wing, and, once it was decided that the boy would pursue a legal career, he set about preparing him for it.

Albert left Lurgan College in 1879 and was articled the day after leaving school to the law firm of Maclean, Boyle, and Maclean in Dublin. Kirkpatrick had inspired him to continue his general education, and most evenings were set aside for the study of literature, composition, logic and history. In 1881 he joined the Belmont Literary Society and was soon considered one of their best speakers. One member predicted that, 'Since Mr Lewis joined the Society his matrimonial prospects have gone up 20 per cent,' little knowing that they had been quite high since he first met Miss Edie Macown when he went off to Lurgan. Both, it seems, were more 'in love with love' than with one another, and by 1884 Edie had faded out of Albert's life.

The following year Albert qualified as a solicitor and, after a brief partnership, started a practice of his own in Belfast which he conducted with uniform success for the rest of his life.

On returning to Belfast, Albert was united not only with his family but with their neighbours, the Hamiltons. When the Lewises moved to Lower Sydenham in 1870 they had become members of the parish of St Mark, Dundela. Four years later the church acquired a new rector, the Reverend Thomas Hamilton. Richard Lewis was always a stern critic of Thomas Hamilton's sermons, but the young Lewises and Hamiltons became warm friends immediately. Whereas the Lewises sprang from Welsh farmers and were, despite their evangelical Christianity, materially minded, the Hamiltons were a family of reputable antiquity with a strong ecclesiastical tradition.

The Irish branch of the Hamilton family was descended from one Hugh Hamilton who settled at Lisbane, Co. Down, in the time of James I and was one of the Hamiltons of Evandale, of whom Sir James Hamilton of Finnart (d. 1540) was an ancestor. His great-great-grandson (Thomas's grandfather) was Hugh Hamilton (1729–1805), successively a Fellow of Trinity College, Dublin, Dean of Armagh, Bishop of Clonfert, and, finally, Bishop of Ossory.

Thomas, who was born in 1826, took a First in Theology at Trinity College, Dublin, in 1848 and was made deacon in the same year. He was much afflicted with his throat and in 1850 set out with his family on a grand tour of Europe. Two years later he took another trip for his health, this time to India, where he was ordained priest in 1853. On his return to England the following year, Thomas was appointed chaplain in the Royal Navy and served with the Baltic squadron of the fleet throughout the Crimean War. In 1859 he married Mary Warren, the daughter of Sir John Borlasse Warren, by whom he had four children: Lilian,

Florence Augusta, Hugh and Augustus. From 1870 until 1874 Thomas was chaplain of Holy Trinity Church, Rome, after which he returned to Ireland and took up the incumbency of St Mark, Dundela.

'Through the Warrens the blood went back to a Norman knight whose bones lie at Battle Abbey,' wrote Lewis in *Surprised by Joy*. This was the very 'William of Warenne' of Kipling's poem 'The Land' – and it seems a pleasant coincidence that the author of *Puck of Pook's Hill* owned and wrote his series of tales about the land which had once belonged to an ancestor of the author of *The Lion, the Witch and the Wardrobe*.

Hamilton was an impressive and eloquent preacher, and during many of his sermons was often seen to be shedding tears in the pulpit ('one of his weepy ones today,' the Lewises would say). His religion was, unfortunately, marred by his intense bigotry towards Roman Catholics whom he considered the Devil's own children. He was also especially sensitive to swearing and in his naval journals he often recorded how he took a sailor aside to whisper some admonition in his ear. Once when returning to his ship in the captain's gig, in a dangerous sea, he heard the officer in charge rebuke one of the crew with an oath. Hamilton immediately admonished the officer publicly. Afterwards the captain remonstrated with his chaplain, taking the view that the seriousness of the emergency excused the officer's slip. 'Captain,' replied Hamilton, 'if you found yourself in the presence of the enemy, what would you do?' 'Well, I suppose my duty,' said the captain. 'And I, Captain, was in the presence of *my* enemy, and I did *my* duty,' was Hamilton's retort. On the positive side of the account can be added the fact that Thomas Hamilton volunteered unhesitatingly for duty in the Baltic cholera camp at a time when deaths from that disease were of daily occurrence in the fleet.

Hamilton's wife, Mary Warren, was infinitely his superior in energy and intelligence. This clever and aristocratic woman was a typical daughter of a Southern Irish seigneur of a century ago, and the Rectory at Dundela reflected her tastes. The following account comes from one of her grandsons:

The house was typical of the woman: infested with cats (which were however rigorously excluded from the study), their presence was immediately apparent to the nose of the visitor when the slatternly servant opened the front door. Supposing him to have been invited to dine, he would find himself in a dirty drawing room, adorned with rare specimens of glass, china and silver. The hand which his hostess extended to him would gleam with valuable rings, but would bear too evident traces of her enthusiasm as a poultry keeper. The announcement of dinner was the signal for a preconcerted rush on the part of the family, the object of which was to ensure the unfortunate guest the chair which had only three sound legs. The dinner, in spite of the orders of the head of the house, was apt to be thoroughly in keeping with the general style of the establishment, and the visitor, having partaken of a perfectly cooked salmon off a chipped kitchen dish, would probably be offered an execrably mangled chop, served in a collector's piece of Sheffield plate.

Despite this unusual home life, Hamilton tried to ensure that his children received a good education. He was particularly successful with his second daughter, Florence (or 'Flora'), who proved to be a brilliant mathematician. At the same time that Albert was preparing for the Bar, Flora was reading Mathematics at the Queen's College in Belfast. In 1880 the eighteen-year-old Flora took her first degree at Queen's. In another examination the following year, she passed with First Class Honours in Geometry and Algebra. She remained at Queen's College until she was 23 when, in 1885, she passed the second university examination and obtained First Class Honours in Logic and Second Class Honours in Mathematics.

Albert had long been a favourite of Thomas and Mary Hamilton – especially of the latter who liked discussing politics with him. He, however, was far more interested in Flora than in her parents, and in 1886 he made his feelings known to her. Flora made it at once clear that she could never have 'anything but friendship to give in exchange' and urged him to stop writing to her. Though they lived only a mile apart, the correspondence continued. In 1889 Flora began writing magazine articles and, because of his superior knowledge of English literature, she found in Albert an able and flattering critic. Hamilton, with considerable astuteness, realized that Albert's attachment to his daughter could be made to serve his own purposes. He was a man much addicted to short jaunts or holidays and in the unfortunate Albert he found not only a courier but, on many occasions, a disbursing officer. 'I'm a mere parcel,' he would say genially, leaving Albert to make all the arrangements. Never had a Jacob served more arduously for his Rachel than did Albert, and he was at last rewarded for his patience. In 1893 Flora agreed to marry him, and in her cool-headed and matter-of-fact way, she wrote: 'I wonder do I love you? I am not quite sure. I know that at least I am very fond of you, and that I should never think of loving anyone else.'

After a year's engagement, during which many love letters were exchanged, Albert and Flora were married. The wedding was celebrated on 29 August 1894 at St Mark's Church, Dundela. The reception was held immediately afterwards in the Royal Avenue Hotel, and Albert's somewhat disappointed father-in-law was heard to say, 'Now that he's got what he wanted, there'll be no more jaunts.'

Albert and Flora went to North Wales for their honeymoon, after which they returned to Belfast and settled at Dundela Villas, one of a pair of semi-detached houses within a mile of Albert's old home. It is in this house that their first son, Warren Hamilton, was born on 16 June 1895, and their second son, Clive Staples, on 29 November 1898.

I. EARLY DAYS

If any star danced at the birth of Clive Staples Lewis on 29 November 1898 in one of the semi-detached Dundela Villas near the outskirts of Belfast, the mists of time – and the predominant drizzle of Northern Ireland – have obscured it.

His brother Warren, three years old at the time, wrote, 'Of his arrival I remember nothing, though no doubt I was introduced to him, and it was only by degrees that I became dimly conscious of him as a vociferous disturber of my domestic peace.'

The natural jealousy of the newcomer died away as soon as babyhood ended, and the encumbrance was able to grow into a companion. Clive seems to have matured with commendable speed, not only talking, but expressing his preferences with typical decisiveness before he was two.

The first ten years of his childhood differed little from that of any average child in a similar period and setting. Early delights were those of rail travel each summer to and from nearby seaside resorts: '. . . the selection of toys to be taken, the bustle of packing, and then the great moment when the cab arrived to take us to the station. Then came the glorious excitement of the train journey, and, supreme bliss, the first sight of the sea.'

This month by the sea each year was their only holiday, and the single variation came in August 1907 when Mrs Lewis took the two boys to Berneval, near Dieppe, in northern France – Clive's only holiday abroad until he went to Greece in 1960. Otherwise, as they grew older, they could bicycle out for the day into the country, and occasionally visit friends or relations at no great distance.

About his early years Clive Lewis remembered with most gratitude, after 'good parents, good food and a garden (which then seemed large) to play in, two other blessings': first, his nurse Lizzie Endicott 'in whom even the exacting memory of childhood can discover no flaw – nothing but kindness, gaiety and good sense. . . . The other blessing was my brother. Though three years my senior, he never seemed to be an elder brother; we were allies, not to say confederates from the first.'

The biggest change in their lives during Clive's first ten years was the building of the 'New House' – Little Lea – and the move into it in April 1905. This was on the very edge of suburbia: 'On one side it was within twenty minutes' walk of a tram stop, on the other within a mile of what was indisputably open hilly farmland.' And as they both had bicycles, the real country, which they now discovered for the first time, was only a few minutes' ride away from their own front door. It was during these early 'golden years' before boarding-school that Clive developed his passionate love of Co. Down which he retained all his life.

Besides this delight there was, as Warren records, 'the new house itself which, though perhaps the worst designed house I ever saw, was for that very reason a child's delight. On the top floor, cupboard-like doors opened into huge, dark, wasted spaces under the roof, tunnel-like passages through which children could crawl, connecting space with space.' 'The New House is almost a major character in my story,' wrote Clive years later in *Surprised by Joy*. 'I am a product of long corridors, empty sunlit rooms, upstair indoor silences, attics explored in solitude, distant noises of gurgling cisterns and pipes, and the noise of wind under the tiles.' And he in turn wove these recollections into much that he was to write, from *Dymer* to *The Magician's Nephew*.

The house was full of books – 'I had always the same certainty of finding a book that was new to me as a man who walks into a field has of finding a new blade of grass' – though all of these were the works of novelists, historians, essayists and biographers. Neither of Clive Lewis's parents 'had the least taste for that kind of literature to which my allegiance was given the moment I could choose books for myself. Neither had ever listened for the horns of elfland. There was no copy of Keats or Shelley in the house, and the copy of Coleridge was never (to my knowledge) opened. If I am a romantic, my parents bear no responsibility for it.'

But even from his earliest days 'Jack' Lewis (at the age of four he had suddenly announced that his name was Jacksie – soon shortened into Jack – and refused to answer to any other ever after) had been able to find chinks at least in the magic casements – long before he could fling them wide and venture out over the perilous seas in the faery lands forlorn of which he was to add not a few to the literary atlas. To begin with, Lizzie Endicott would tell him fairy tales of her own country – of leprechauns with their pots of buried gold, of the Daoine Sidh, and of the Isle of Mell Moy which was to make him such an enthusiastic reader of James Stephens and the early Yeats.

Then came the early Beatrix Potter volumes, hot from the press. *Squirrel Nutkin*, his favourite, was published in 1903 before he was five – the book which gave him his first experience of 'sweet desire' as described in *Surprised by Joy*. 'I liked the Beatrix Potter illustrations at a time when the idea of humanized animals fascinated me perhaps even more than it fascinates most children,' he wrote in *An Experiment in Criticism* (1961); and he followed up this fascination through the pages of old volumes of *Punch* with their animal cartoons by Tenniel and Sambourne and Partridge, besides those in Lewis Carroll, and in the old Dalziel illustrations to *Mother Goose* of which a copy of the 1895 reprint had been given to Warren.

The first real introduction to romance came by chance, by way of a copy of *A Connecticut Yankee in King Arthur's Court* in which he was able to taste something of the true Logres even through Mark Twain's vulgar ridicule of his great original. But this was followed by an even more blessed discovery: the monthly *Strand Magazine* was serializing Conan Doyle's *Sir Nigel* from December 1905 to December 1906 – a real introduction to the world of chivalry. But more important even than Mark Twain's perverted Arthuriad and Doyle's brightly coloured Middle Ages were the serials in the *Strand* by E. Nesbit with H. R. Millar's superb and evocative illustrations: *Five Children – and It* (April to December 1902),

The Phoenix and the Carpet (July 1903 to June 1904), and *The Story of the Amulet* (May 1905 to April 1906). 'The last did most for me,' he recollected in 1955. 'It first opened my eyes to antiquity, the "dark backward and abysm of time". I can still re-read it with delight.'

This naturally leads on to the stories which Clive Lewis began writing before he was six and continued to elaborate for the next half-dozen years or more. After the move to Little Lea, he soon 'staked out a claim to one of the attics' and made it his 'study', decorating the walls with pictures of his own making or cut from brightly coloured Christmas numbers of magazines. 'Here,' he records, 'my first stories were written, and illustrated, with enormous satisfaction. They were an attempt to combine my two chief literary pleasures – "dressed animals" and "knights-in-armour". As a result, I wrote about chivalrous mice and rabbits who rode out in complete mail to kill not giants but cats.'

It is tempting to look here for the origin of such characters as Reepicheep the chivalric Talking Mouse, one of the most successfully developed among the higher animals of Narnia. But when discussing stories made up in childhood and their effect, or otherwise, on those written later, he told Green categorically that none of the characters or adventures in the Narnian stories were drawn from the Animal-Land of his own childhood inventions. The whole spirit of Narnia is different, as he also pointed out in *Surprised by Joy*: 'Animal-Land had nothing whatever in common with Narnia except the anthropomorphic beasts. Animal-Land, by its whole quality, excluded the least hint of wonder . . . in mapping and chronicling Animal-Land I was training myself to be a novelist. Note well, a novelist; not a poet. My invented world was full (for me) of interest, bustle, humour and character; but there was no poetry, even no romance in it. It was almost astonishingly prosaic.' Moreover, the Animal-Land which came into action in the holidays when Warren was at home from his English boarding-school 'was a modern Animal-Land; it had to have trains and steamships if it was to be a country shared with him. It followed, of course, that the medieval Animal-Land about which I wrote my stories must be the same country at an earlier period; and of course the two periods must be properly connected. This led me from romancing to historiography: I set about writing a full history of Animal-Land.' History led to geography: the world was re-mapped with Warren's 'India' as an island across the sea from Animal-Land, 'And those parts of that world which we regarded as our own – Animal-Land and India – were increasingly peopled with consistent characters,' and came to be known generally as 'Boxen'.

Many of Lewis's Boxonian stories are still extant, though most of these are from the later period, written between the ages of twelve and fourteen, when they became novels about minor characters rather than straight 'histories'. While they show great precocity, there is little evidence of anything else and hardly any foreshadowing of what was to come: they are interesting as the earliest works of C. S. Lewis – and intensely dull. This is largely due to the careful banishment of the poetic, the romantic and the imaginative elements – and to the extraordinary absorption with politics. This has been explained by Warren Lewis in his Introduction to the *Letters*, where he describes the continuous political discussions current in Ireland at the time, mainly diatribes against the government of the day between men of the same political persuasions – and vituperative and unexplained condemnation of all who differed from them in politics or religion.

'Any ordinary parent,' Warren concludes, 'would have sent us boys off to amuse ourselves elsewhere when one of these symposiums took place, but not my father; he would have thought it uncivil to the guest. Consequently we had to sit in silence while the torrent of vituperation flowed over our heads. The result in Jack's case was to convince him firstly that "grown-up" conversation and politics were one and the same thing, and that therefore he must give everything he wrote a political framework; and secondly to disgust him with the very word "politics" before he was out of his teens.'

Moreover, although the Boxonian characters are 'dressed animals', there is no attempt to keep up the fiction, and without the illustrations it would often be hard to remember that, for example,

Lord John Big is a frog, James Bar a bear, Macgoullah a horse, and Viscount Puddiphat an owl. And unfortunately none of the early stories of 'knights-in-armour' (even if the knights were dressed animals) seem to have survived, though there are a few early attempts at verse concerning 'Knights and Ladyes'.

Meanwhile the outward life went on more or less as usual. Warren departed to boarding-school in England, while Clive was taught at Little Lea by a governess called Miss Harper: 'She is fairly nice *for* a governess, but all of them are the same,' he confided to his first diary at the end of 1907, in which he describes himself as 'like most boys of nine, and I am like Papy, bad temper, thick lips, thin and generally wearing a jersey'.

Other diary scraps describe the rest of the household: his grandfather, Richard Lewis (1832–1908), 'who lives in a little room of his own upstairs'; Maude the housemaid and Martha the cook; several pets, 'a dog called Tim, a black and white mouse called Tommy, and lastly a canary called Peter.' The entry for Thursday, 5 March 1908 is typical – except for the unexpected item with which it concludes: 'I rise. The lawn is white with frost. I have breakfast. Get my coat and cap and see Papy off [to the office]. Miss Harper comes. Lessons. [The next entry translates the opening sentence of *De Bello Gallico*.] Dinner. I am carpentring at a sword. I read "Paradise Lost", reflections there-on.'

We do not know what these reflections were, nor how much of the poem which was to mean so much to him in later life was either read or understood by him in his tenth year; but even as he wrote, his own paradise was on the verge of being lost. 'There came a night when I was ill and crying both with headache and toothache and distressed because my mother did not come to me,' he wrote in *Surprised by Joy*. 'That was because she was ill too; and what was odd was that there were several doctors in her room, and voices and comings and goings all over the house and doors shutting and opening. It seemed to last for hours. And then my father, in tears, came into my room and began to try to convey to my terrified mind things it had never conceived before. It was in fact cancer and followed the usual course; an operation (they operated in the patient's house in those days), an apparent convalescence, a return of the disease, increasing pain, and death [on 23 August 1908]. My father never fully recovered from this loss.'

The effect of Flora's death on Albert Lewis was to alienate him from his two sons just at the time when mutual comfort was most needed. His nerves had never been of the steadiest and his emotions had always been uncontrolled: now he began to speak wildly and act unjustly. To children just entering on their teens the sight of adult grief and fear is apt to produce revulsion rather than sympathy, and adult loss of control is put down to unkindness rather than to its true cause. Warren and Clive lost their mother slowly as her last illness shut them further and further away from her. When she was dead their father was incapable of taking her place and had already forfeited a great deal of his own, without knowing it. They were driven to rely more and more exclusively on each other for all that made life bearable, to have confidence only in each other – 'two frightened urchins huddled for warmth in a bleak world,' as one of them was to write in *Surprised by Joy*. And he continues: 'With my mother's death all settled happiness, all that was tranquil and reliable, disappeared from my life. There was to be much fun, many pleasures, many stabs of Joy; but no more of the old security. It was sea and islands now; the great continent had sunk like Atlantis.'

The first island to be visited by 'Jack' Lewis after his mother's death was one of the unpleasantest that he was to experience. Albert Lewis was probably wise to send him away from the shadow of loss at home, and strive to fill his life with the new and absorbing experiences of school life: but of all the schools in the British Isles he seems to have chosen the very worst.

Wynyard School, Hertfordshire, and its ogre of a headmaster have been described fully in *Surprised by Joy* (as 'Belsen') and little more need be said of them here, save to state that the contemporary evidence of diaries and letters fully bears out the recollections of later years.

When Warren Lewis entered the school in May 1905 it had already begun the easy descent to Avernus which was precipitated by a law case in 1901 when the headmaster, the Reverend Robert Capron (1851–1911), treated a boy with such brutality that the father brought a High Court action against him, which was settled out of court and against the defendant. Apart from the rapidly developing mania for inflicting punishment, Capron seems to have run the school very much on the lines of Crichton House described by F. Anstey in *Vice Versa*, which Lewis called 'the only truthful school story in existence'. But it was an altogether smaller and – towards the end – more squalid affair, though Capron, like Anstey's Dr Grimstone, seems to have begun as a competent teacher whose pupils at one time gained scholarships to public schools. By the time the Lewis boys were entrusted to his care, however, the instruction had become 'at once brutalizing and intellectually stupefying', little was taught and still less remembered.

'In spite of Capron's policy of terror,' wrote Warren, 'the school was slack and inefficient, and the time-table, if such it could be called, ridiculous. When not saying lessons, the boys spent the whole of school working out sums on slates; of this endless arithmetic there was little or no supervision. Of the remaining subjects, English and Latin consisted, the first solely and the second mainly, of grammar. History was a ceaseless circuit of the late Middle Ages; Geography was a meaningless list of rivers, towns, imports and exports.'

There was no school library at Wynyard, but the boys were by no means illiterate, though Warren and Clive seem to have had better taste than most of their companions. A 'Club for getting monthly magazines' which they formed during Clive's first term shows this: the other boys' contributions were the *Captain*, the *Boy's Own Paper*, the *Wide World*, the *Royal*, and the *London Magazine*, but Warren's choice was *Pearson's* and Clive's the *Strand*. As they all shared each other's magazines, Clive found himself reading 'twaddling school-stories', which he dismissed later as 'mere wish-fulfilment of the hero' – surely forgiveable in a school such as Mr Capron's establishment. The *Strand*, however, was offering at this time E. Nesbit's excellent pastiches of imagination and history, *The House of Arden* and *Harding's Luck*, with the odd Sherlock Holmes story and A. E. W. Mason's *At the Villa Rose* for more adult excitement, while Hall Caine's semi-religious thriller *The White Prophet* may have led him on to the taste for romances of the early Christians in Rome which he developed at this time. These he found in Sienkiewicz's *Quo Vadis?* (1898), Dean Farrar's *Darkness and Dawn: or, Scenes in the Days of Nero* (1891), Whyte-Melville's *The Gladiators: a Tale of Rome and Judaea* (1863), and Lew Wallace's *Ben Hur: A Tale of the Christ* (1880).

'They were mostly, as literature, rather bad books,' he decided. 'What wore better, and what I took to at the same time, is the work of Rider Haggard.' *The Ghost Kings* was running as a serial in *Pearson's*, and *Pearl Maiden, a Tale of the Fall of Jerusalem* (1903) would have come with the early Christians stories. He also fell for a while under the spell of H. G. Wells's science-fiction – a taste which did not last, though he was still reading Haggard with enjoyment at the end of his life.

It is curious, however, that Lewis should have missed *The Wind in the Willows* which came out in 1908 during his first term at Wynyard, at a time when his interest in 'dressed animals' was at its height in the heyday of Boxen. He read neither that nor E. Nesbit's Bastable stories until he was in his twenties – but 'I do not think I have enjoyed them any the less on that account.'

Boxen was not, however, his only literary concern at the time. A fragment of a historical novel written in the summer of 1909 still survives, called *The Ajimywanian War* – so dull that it might be an imitation of the dullest history book in use at Wynyard. He was also attempting another diary, or 'Autobiography' as he calls it, of his experiences among the 'five boarders at this ridiculous little "select academy for young gentlemen" – Squiffy [Field], Bowser, Mears, Jeyes and me . . . Oldy and his son Wyn are the only masters here, and Wyn can't teach for nuts either.' But that too petered out after a week.

During his first year at Wynyard Clive had written desperately to his father to be taken away: 'We simply CANNOT wait in this hole till the end of term'; but the fear of losing his few remaining pupils curbed some of Capron's excesses in the rapidly shrinking – and sinking – establishment, and Capron's son seems to have been trying to improve relations with the parents by writing solicitously about their sons: 'Jacko appears to be very bright and happy this term,' he was assuring Albert Lewis. 'His health is excellent.' He seems, nevertheless, to have suffered from a weak chest throughout childhood, though the removal of adenoids at the beginning of 1909 may have helped him to survive the following winter without any illness.

On his way back to Wynyard in January 1910 his second cousin on his mother's side, Hope Ewart, took Clive to see *Peter Pan* in London, which impressed him deeply and remained vivid in his memory; theatre-going in Belfast consisted only of musical comedies and vaudeville beyond which Albert Lewis did not aspire.

This cousin was a member of a family that meant much to the two motherless boys. The younger describes their house in *Surprised by Joy* as 'Mountbracken'. It was actually Glenmacken, the home of Sir William Quartus Ewart (1844–1919) whose wife, wrote Lewis, was 'my mother's first cousin and perhaps my mother's dearest friend, and it was no doubt for my mother's sake that she took upon herself the heroic task of civilizing my brother and me. We had a standing invitation to lunch at Mountbracken whenever we were at home; to this, almost entirely, we owe it that we did not grow up savages. The debt is not only to Lady E[wart] ("Cousin Mary") but to her whole family; walks, motor-drives (in those days an exciting novelty), picnics, and invitations to the theatre were showered on us, year after year, with a kindness which our rawness, our noise, and our unpunctuality never seemed to weary. We were at home there almost as much as in our own home, but with this great difference, that a certain standard of manners had to be kept up. Whatever I know (it is not much) of courtesy and *savoir faire* I learned at Mountbracken.'

Wynyard having collapsed in the summer of 1910 (Capron was certified insane and died two years later), a new school was needed for Clive; Warren was already at Malvern College. Albert Lewis decided that he should go to Campbell College not two miles from Little Lea – 'which had been founded with the express purpose of giving Ulster boys all the advantages of a public school education without the trouble of crossing the Irish Sea.' It was arranged that he should go as a boarder, but with the privilege of an *exeat* to come home every Sunday.

Although the complete lack of quiet or privacy was trying – he described it as 'very like living permanently in a large railway station' – Clive found Campbell College a great improvement on Wynyard, and really began to enjoy learning, and to remember what he learnt. He was particularly grateful to an 'excellent master whom we called Octie' (J. A. McNeill) who introduced him in form to Arnold's *Sohrab and Rustum*: 'I loved the poem at first sight and have loved it ever since.'

But his stay at Campbell was to be brief: on 13 November 1910 Albert Lewis was writing to Warren at Malvern: 'When Jacko came home this morning he had such a frightful cough that I had Dr Leslie up to examine him. As a result, Leslie has advised me not to send him back to school for some days'; and he went on to ask Warren to find out about Cherbourg, a preparatory school at Malvern, as 'I am strongly inclined to send Jacko there until he's old enough to go to the College.'

After two glorious months of peace and quiet at home, reading ever reading – at this time largely fairy tales – the invalid was deemed well enough to begin at Cherbourg. And accordingly he was writing to his father near the end of January 1911: 'Warnie and I arrived safely at Malvern after a splendid journey. Cherbourg is quite a nice place. There are 17 chaps here. There are three masters, Mr Allen, Mr Palmer and Mr Jones, who is *very* fat . . . Malvern is one of the nicest English towns I have seen yet. The hills are beautiful, but of course not so nice as ours.'

The school was not as small as would appear from this as there were day boys as well as the seventeen boarders; and although his letters and odd scraps of diary are full of criticism of the masters, and often of the school itself, Lewis seems to have been reasonably happy at Cherbourg and recorded that 'here indeed my education really began. The Headmaster [Arthur C. Allen] was a clever and patient teacher; under him I rapidly found my feet in Latin and English, and even began to be looked on as a promising candidate for a scholarship at the College.'

In *Surprised by Joy* Lewis goes on to tell how he lost his faith during his terms at Cherbourg, sparked off by the esoteric religious flounderings of the matron, Miss Cowie. Other reasons joined to make him an apostate – 'dropping my faith with no sense of loss but with the greatest relief.' Intense preoccupation with prayer had made prayer an increasingly unendurable penance; and a natural and induced pessimism had grown up from his own manual clumsiness, his mother's death, the miseries of Wynyard, and his father's exaggerated statements as to the difficulty of managing 'to avoid the workhouse.'

Another cause had its roots in the very brilliance of Lewis's mind, which began suddenly to blossom under the influence of the excellent teaching at Cherbourg, and in particular the classical authors. 'Here, especially in Virgil, one was presented with a mass of religious ideas; and all teachers and editors took it for granted from the outset that these religious ideas were sheer illusion. No one ever attempted to show in what sense Christianity fulfilled Paganism or Paganism prefigured Christianity. The accepted position seemed to be that religions were normally a mere farrago of nonsense, though our own, by a fortunate exception, was exactly true. . . . But on what grounds could I believe in this exception? . . . I was very anxious not to.'

Other influences were also at hand to shake his faith. In May 1912 a new master came to Cherbourg – whom we may leave in the decent obscurity of his nickname 'Pogo' – whose evil effects on the adolescent mind are well described in *Surprised by Joy*. At the same time came the sudden upsurge of puberty and an easy surrender to sexual temptation. 'But this is amply accounted for by the age I had then reached and by my recent, in a sense deliberate, withdrawal of myself from Divine protection. I do not believe Pogo had anything to do with it. . . . What attacked me through

Pogo was not the Flesh (I had that of my own) but the World: the desire for glitter, swagger, distinction, the desire to be in the know. . . . I began to labour very hard to make myself into a fop, a cad, and a snob.

'Pogo's communications, however much they helped to vulgarize my mind, had no such electric effect on my senses as the dancing mistress, nor as Bekker's [sic] *Charicles*, which was given me for a prize. [This was *Charicles, or Illustrations of the Private Life of the Ancient Greeks* (1840) by the German archaeologist Wilhelm Becker (1796–1846), written in fictional form, with a scholarly "excursus" following each chapter and footnotes citing his original Greek authorities. The passage in question was probably the scene in Corinth with accompanying excursus on the Heterae.] I never thought that dancing mistress as beautiful as my cousin G. [Gundreda Ewart], but she was the first woman I ever "looked upon to lust after her"; assuredly through no fault of her own.'

Side by side with the awakening of carnal and worldly desires came what Lewis described as the real romantic passion of his life. It came with the sudden overwhelming return of 'Joy' – the pang of sweet desire for the Unknown – when he chanced upon the Christmas number of the *Bookman* for December 1911 with a coloured supplement reproducing several of Arthur Rackham's illustrations to *Siegfried and the Twilight of the Gods* in a loosely poetic version made by Margaret Armour.

'A moment later, as the poet says, "The sky had turned round," ' as Lewis records in *Surprised by Joy*. 'I had never heard of Wagner, nor of Siegfried. I thought the Twilight of the Gods meant the twilight in which the gods lived. How did I know, at once and beyond question, that this was no Celtic, or silvan, or terrestrial twilight? But so it was. Pure "Northernness" engulfed me: a vision of huge, clear spaces hanging above the Atlantic in the endless twilight of Northern summer, remoteness, severity . . . and almost at the same moment I knew that I had met this before, long, long ago (it hardly seems longer now) in *Tegner's Drapa*, that Siegfried (whatever it might be) belonged to the same world as Balder and the sunward-sailing cranes.'

Lewis was here harking back to a chance reading several years earlier of Longfellow's poem based on the Swedish poet Esaias Tegner's version (1825) of *Frithiof's Saga*, which begins

> I heard a voice, that cried,
> 'Balder the Beautiful
> Is dead, is dead!'
> And through the misty air
> Passed like the mournful cry
> Of sunward sailing cranes.

This had been the last time he experienced Joy before the Dark Ages in the 'Concentration Camp' of Wynyard.

The craze for all things 'Northern' which followed this great moment of revelation and the rediscovery of Joy became the most important thing in Lewis's life for the next two or three years – he describes it as almost a double life, particularly during the unpleasant year at Malvern College (1913–14), when the mental ecstasy and the physical purgatory alternated with dizzying rapidity.

By the summer of 1912 Lewis had discovered the works of Wagner by means of gramophone records. He and Warren now had a gramophone and 'gramophone catalogues were already one of my favourite forms of reading; but I had never remotely dreamed that the records from Grand Opera with their queer German or Italian names could have anything to do with me.' But a magazine called the *Soundbox* was doing synopses of great operas week by week, and it now did the whole *Ring*. 'I read in a rapture and discovered who Siegfried was and what was the "twilight" of the gods.' On the strength of this he began to write a poem on the Wagnerian version of the Nibelung story, and to collect records of the operas.

Later that summer Lewis came across an actual copy of the illustrated *Siegfried and the Twilight of the Gods* on the drawing-room table of his cousin Hope Ewart (now Mrs George Harding) during a visit to her home at Dundrum near Dublin, and found that the Rackham pictures 'which seemed to me then to be the very music made visible, plunged me a few fathoms deeper into my delight. I have seldom coveted anything as I coveted that book' – and he was able to buy the cheaper edition shortly afterwards.

This visit to Dundrum seems to have merged in his memory with one the following August when he and Warren were bicycling 'via Glendalough and the Vale of Avoca through the most glorious scenery possible' when he came to record how 'this imaginative Renaissance almost at once produced a new appreciation of external nature. At first, I think, this was parasitic on the literary and musical experiences. On that holiday at Dundrum, cycling among the Wicklow mountains, I was almost involuntarily looking for scenes that might belong to the Wagnerian world . . . But soon (I cannot say how soon) nature ceased to be a mere reminder of books, became herself the medium of the real joy.'

In this great Northern Renaissance Lewis found everything else dwarfed in proportion. 'If the Northernness seemed then a bigger thing than my religion, that may partly have been because my attitude towards it contained elements which my religion ought to have contained and did not.' Years later, in a lecture to the Socratic Club at Oxford, he confessed that: 'If Christianity *is* only a mythology, then I find that the mythology I believe in is not the mythology I like best. I like Greek mythology much better: Irish better still: Norse best of all.' And in another lecture he described himself as one who loved Balder before he loved Christ.

Meanwhile Lewis was progressing well at school. His first printed works, two undistinguished essays, appeared in the *Cherbourg School Magazine*; he began to take an interest in the Shakespearean productions of Frank Benson's company whenever it visited Malvern, and he was becoming a likely candidate for a scholarship to the College.

He was to take the entrance examination in June 1913, but 'was obliged to retire to bed with rather a high temperature.' However, Canon James, the headmaster, sent the papers over to Cherbourg, and Mr Allen could write to Albert Lewis on 8 June: 'I am so glad to be able to tell you that your son has been recommended for a Junior Scholarship. This is very satisfactory, as his work was of course much handicapped by being done in bed, when he was feeling far from well.' Warren commented that 'in the circumstances I am inclined to rate his obtaining a Scholarship as the greatest triumph of his career,' while Hope Harding wrote to Albert Lewis: 'We were delighted to hear the news, and have wired to Jacko to tell him so. I can't say I'm surprised, however, for I always knew he was a remarkable boy, besides being one of the most lovable I ever came across. George and I are looking forward to the boys' visit in the summer holidays very much.'

Lewis bade farewell to Cherbourg School with his first published poem, which appeared in the school magazine on 29 July 1913: 'Quam Bene Saturno', after Tibullus [I.iii.35–50], beginning

> Alas! What happy days were those
> When Saturn ruled a peaceful race,
> Or yet the foolish mortals chose
> With roads to track the world's broad face . . .

Certainly, if the Age of Saturn still lingered during the summer holiday at Dundrum when the Valkyries seemed to be riding over the Mountains of Mourne and Fafair the dragon guarded the Rhine Gold in a cave above the Vale of Avoca, the reign of Jove was about to claim Clive Lewis 'with grim Array' when he arrived for his first term at Malvern College on 18 September 1913.

He went expecting almost a heaven on earth compared with his earlier experiences of school. For Warren, who had left the previous term and was cramming for a year before going to Sandhurst, it had been 'a place in which it was bliss to be alive and to be young was very heaven,' and he had not stinted in singing its praises. But Warren was a cheery extrovert; good enough at games, the type of boy to be readily popular with his companions – and not particularly interested in learning, while Clive was his direct antithesis in all these respects.

To begin with he wrote hopefully to his father: 'So far everything has been very pleasant indeed. Luckily I am going to get a study out of which the old occupants are moving today. There will be three other people in it – Hardman, Anderson and Lodge.' A week later: 'The work here is very heavy going, and it is rather hard to find time for it in the breathless life we lead here. So far that "breathlessness" is the worst feature of the place. You never get a "wink of peace". It is a perpetual rush at high pressure, with short intervals spent in waiting for another bell . . .'

But near the end of term Warren came back for a House Supper, 'a noisy, cheerful function, of which all I remember is Jack's gloom and boredom glaringly obvious to all, and not tending to increase his popularity with the House. On 22 December he and I set off together for the last time on the old, well-loved journey to Belfast via Liverpool,' described with such affectionate nostalgia in *Surprised by Joy*.

Lewis was ill again during the holidays and forced to return to school a fortnight late – at which he did not repine, but buried himself in his dream-world of literature 'of legendary loves and magic fears'. But he found the transition from 'the warmth and softness and dignity of his home life to the privations, the raw and sordid ugliness of school' – from the copy of *The Rhinegold and the Valkyries* which his father had given him at Christmas to match *Siegfried and the Twilight of the Gods* – upset him even more than the previous term had done. Even the removal to a better study, with Hardman and W. E. H. Quennell as companions, was only a temporary alleviation. By 18 March he was writing to his father: 'Not only does this persecution get harder to bear as time goes on, but it is actually getting more severe. As for the work, indeed, things are now much brighter, and I have been getting on all right since half term. But, out of school, life gets more and more dreary; all the prefects detest me and lose no opportunity of venting their spite . . . Please take me out of this as soon as possible, but don't, whatever you do, write to the James [Canon James, the headmaster] or the Old Boy [the Reverend T. Spear, housemaster], as that would only make things worse.'

Albert Lewis reacted with unexpected good sense and moderation. 'He is very uncomfortable at Malvern,' he wrote to Warren. 'He is not popular with the prefects apparently, and gets more than a fair share of the fagging and bullying. In a word, the thing is a failure and must be ended. His letters make me unhappy . . . I suppose the best thing I can do is to send him to "Kirk" after next term.'

Warren agreed, though expressing considerable natural bitterness and blaming Clive for much of his own unhappiness – he 'started with everything in his favour, and if he has made himself unpopular, he has only himself to thank for it . . . I feel it intensely that my brother should be a social outcast in the House where I was so happy.' But looking back with hindsight fifty years later, he wrote in his Preface to the *Letters*: 'The fact is that he should never have been sent to a public school at all. Already, at fourteen, his intelligence was such that he would have fitted in better among undergraduates than among schoolboys; and by his temperament he was bound to be a misfit, a heretic, an object of suspicion within the collective-minded and standardizing Public School system. He was, indeed, lucky to leave Malvern before the power of this system had done him any lasting damage.'

In *Surprised by Joy* Lewis sums up his troubles at Malvern and his dislike of the whole atmosphere of the place and all it stood for, firstly by stressing his utter exhaustion there: 'I was tired, dog-tired, cab-horse tired, tired (almost) like a child in a factory.' This was partly due to his age, he had for the moment rather outgrown his strength, and to sleeplessness caused by trouble with his teeth; but also to the fagging system which made it possible for an unpopular boy to be fagged out of virtually all his spare time – and much time, too, that should have been spent on preparation for the next lessons. 'And remember,' he added, 'that, even without fagging, a school day contains hardly any leisure for a boy who does not like games. For him, to pass from the form-room to the playing field is simply to exchange work in which he can take some interest for work in which he can take none, in which failure is more severely punished, and in which (worst of all) he must feign an interest.

'I think that this feigning, this ceaseless pretence of interest in matters to me supremely boring, was what wore me out more than anything else. . . . For games (and gallantry) were the only subjects, and I cared for neither. . . . Spiritually speaking, the deadly thing was that school life was a life almost wholly dominated by the social struggle; to get on, to arrive, or, having reached the top, to remain there, was the absorbing preoccupation.'

But of 'Tarting' and 'Bloodery' Lewis has written, perhaps too much, in *Surprised by Joy*: they were temptations that did not move him more than as his first and worst experience of the 'Inner Ring' which he was to attack so fiercely in later life.

His study-mate, 'Hardman' – now Air Chief Marshal Sir Donald Hardman, C.B.E., K.C.B., D.F.C. – writes on the whole picture given in *Surprised by Joy*: 'In a word it is in my view unbalanced and exaggerated. This is not to say that some of the practices and customs he complains of did not exist; they did, but Lewis has blown them up out of all proportion. "Tarting" did exist, but I'm sure, to nothing like the extent that he makes out. He has a good deal to say about fagging; it could at times be very irritating, but we took it as all in the day's work and I have never known it leave these scars on anyone else. Every House must have its good and lean years in House Prefects and we were not particularly blessed with ours in Lewis's day. Even so, I am sure that he was not unhappy all the time. I can remember going with him for long walks on Sundays when he was in the gayest of moods – story telling and mimicking people. It is surprising that he should forget the happy times and remember only the unhappy ones.'

However, Lewis does record that there were 'two blessings' at Malvern 'that wore no disguise': one was 'the Grundy' – the school library, 'not only because it was a library, but because it was a sanctuary'; and the other was 'my form master, Smewgy as we called him.' This was Harry Wakelyn Smith who taught Classics and English to the Upper Fifth during most of his time at Malvern, from 1885 until his death in 1918, who is well and lovingly described in *Surprised by Joy*.

Lewis kept secret the fact that he was leaving Malvern after the summer term of 1914. But before he went he wrote some verses in imitation of Ovid's *Pars estis pauci* [*Ex Ponto*, III.ii.25 et seq.] in the metre of the last chorus of *Atalanta in Calydon*. 'They were top of the form and well spoken of by Smewgy', he wrote when

enclosing them to his father; and they read almost as a farewell to
Smewgy himself:

> Of the host whom I named
> As friends, ye alone
> Dear few! were ashamed
> In troubles unknown
> To leave me deserted, but boldly ye cherished my cause as your own. . . .
>
> But nay! for the days
> Of a mortal are few;
> Shall they limit your praise,
> Nay rather to you
> Each new generation shall offer – if aught be remembered – your due. . . .

When looking back on what he had just written in *Surprised by
Joy* about the miseries of his year at Malvern, Lewis continued:
'I find myself exclaiming, "Lies, lies! This was really a period of
ecstasy. It consisted chiefly of moments when you were too happy
to speak, when gods and heroes rioted through your head, when
Satyrs danced and Maenads roamed on the mountains, when
Brynhild and Sieglinde, Deirdre, Maeve and Helen were all about
you, till sometimes you felt that it might break you with mere
richness." . . . All this is true, but it does not make the other
version a lie. I am telling a story of two lives. . . . When I remember
my inner life I see that everything mentioned in the last two
chapters [about Malvern] was merely a coarse curtain which at
any moment might be drawn aside to reveal all the heavens I then
knew. The same duality perplexes the story of my home life . . .'

Lewis goes on to describe at some length his father's character
and the reasons why life at home was becoming progressively more
difficult. Briefly, Albert Lewis erred through a combination of
egocentricity and sheer affection for his sons. He enjoyed their
company so much that when he was in the house he insisted on
being with them all the time: if they had a visitor of their own age,
or wanted to read or study quietly by themselves, he allowed it to
make no difference. But with them he must dominate the conversation and impose his own interests at the expense of theirs,
usually failing to take in anything they said to him, due to the

illogicality and effervescence of his mind. Only when their father was away at work could Warren and Clive retire to 'the little end room' to read and write and chronicle the endless episodes in the history of Boxen.

But the Boxonian days came to an end in 1913 when Warren left Malvern for a crammer who helped him win a prize cadetship at Sandhurst the following year, and Clive was indeed already deep in 'Northernness', exploring more deeply than the late Teutonic version of the Nibelung saga adapted by Wagner, and finding his way into the genuine Norse and Icelandic originals of saga and Eddic literature. 'I passed on from Wagner,' he says, 'to everything else I could get hold of about Norse mythology, *Myths of the Norsemen* [by H. A. Guerber], *Myths and Legends of the Teutonic Race* [presumably *Teutonic Myth and Legend*, by Donald A. Mackenzie], Mallet's *Northern Antiquities*.' This last he obtained in the old Bohn Library edition, with an appendix containing most of the *Prose Edda*, which he found the most stimulating discovery so far.

At Malvern he found a copy of the *Corpus Poeticum Boreale* (1881), F. York Powell's great edition of all the mythological poems in the *Elder Edda* – 'and tried vainly but happily to hammer out the originals from the translation at the bottom of the page.' This was during the summer term of 1914, by which time Lewis was deep in one of the most remarkable of his early works, 'a tragedy, Norse in subject and Greek in form. It was called *Loki Bound* and was as classical as any Humanist could have desired . . . The main contrast in my play was between the sad wisdom of Loki and the brutal orthodoxy of Thor. . . . Thor was, in fact, the symbol of the Bloods [at Malvern] . . . Loki was a projection of myself; he voiced that sense of priggish superiority whereby I was, unfortunately, beginning to compensate myself for my unhappiness.'

He had already begun to write this play when he first made friends with Arthur Greeves in April 1914, as graphically described in *Surprised by Joy*, and found another who shared his delight in things Northern. They discovered 'in a torrent of questions that we liked not only the same thing, but the same parts of it and in the same way; that both knew the stab of Joy and that, for both, the arrow was shot from the North.'

Arthur Greeves (1895–1968) was the youngest of the five children of Joseph Greeves, the nearest neighbour of the Lewises at Little Lea. Arthur had been a casual acquaintance of the Lewis boys for most of their lives, but only from 1914 did he begin to become, as Clive wrote in 1933, 'after my brother, my oldest and most intimate friend'. And in that same year Warren wrote of him that 'his circumstances have been such that he has never been compelled to face the issues of life . . . But it would be unfair to blame him, for his character is the result of an accident of his youth – while he was still a boy a doctor diagnosed him as suffering from a weak heart, and by the time the diagnosis was disproved, he was already a confirmed valetudinarian. At the plastic age he was exempted from the discipline of school and the preoccupations of a career, made into an invalid by his mother, whose favourite he is, and encouraged to float rudderless and motiveless down the years.'

The friendship with Arthur Greeves came exactly at the right moment. There was a temporary shadow cast by Malvern over Clive's intimacy with Warren – who, anyhow, was now an army cadet at Aldershot with new interests of his own, and very short leaves; moreover the Great War, breaking out in August 1914, accelerated his training and would soon carry him off to France as an officer in the Royal Army Service Corps.

It was not without much heart-searching and discussion with Warren that Albert Lewis took Clive away from Malvern, realized that no public school would suit him, decided against sending him back to Campbell College, and entrusted him to 'Kirk', the crammer in Surrey who had helped Warren into Sandhurst.

William T. Kirkpatrick (1848–1921), whose teaching was to have more far-reaching effects on C. S. Lewis than anyone else with whom he came in contact, is fully described – as are his original and in this case at least most effective methods of teaching – in *Surprised by Joy*; and his most outstanding characteristics are lovingly reproduced in the person of MacPhee in *That Hideous Strength*. He had been headmaster of Lurgan College from 1874 until he retired in 1899. Albert Lewis was one of his pupils there and afterwards became his solicitor. On retiring, Kirkpatrick began to take private pupils, and by 1912 he and his wife were settled at Gastons, Great Bookham, Surrey.

And there Clive Lewis found him early in September 1914 when he arrived to begin his real education: 'He was over six feet tall, very shabbily dressed (like a gardener, I thought), lean as a rake, and immensely muscular. His wrinkled face seemed to consist entirely of muscles, so far as it was visible; for he wore moustache and side whiskers with a clean-shaven chin . . . If ever a man came near to being a purely logical entity, that man was Kirk,' Lewis decided, and his own acutely logical mind was to a great extent formed and sharpened by Kirkpatrick's. Kirkpatrick's outstanding conviction was that language was given to man solely for the purpose of communicating or discovering truth. The general banalities and 'small-talk' of most people did not enter into his calculations. 'The most casual remark was taken as a summons to disputation.' To a mere 'torrent of verbiage' he would cry 'Stop!', not from impatience, but because it was leading nowhere. More sensible observations might be interrupted by 'Excuse!', ushering in some parenthetical comment. Full approval would be encouraged by 'I hear you' – but usually followed by refutation: 'Had I read this? Had I studied that? Had I any statistical evidence? And so to the almost inevitable conclusion: "Do you not see then that you had no right . . ." '

'Some boys would not have liked it,' Lewis comments, 'to me it was red beef and strong beer'; and, toned down and adapted to possible equals rather than pupils, this became his own method of argument, his own idea of conversation throughout life. Who among his friends cannot still see him swing round with the light of good-humoured battle in his eyes on spotting a loose or too casual pronouncement, and hear his exultant cry of 'I challenge that!'? The Christian virtue that he found hardest to acquire was to suffer fools gladly; for years he failed to realize that the Kirk treatment might upset or offend; but at last he was able to turn it to glorious use, when the silliest dinner-table remark could be taken by him and manipulated gently and followed to conclusions of which you had never dreamed – and yet leaving you with the warm glow of undeserved pride at having initiated such a profoundly interesting discussion.

Kirkpatrick's methods of instruction were 'red beef and strong beer' too. Not only had Lewis been grounded more securely than he knew at Cherbourg and Malvern, but he had been blessed with a brain ready at the right stimulus to develop those prodigious powers of memory and applied knowledge which the late Austin Farrer described as perhaps the greatest and most amazing in his generation. And so he was able to benefit fully from Kirkpatrick's rather 'sink or swim' method – which may, however, have been applied intentionally to a pupil whose unusual capabilities and capacity for learning he had sized up at once.

Lewis arrived at Bookham on Saturday, 19 September 1914, and two days later he was flung straight into Homer, of whom he had never read a word, nor had any introduction to the Epic dialect, having only studied the straight Attic of Xenophon and the dramatists. Kirkpatrick's method was to read aloud twenty lines or so of the Greek, translate, with a few comments and explanations for another hundred lines, and then leave his pupil to go over it with the aid of a lexicon, and make sense of as much of it as he could. It worked with Lewis, who had no difficulty in memorizing every word as he looked up its meaning. Kirkpatrick at this stage seemed to value speed more than absolute accuracy, and Lewis soon found himself understanding what he read without translating it, beginning to think in Greek: 'That,' he commented, 'is the great Rubicon to cross in learning any language.' And so, 'Day after day and month after month, we drove gloriously onward,' till the music of Homer 'and the clear, bitter brightness that lives in almost every formula had become part of me.'

'After a week's trial, I have come to the conclusion that I am going to have the time of my life,' Lewis wrote to Arthur Greeves.

And a little later: 'As for my average Bookham day, there is not much to tell. Breakfast at 8.00, where I am glad to see good Irish soda bread on the table, begins the day. I then proceed to take the air till 9.15, when I come in and have the honour of reading that glorious *Iliad*, which I will not insult with my poor praise. 11–11.15 is a little break, and then go on with Latin until luncheon at 1.00. From 1–5.00 the time is at my own disposal to read, or write or moon about in the golden tinted woods and valleys of this country. 5–7 we work again. 7.30 dinner. After that I have the pleasant task of English Literature mapped out by Himself. Of course that doesn't include novels, which I read at other times. I am at present occupied (as Eng. Lit.) with Buckle's *Civilization of England*, and (of my own accord) Ibsen's plays.'

This routine became the archetype of a 'normal day' as he would choose his days to be: 'if I could please myself I would always live as I lived there'; and indeed throughout his subsequent life at Oxford and Cambridge he continued whenever possible to follow this schedule as far as circumstances would allow – the main variation being that in time more evenings were spent in talk with friends or at meetings of various literary or other societies than in reading.

Another habit contracted at Bookham was reading 'suitable' books during afternoon tea, which he held should be taken alone. 'It would be a kind of blasphemy to read poetry at table: what one wants is a gossipy, formless book which can be opened anywhere,' and his usual choice was Boswell, Herodotus, Burton, *Tristram Shandy*, *The Essays of Elia* or Andrew Lang's *History of English Literature*.

The two and a half years thus initiated at Great Bookham, while among the most important in forming the C. S. Lewis who was to be, were years of peace and content such as he was hardly to know again; but they were years of mental development fed by literary discovery and sound learning. Very little actually happened in the biographical sense, beyond holidays in Ireland and occasional visits from Warren on leave from the Western Front.

During this time he wrote almost weekly letters to Arthur

Greeves, telling mainly of the books that he was reading, many of them landmarks of importance when viewed in the light of his future career. Thus, in November 1914 he was discovering William Morris, both the poems and the prose romances; in January 1915 he first read the *Morte Darthur* – 'it has opened up a new world to me,' in January 1916 *The Faerie Queene* and *Grettir the Strong*. A diary kept for three weeks in July 1915 shows him reading *Prometheus Bound* in the original Greek, 'a red letter day in my life', Keats, Ruskin, Horace, Aristotle and Virginia Woolf. And he was celebrating these delights in verse:

> And while the rain is on the leads
> What songcraft sweet shall be our fare?
> The tale where Spenser's magic sheds
> A slumbrous sweetness on the air
> Of charmed lands, and Horace fair,
> And Malory who told the end
> Of Arthur, and the trumpet blare
> Of him who sang Patroklos' friend . . .

At the end of February 1916 (he mistakenly dates it August 1915 in *Surprised by Joy*) Lewis made one of the literary discoveries which, he maintained, left the deepest and most enduring impression on both his literary and his spiritual life. 'I have had a great literary experience this week,' he wrote to Arthur Greeves. 'I have discovered yet another author to add to our circle – our very own set: never since I first read *The Well at the World's End* have I enjoyed a book so much – and indeed I think my new "find" is quite as good as Malory or Morris himself. The book, to get to the point, is George MacDonald's "Faerie Romance", *Phantastes*, which I picked up by hazard in a rather tired Everyman copy on our station bookstall last Saturday.'

Thirty years later, in the introduction to a selection from his works, Lewis wrote of George MacDonald, 'I have never concealed the fact that I regard him as my master; indeed, I fancy I have never written a book in which I did not quote from him,' and after describing the purchase of *Phantastes*, he continues, 'A few hours later I knew that I had crossed a great frontier. I had already been waist deep in Romanticism; and likely enough, at any moment, to flounder into its darker and more evil forms, slithering down the steep descent that leads from the love of strangeness to that of eccentricity, and thence to that of perversity. Now *Phantastes* was romantic enough in all conscience; but there was a difference. Nothing was at that time further from my thoughts than Christianity and I therefore had no notion what this difference really was. I was only aware that if this new world was strange, it was also homely and humble; that if this was a dream, it was a dream in which one at least felt strangely vigilant; that the whole book had about it a sort of cool, morning innocence, and also, quite unmistakably, a certain quality of Death, *good* Death. What it actually did to me was to convert, even to baptize (that was where the Death came in) my imagination. It did nothing to my intellect nor (at that time) to my conscience. Their turn came far later with the help of many other books and men.'

This was the highlight among Lewis's literary discoveries at Bookham, but he continued with his explorations and was soon reporting with enthusiasm to Greeves on his first reading of *Sir Gawain and the Green Knight* and *Beowulf* (both still in translation), Chaucer, Sidney, *Tristan* (in French, so presumably the medieval 'prose' *Tristan* credited to Helie de Borron), *The Song of Roland*, the *Argonautica* of Apollonius Rhodius (in Greek) – which he compared unfavourably with *The Life and Death of Jason* – *Paradise Lost*, and *Comus* – 'an absolute dream of delight' – Shakespeare's fairy and romantic plays, and a curious work called *Letters from Hell*, written in Danish by Valdemar Adolph Thisted in 1866, and translated by Julie Sutter in 1885 with an introduction by MacDonald, which may later have given him the idea (though none of the contents) for *The Screwtape Letters*.

On the more conventionally academic side he was progressing amazingly and Kirkpatrick was writing to Albert Lewis as early as January 1915: 'He was born with the literary temperament and we have to face that fact with all it implies. This is not a case of early precocity showing itself in rapid assimilation of knowledge and followed by subsequent indifference or torpor. As I said before, it is the maturity and originality of his literary judgements which is so unusual and surprising. By an unerring instinct he detects first rate quality in literary workmanship, and the second rate does not interest him in any way.' On 28 March he added that, while still rather behind with Greek grammar, he 'has a sort of genius for translating . . . He has read more classics in the time than any boy I ever had, and that too very carefully and exactly. In Homer his achievement is unique – 13 books or more of the *Iliad* and 9 of the *Odyssey*. It will not surprise you to learn that in the Sophoclean drama, which attains a high level in poetic expression, especially in the lyric portions, he could beat me easily in the happy choice of words and phrases . . . He is the most brilliant translator of Greek plays I have ever met.'

As Lewis's time at Bookham drew towards an end much discussion passed between Kirkpatrick and Albert Lewis with regard to his future. There were suggestions that he should take up law, or join the Regular Army; but Kirkpatrick's settled opinion, with which Lewis himself was only too eager to agree, was that he should proceed to the university with the idea of an ultimate fellowship, or failing that of becoming a schoolmaster – though his own private ambition was to be a poet and romance writer.

But this was 1916, and with the war going badly for the Allies, conscription had come in. Lewis discovered that, as an Irishman, he could claim exemption. But he was determined to serve, and this at least gave him the opportunity to enlist voluntarily. If he passed into Oxford he would be able to join the Officers' Training Corps and get a commission as soon as his papers came through.

Accordingly, on 4 December 1916 he reached Oxford for the first time, to sit for a scholarship examination, and found comfortable lodgings in 'the first house on the right as you turn into Mansfield Road out of Holywell.' 'This place has surpassed my wildest dreams,' he wrote, 'I never saw anything so beautiful, especially on these frosty moonlight nights; though the Hall at Oriel, where we do the papers, is fearfully cold at about four o'clock in the afternoons. We have most of us tried with varying success to write in our gloves.'

Any fears of the result he may have had were groundless, for shortly after reaching Belfast for his Christmas holidays Lewis received a letter from Reginald W. Macan, Master of University College, informing him that 'This College elects you to a Scholarship (New College having passed you over)'; and *The Times* of 14 December listed amongst the successful candidates, besides 'Clive S. Lewis, University College', 'Alfred C. Harwood, Christ Church', and 'Arthur Owen Barfield, Wadham College', who were soon to be among his closest friends.

Although now a Scholar of Univ., Lewis was not yet officially a member of Oxford University, as he had still to pass Responsions, the entrance examination. This included elementary mathematics as a compulsory subject, and at the end of January 1917 he returned to Bookham for another term to see if Kirkpatrick could instil a sufficient amount of 'the low cunning of Algebra' into him, mathematics being a subject which he seemed continually incapable of mastering.

On the way he visited Oxford again, this time for an interview with the Master of Univ., who, he reported to his father, 'was a clean-shaven, white-haired, jolly old man, and was very nice indeed. He treated me to about half an hour's "Oxford manner" and then came gradually round to my own business. Since writing last, he has made enquiries, and it seems that if I pass Responsions in March I could "come up" in the following term and join the O.T.C.'

At Bookham, besides the hated algebra, Lewis extended his studies to German and Italian. The former he found difficult – Chamisso and Fouqué he enjoyed, but Goethe was still beyond him; Italian, on the other hand, came easily to so proficient a Latinist – 'by the end of term I should be able to read it as easily as French.'

The weekly letters to Arthur Greeves continued as before, full of what he was reading, writing and thinking. A prose romance called *Bleheris* had been on the stocks the previous term, but this was now cast aside in favour of a new idea which was to take final form ten years later as *Dymer*. This was at first also in prose, but in modern English as opposed to the archaic style devised by Morris in which his previous efforts had been couched. There was also a narrative poem, 'The Childhood of Medea', which 'will leave off where most poems about her begin – shortly after her meeting with Jason. It will describe her lonely, frightened childhood away in a castle with the terrible old king her father, and how she is gradually made to learn magic against her will.'

Greeves was also planning stories (which he seems never to have written) and was discussing the charms of actual women who were the prototypes of his heroines; but Lewis was still more interested in

> The land where I shall never be,
> The love that I shall never see,

and went on to disclaim authorship of the couplet (which was later to appear, still anonymously, on the title page of *Spirits in Bondage*): 'a beauty, isn't it, but NOT by me – I wish it were. Andrew Lang quotes it somewhere, but I have never been able to discover the author. Whoever it be, he deserves immortality for these two lines alone.' (The lines, slightly misquoted, were in fact from a poem by Lang himself, inspired by a prose passage from Baudelaire, which he quotes on p. 579 of his *History of English Literature*.)

Religion was also discussed occasionally, though only Greeves, who was a Christian, raised the subject. Lewis was still a determined atheist, and when challenged took up his stand in the anthropological field, citing 'dying gods' and 'fertility rites' from Lang's *Myth, Ritual and Religion* and Frazer's *The Golden Bough*. 'All religions, that is all mythologies, to give them their proper name, are merely man's own invention – Christ as much as Loki,' he wrote to Greeves on 12 October 1916; and he had allowed himself to be confirmed on 6 December 1914 merely to please his father and avoid endless argument. 'As to the immortality of the soul,' he continued in the letter to Greeves, 'though it is a fascinating theme for day-dreaming, I neither believe nor disbelieve: I simply don't know anything at all, there is no evidence either way' – which agnosticism he enshrined in a poem written in 1917 which ends:

> I think, if it be truth, as some have taught
> That these frail seeds of being are not caught
> And blown upon the cosmic winds in vain
> After our death, but bound in one again
> Somewhere, we know not how, they live and thrive
> Forever, and the proud gods will not give
> The comfortable doom of quiet sleep,
> Then doubt not but that from the starry deep
> And utmost spaces lit by suns unknown
> We should return again whence we were flown,
> Leaving the bauble of a sainted crown,
> To walk and talk upon the hills of Down.

II. OXFORD: THE WAR AND AFTER

Clive Lewis returned to Oxford on 20 March 1917, lodged in the same digs as before, and presented himself to take Responsions. In this exam he was 'handsomely ploughed', on account of his inability to cope satisfactorily with mathematics – in particular algebra. In spite of this, however, he was allowed to come into residence in the Trinity Term so as to be able to pass into the Army by way of the University Officers' Training Corps. From the academic point of view he was supposed to be reading for Responsions, and even went for algebra lessons to J. E. Campbell of Hertford College. But he never, in fact, passed Responsions; and after the war was able to take up his scholarship at Univ. without having done so, ex-servicemen being exempted from any need to pass it. 'Otherwise,' he commented, 'I should have had to abandon the idea of going to Oxford.'

On Thursday, 26 April, after a three-week holiday in Belfast, he arrived at University College for his brief interlude before going into the Army – and fell straightway under the spell of Oxford, writing long, lyrical descriptions to Arthur Greeves of all that he was doing and seeing and reading.

'The place is on the whole absolutely ripping,' he wrote. 'If only you saw the quad on these moonlit nights with the long shadows lying half across the level perfect grass and the tangle of towers and spires beyond in the dark!' He had rooms overlooking the Front Quad that were still filled with the furniture of some pre-war member of the college still at the front, or perhaps long dead. 'It is getting to be quite homely to me, this room, especially when I come back to it by firelight and find the kettle boiling. How I love kettles! Dinner is not in Hall now, as there are only twelve men in College, but in a small lecture room, and the dons don't turn up. For all other meals the scout brings you your cover in your rooms.'

Very soon Lewis discovered the river, going boating on most afternoons, bathing at 'Parson's Pleasure' 'without the tiresome convention of bathing things,' and generally revelling in the usual delights of a first Summer Term. Soon, too, he discovered the bookshops – many more than now, and all still independent.

And also he made the acquaintance of the College library, and 'still better is the Library of the Union Society (a club everyone belongs to) . . . an admirable library where I have passed many happy hours and hope to pass many more.'

The happy time at Univ. came to an end early in June when Lewis was suddenly drafted into a cadet battalion. He was, however, fortunate in that the battalion was quartered in Keble College, so that he was, in fact, to remain in Oxford for another three months. Directly after his move he wrote to his father, 'at first when I left my own snug quarters and my own friends at Univ. for a carpetless little cell with two beds (minus sheets or pillows) at Keble, and got into a Tommy's uniform, I will not deny that I thought myself very ill used.'

'Though the work is very hard and not very interesting, I am quite reconciled to my lot. It is doing me a lot of good,' he confided to Greeves a little later. 'I have made a number of excellent friends. My room-mate Moore (of Clifton) is quite a good fellow, tho' a little too childish and virtuous for "common nature's daily food". The advantages of being in Oxford are very great as I can get weekend leave (from 1 o'clock Saturday till 11 p.m. Sunday) and go to Univ. where I enjoy the rare luxury of sheets and a long sleep. . . .

'I am in a strangely productive mood at present and spend my few moments of spare time in scribbling verse. When my four months course in the cadet battalion is at an end, I shall, supposing I get a commission all right, have a four weeks leave before joining my regiment. During it I propose to get together all the stuff I have perpetrated and see if any kind publisher would like to take it. After that, if the fates decide to kill me at the front,

I shall enjoy a nine days immortality while friends who know nothing about poetry imagine that I must have been a genius – what usually happens in such cases. In the meantime my address is – No. 738 Cadet C. S. Lewis, "E" Company, Keble College, Oxford.'

The double life was now drawing to a close: 'This weekend, I am again spending in Univ.,' he wrote to Greeves about 10 July. 'Do you know, I am more homesick for the College than ever I was for Little Lea. I love every stone in it.'

After a brief leave in Belfast (9–11 August) Lewis was writing to his father on 27 August 1917: 'You must have been wondering what had come over me, but I hope that the crowded time I have been having since I left home will serve as some excuse. First of all came the week at Warwick, which was a nightmare . . .

'We came back on Saturday, and the following weekend I spent with Moore at the digs of his mother who, as I mentioned, is staying at Oxford. I like her immensely and thoroughly enjoyed myself. On Wednesday as you know, Warnie was up here and we had a most enjoyable afternoon and evening together, chiefly at my rooms in Univ. How I wish you could have been there too. But please God I shall be able to see you at Oxford and show you my "sacred city" in happier times.'

'The next amusement on our programme,' he wrote a fortnight later, 'is a three-day bivouac up in the Wytham hills. As it has rained all the time for two or three days, our model trenches up there will provide a very unnecessarily good imitation of Flanders mud. You know how I always disapproved of realism in art!'

This was followed by an exam, which seems to have been little more than a formality; and on 25 September 1917 Albert Lewis noted that Clive was 'gazetted to Third Battalion, Somerset Light Infantry'; and on Saturday, 29 September 1917, 'Jacks got one month's leave from this date from officer cadet corps, Oxford. Went to stay with a chum named Moore and his mother. Came home on 12th October.'

At the end of his leave, Lewis was posted to Crownhill near Plymouth, whence he wrote to Arthur Greeves during November:

'I am quite fairly comfortable here, we are in huts: but I have a room to myself with a fire in it and so am quite snug.' But suddenly the dreaded summons to the front reached him. At 5.55 p.m. on 15 November 1917 he wired desperately to his father: 'Have arrived Bristol on 48 hours leave. Report Southampton Saturday. Can you come Bristol. If so meet at Station. Reply Mrs Moore's address 56 Ravenswood Road, Redlands, Bristol. Jack.'

'No one in Great Britain getting Jack's wire would have had a moment's doubt that he was on the eve of embarkation for overseas service,' writes Warren. But Albert Lewis simply wired back: 'Don't understand telegram. Please write.' Even more desperately Clive Lewis wired back at 11.20 a.m. the following morning: 'Orders France. Reporting Southampton 4 p.m. Saturday. If coming wire immediately.'

Albert Lewis did not come, and Clive crossed to France on 17 November 1917. 'I am at present in billets in a certain rather battered town somewhere behind the line,' he wrote to his father on 13 December. At the beginning of February 1918 Lewis 'had the good luck to fall sick with what the troops called "trench fever" and the doctors P.U.O. (Pyrexia, unknown origin) and was sent for a wholly delightful three weeks to hospital at Le Tréport.'

He remained in hospital for the rest of the month, with one slight relapse early on, writing more and more nostalgic letters to Arthur Greeves about their quiet days together in Belfast and his own brief stay in Oxford.

He returned to the front on 28 February, but was out of the immediate fighting area when the Germans launched their great spring offensive on 21 March with all the additional troops withdrawn from the Eastern Front after the collapse of revolution-ridden Russia.

This, perhaps the worst crisis of the war, galvanized the War Cabinet into action at last. Lloyd George took over the direction of the War Office on 23 March and was soon transporting 30,000 men a day to France. Haig had said that he could only hold the Germans for eighteen days without the reserve: Lloyd George got them over to him within a week. Nevertheless, the Allies were not merely retreating, they were disintegrating. On 3 April Foch took over supreme command of the Allied Armies (his position was made official on 14 April) and was slowly able to halt the advance when the Germans were within forty miles of Paris. 'With our backs to the wall and believing in the justice of our cause, each must fight to the end,' cried Haig, speaking for the British forces of which he was still in supreme command, when the second German *putsch* came (9–25 April) – and the great salient stretched without breaking, and Ludendorff drew back slowly and sullenly towards ultimate defeat.

This was the brief portion of the war in which Lewis took part. From 21 March until 15 April he must have been in or near the front line. 'Until the great German attack came in the spring we had a pretty quiet time,' he recorded in *Surprised by Joy*. 'Even then they attacked not us but the Canadians on our right, merely "keeping us quiet" by pouring shells into our line about three a minute all day. . . . Through the winter, weariness and water were our chief enemies. I have gone to sleep marching and woken up again and found myself marching still. One walked in the trenches in thigh gum boots with water above the knee; one remembers the icy stream welling up inside the boot when you punctured it on concealed barbed wire. . . . I came to know and pity and reverence the ordinary man: particularly dear Sergeant Ayres, who was (I suppose) killed by the same shell that wounded me. I was a futile officer (they gave commissions too easily then), a puppet moved about by him, and he turned this ridiculous and painful relation into something beautiful, became to me almost like a father. But for the rest, the war – the frights, the cold, the smell of H.E., the horribly smashed men still moving like half-crushed beetles, the sitting or standing corpses, the landscape of sheer earth without a blade of grass, the boots worn day and night until they seemed to grow to your feet – all this shows rarely and faintly in memory. It is too cut off from the rest of my experience and often seems to have happened to someone else.'

Lewis was wounded on Mount Bernenchon during the Battle

of Arras on 15 April 1918 – by an English shell exploding where it should not have been. He was able to write a few lines to his father on 17 April, to say that he was in the 'Liverpool Merchants Mobile Hospital, Etaples – Getting on all right but can't write properly yet as my left arm is still tied up and it's hard to manage with one.' And on 14 May: 'I expect to be sent across in a few days time, of course as a stretcher case . . . In one respect I was wrong in my last account of my wounds: the one under my arm is worse than a flesh wound, as the bit of metal which went in there is now in my chest, high up under my "pigeon chest": this however is nothing to worry about as it is doing no harm. They will leave it there and I am told that I can carry it about for the rest of my life without any evil results.'

And he was safely ensconced at Endsleigh Palace Hospital, Endsleigh Gardens, London, by 25 May 1918 – and out of the war, though he did not yet know it.

'I am sitting up in bed in the middle of a red sunset to answer this evening's letter straight away,' he wrote to Greeves on 1 June. 'I am in a vastly comfortable hospital, where we are in separate rooms and have tea in the morning and big broad beds and everything the heart of man could desire; and best of all, in close communication with all the bookshops of London.'

It is at this point in C. S. Lewis's life that his biographers find themselves in difficulties. When about to describe his return to Oxford in January 1919, Lewis says in *Surprised by Joy*: 'But before I say anything of my life there I must warn the reader that one huge and complex episode will be omitted. I have no choice about this reticence. All I can or need say is that my earlier hostility to the emotions was very fully and variously avenged. But even if I were free to toll the story, I doubt if it has much to do with the subject of this book.' In a more civilized age this would be accepted as an absolute embargo on prying further into private affairs. But as so many of Lewis's most personal letters and papers have already been given or willed to public collections, we have no choice but to follow up all the available evidence as far as it will take us.

It does not, in fact, take us very far. Early 'hostility to the emotions', aggravated by his (perhaps exaggerated) revulsion against the unsavoury perversions at Malvern, made Lewis excessively wary of 'the lusts of the flesh'. While he seems to have discussed these pretty freely with Arthur Greeves, and after his conversion spoke of his early sins with understandable detestation (we may add, with perhaps some exaggeration hovering between a touch of subconscious pride at his regeneration and a very real gratitude to God for helping him to achieve it), the available material gives absolutely no concrete evidence of lapses from chastity in the stricter sense.

Undoubtedly Lewis 'fell in love' once or twice in his youth and early manhood, just as naturally as he felt carnal desire for the dancing mistress at Cherbourg – or the various other women whose physical charms, or the lack of them, he discussed with Greeves. Even during the terrible stress of his fifteen months in the Army, several of them with death imminent and probable, he apparently did not waste his pay 'on prostitutes, restaurants and tailors, as the gentiles do.' And none of the more serious love-affairs that he mentions or suggests in letters and diaries seem to have progressed very far.

The only really overwhelming 'love-affair' of his early life, and that to which he may well be referring in *Surprised by Joy*, was of a kind and took so surprising a turn that it can hardly be classified with the ordinary 'lusts of the flesh'. His affection for Mrs Moore – his infatuation, as it seemed to his friends and even to his brother who knew him more intimately than any of them – may have started with that incomprehensible passion which attractive middle-aged women seem occasionally able to inspire in susceptible youths: but it very soon turned from the desire for a mistress into the creation of a mother-substitute – in many ways a father-substitute also.

When Lewis had been ordered to the front and had telegraphed to his father to come and spend his last day in England with him, Albert Lewis had indeed 'misunderstood' the telegram and not come. It might have been a genuine misunderstanding. But in

June 1918, when he lay wounded in hospital in London, Lewis wrote several times begging him to come and see him: 'Come and see me. I am homesick, that is the long and short of it.'

'One would have thought that it would have been impossible to resist such an appeal as this,' wrote Warren Lewis. 'But my father was a very peculiar man in some respects; in none more than in an almost pathological hatred of taking any step which involved a break in the dull routine of his daily existence. Jack remained unvisited, and was deeply hurt at a neglect which he considered inexcusable. Feeling himself to have been rebuffed by his father, he turned to Mrs Moore for the affection which was apparently denied him at home.'

Lewis was moved from London towards the end of July, to a convalescent home in Ashton Court near Clifton, Bristol, which he chose as it was near Mrs Moore – and there were difficulties in the way of getting into one in Northern Ireland. He was supposed to be there for only two months, but an outbreak of infectious disease which caused the home to be isolated, and his own unexpectedly slow recovery from his wounds, kept him there until mid-October, when he was posted to Ludgershall, near Andover, Hampshire.

By this time definite news of Paddy Moore's death had come through, and Albert Lewis wrote to commiserate. Mrs Moore replied on 1 October 1918: 'I just lived my life for my son, and it is very hard to go on now . . . Of the five boys who came out to us so often at Oxford, Jack is the only one left. I feel that I can never do enough for those that are left. Jack has been so good to me. My poor son asked him to look after me if he did not come back. He possesses for a boy of his age such a wonderful power of understanding and sympathy.'

Meanwhile Lewis's first literary venture was taking shape. The embarkation leave in October 1917 had been so curtailed by illness that he was probably able to do little in the way of assembling and copying out his poems during his visit to Belfast. But as soon as he was able to do so in the hospital in London, he set to work on preparing a fair copy that could be typed and sent to a publisher – now with several recent poems to add to those written during the Bookham and Oxford periods – and continued to do so even more industriously when he got to Ashton Court.

About 12 September, Lewis wrote to Greeves from 56 Ravenswood Road, Bristol (Mrs Moore's): 'The best of news! After keeping my MS. for ages Heinemann has actually accepted it. You can imagine how pleased I am, and how eagerly I now look at all Heinemann's books and wonder what mine will be like. I'm afraid the paper will be poor as it always is now in new books. It is going to be called *Spirits in Prison* by Clive Staples and is mainly strung round the idea that I mentioned to you before – that nature is wholly diabolical and malevolent and that God, if he exists, is outside of and in opposition to the cosmic arrangements . . .'

In October he was writing from Pelham Downs Camp, Ludgershall (near Andover): 'No, you were wrong, I have not gone on my leave; I was only out for a night at Mrs Moore's . . . I have now, however, had my Board, over a month late I'm glad to say, and have been sent for further convalescence to a camp here.'

'It is terrible to think how quickly an old order changes and how impossible it is to build it up again exactly the same,' he wrote on 2 November 1918. 'I wonder will there be many changes when we meet again? Maureen [Mrs Moore's daughter] told me the other day that I was greatly changed since she first knew me, but, with the impenetrable reticence of a child, declined to say in what way. I made a journey to London to see Heinemann's [on 26 October]. C. S. Evans, the manager, was very nice to me and quite enthusiastic about the book and especially about one piece. John Galsworthy, he said, had read the MS. and wanted to put this piece ["Death in Battle", *Spirits in Bondage*, pp. 105–6] in a new Quarterly which he is bringing out for disabled soldiers and sailors called *Reveille*: of course I consented . . . So at last dreams come to pass and I have sat in the sanctum of a publisher discussing my own book.'

Spirits in Bondage (the name was changed on account of *A*

Spirit in Prison (1908) by Robert Hichens – a title too similar to that originally chosen) was delayed in publication on account of shortage of cloth for binding, and did not come out until March 1919, after the appearance of 'Death in Battle' in the February number of *Reveille* – C. S. Lewis's first publication, other than contributions to school magazines. He was in good company in the third number of *Reveille*, which included poems by Robert Bridges, Siegfried Sassoon, Robert Graves and Hilaire Belloc; his own poem appeared under the pseudonym 'Clive Hamilton' on which he had finally decided – his own Christian name and his mother's maiden name.

It received no special attention ('graceful and polished,' said *The Times*; 'the work is strongly imagined and never unhealthy, trifling or affected,' according to the *Scotsman*), and Lewis seems to have been rather unduly disappointed. He certainly almost ceased writing lyrics, but turned back none the less to his real literary love, the long narrative poem. While *Spirits in Bondage* was still in the press he was writing to Greeves (on 2 December 1918, from Officers' Command Depot, Eastbourne, to which he had been moved a couple of weeks earlier): 'I have just finished a short narrative, which is a verse version of our old friend *Dymer*, greatly reduced and altered to my new ideas. The main idea is that of development by self-destruction, both of individuals and species . . . I am also at work on a short blank verse scene (you can hardly call it a play) between Tristram and King Mark, and a poem on Ion, which is a failure so far.'

There is no further reference to either the Arthurian or the classical poem, and *Dymer* in any form seems soon to have been set aside, not to be resumed until 1922.

For great changes were coming, though they threw no shadows before. On 8 December, Lewis wrote to his father: 'As you have probably seen in the papers, we are all going to get twelve days "Christmas Leave". I use the inverted commas advisedly, as mine seems likely to be in January . . . I see that we are not to be "discharged", but "demobilized" and kept on the leash for the rest of our lives.' His fear was of being kept in 'Class Z Reserve', as he had volunteered and not been conscripted; but physical unfitness due to his wounds procured him a complete discharge. Over twenty years later the piece of shrapnel had to be removed from his chest, and a further result of his experiences at the front seems to have been a 'distressing weakness' of the bladder from which he suffered for the rest of his life.

Meanwhile Warren Lewis returned to Belfast on leave on 23 December, bitterly disappointed to find that he had once again missed seeing his brother, since their leaves would not overlap. But he was able to record in his diary for 27 December: 'A red letter day. We were sitting in the study about eleven o'clock this morning when we saw a cab coming up the avenue. It was Jack! He has been demobilized, thank God. Needless to say there were great doings. He is looking pretty fit . . . In the evening there was bubbly for dinner in honour of the event: the first time I have ever had champagne at home.'

The festivities over, Lewis was able to return to Oxford early in January to take up his life as an undergraduate where he had left after his one term in the summer of 1917.

'It was a great return and something to be very thankful for,' he wrote to his father on 27 January. 'There is of course already a great difference between this Oxford and the ghost I knew before: true, we are only twenty-eight in College, but we *do* dine in Hall again, the Junior Common Room is no longer swathed in dust sheets, and the old round of lectures, debates, games, and what not is getting under weigh. The re-awakening is a little pathetic: at our first J.C.R. Meeting we read the minutes of the last – 1914. I don't know any little thing that has made me realize the absolute suspension and waste of these years more thoroughly.'

On account of his war service, Lewis was 'deemed to have passed' Responsions and Divinity, and could have proceeded directly to Greats. But in view of his ambition of obtaining a fellowship, his tutor, A. B. Poynton, advised against doing this. Consequently Lewis embarked at once on the 'Honour Mods' course in Greek and Latin literature for the examination in March 1920, before proceeding to the 'Greats' course in which he would specialize in philosophy and ancient history for a 'finals' examination in June 1922.

Meanwhile Oxford was returning to its normal routine and Lewis was falling into it very happily. He would spend all morning working in the college library or attending lectures; he usually lunched and spent the afternoon with Mrs Moore, who had taken lodgings in Oxford, returning to college for Hall dinner, and work in his rooms, where he was able to have a fire only in the evenings owing to the coal shortage.

Among lectures which he was attending, he was particularly impressed by Cyril Bailey on Lucretius, and, as he wrote to Greeves, 'a piece of good luck – I go to lectures by Gilbert Murray twice a week on Euripides' *Bacchae*: luckily I have read it before and can therefore give him a fuller attention: it is a very weird play (you have read his translation, have you not?) and he is a real inspiration – quite as good as his best books.'

Lewis did not concern himself with games, but a leisure activity in which he early took part was the literary and debating society of the college, 'The Martlets' – one of the older and more permanent societies of its kind, and one that 'alone of College Clubs has its minutes preserved in the Bodleian.' The society was limited to twelve members, but Lewis was asked to join and become secretary, 'the reason being, of course, that my proposer, Edwards, was afraid of getting the job himself'; two years later he was elected president.

Other contemporaries who were members of the Martlets included Cyril Hartmann, Rodney Pasley and E. F. Watling (translator of Sophocles for the Penguin Classics), and they became his friends during their time at Univ. Lewis's first paper (12 March 1919) was on William Morris – the subject of almost the last he ever gave to the club, on 5 November 1937; his second was that published in *Rehabilitations* in 1939. Other subjects on which he spoke as an undergraduate included 'Narrative Poetry' and 'Spenser', and after he had become a don he returned to give papers on 'James Stephens', 'Boswell', 'The Personal Heresy in Poetics', 'Is

Literature an Art?' and finally 'The Kappa Element in Romance' (14 November 1940), which formed the basis of his essay 'On Stories', finally expanded into *An Experiment in Criticism* in 1961.

Other events of Lewis's first term included dining with the Master, reading Grace in Hall, and attending tutorials. 'As time goes on,' he wrote to his father, 'I appreciate my hours with Poynton more and more. After Smewgy and Kirk I must be rather spoiled in the way of tutors, but this man comes up to either of them.' And indeed Lewis was singularly fortunate in this particular at Oxford, Poynton being followed by E. F. Carritt for philosophy, and F. P. Wilson and George Gordon when he came to read for the English School: and a man's success at Oxford can often be made or marred by his tutors.

When term ended on 17 March 1919 Lewis stayed up working for a week, and then went to Bristol to help Mrs Moore move house, but got over to Belfast for part of the vacation. The 'entanglement' with Mrs Moore was by now causing his father considerable anxiety, and he was writing to Warren on 20 May, a month after Lewis had returned to Oxford (via Bristol again): 'I confess I do not know what to do about Jack's affair. It worries and depresses me greatly. All I know about the lady is that she is old enough to be his mother, and that she is in poor circumstances. I also know that Jacks has frequently drawn cheques in her favour running up to £10 – for what I don't know. If Jacks were not an impetuous kindhearted creature who could be cajoled by any woman who had been through the mill, I should not be so uneasy.'

However innocent Lewis's involvement with Mrs Moore might be, he felt that it would be quite impossible to explain it to his father. He had for years been led into taking the easy course and lying to him when lies seemed the only way of keeping the family peace, and now he fell back on simple deceit in an attempt to keep his father reasonably happy in his parental paradise.

But duplicity led to the inevitable result, and during the following vacation it came to an open quarrel. Albert Lewis, as his own diary shows, was in the habit of reading any letters to his son that he could lay hands on when he was out of the way – and when he incautiously revealed this during an argument over money, Lewis 'weighed in with a few home truths.'

The quarrel rankled for some months: Lewis made unnecessarily scathing remarks about his father in letters to Greeves, and Albert Lewis lamented the 'estrangement from Jacks' in his diary, blaming himself for not having visited him when wounded, but maintaining that this was unavoidable – and certainly insufficient reason for his son to declare that 'he doesn't respect me: that he doesn't trust me, though he cares for me in a way.' The clash of temperaments was too extreme for any real mutual understanding – and had been so for years. But in fact the quarrel cleared the air considerably, and within a year or so Lewis and his father seem to have been back again on much the same terms as before. The visits to Little Lea were resumed, though now much shortened, and both they and the weekly letter became less of an imposition.

Moreover, in spite of his disapproval of the association with Mrs Moore and his only half-hearted approval of the academic life, Albert Lewis not only continued his son's allowance, but when the scholarship at Univ. came to an end, he promised to finance him for three more years while he tried for various fellowships and lecturing appointments – and this in spite of his almost pathological conviction that, well-to-do though he was, he hovered continually on the edge of bankruptcy. Without his father's aid, Lewis could never have hung on at Oxford until he obtained the fellowship which allowed him to follow the one course of life which gave the opportunity for the full expression of his genius.

But this was far in the future when Lewis returned to Oxford at the end of April 1919 to occupy a new set of rooms at Univ. into which he had begun to move at the end of the previous term. He had distempered the walls 'a nice quiet greyish blue' on which his Dürer prints looked well, and procured 'one good piece of furniture, a small bookcase of dark oak. You would agree with me,' he wrote to Arthur Greeves, 'in liking the beam in the ceiling and the deep windows, and the old tree that taps against them recalling *Phantastes* and *Wuthering Heights*. When it gets into leaf I shall look out into a mass of greenery with glimpses of the old walls across and of the grass below.' In spite of his concentrated work for Mods, Lewis was able to fit in some literary work, and he continues: 'I have nearly finished the Venus poem and am full of ideas for another, which Gilbert Murray gave me the hint of in a lecture – a very curious legend about Helen, whom Simon Magus, a gnostic magician mentioned in the Acts, found living as a very earthly person in Antioch and gradually recalled to her who she was and took her up to Zeus again, reborn: on their way they had to fight "the Dynasties" or planets – the evil powers that hold the heaven, between us and something really friendly beyond. I have written some of it, but of course I get hardly any time either for reading or writing.'

Nothing remains of the poem about Helen, but Lewis may have drawn something from his recollections of it near the end of his life when he began his unfinished romance *After Ten Years* about her adventures as a worn and middle-aged woman after the fall of Troy. As for Simon Magus's 'Dynasties', they surely contributed something to the Oyeseru and the Eldila (good and bad) in *Out of the Silent Planet* and its sequels.

In spite of continuing with his ambition to become a poet, Lewis did not submit any poems to the various undergraduate periodicals and volumes of Oxford poetry of his day. Oxford after the First World War (as after the Second) produced a generation of undergraduates with unusually high artistic gifts. 'As nearly everyone here is a poet himself, they have naturally no time left for lionizing others,' he wrote to his father on 25 May 1919. 'Indeed, the current literary set is one I could not afford to live in anyway, and though many of them have kindly bought copies of [*Spirits in Bondage*], their tastes run rather to modernism, *vers libre*, and that sort of thing. I have a holy terror of coteries . . .'

Yet in spite of his professed dislike for coteries, Lewis was trying to form something of the sort at the time of this letter, with two of his Univ. friends, Cyril Hartmann and Rodney Pasley. 'I don't think anything, even an undergraduate clique, can live on denials,' he was writing to Hartmann from Little Lea on 25 July;

and later in the correspondence, 'It is no use to attack "The Swiss Family Sitwell" unless we offer something in its place – not perhaps actual work – for we are likely to do that in any case – but at least some new and definite formula. Is it possible to find some common ground, other than mere dislike of eccentricity on which to meet? . . . I agree that we should not form ourselves into a definite society. Above all we must not take ourselves too seriously . . . Could people not circulate their things in manuscript and then face an informal meeting in which the others would discuss the victim, who of course could defend himself?'

The correspondence continued at some length throughout the Long Vacation of 1919, but little came of it, though Lewis's involvement in the movement is of interest as showing his early reaction against 'modernism' in literature which he never fully overcame, and that his thoughts were already turning towards the formation of the kind of unofficial literary group which found fruition years later in 'The Inklings'.

And indeed Lewis very soon lost contact with the literary movements of the younger members of the university. He was able to give little time to poetry or social activities until the summer of 1920, since he was reading hard for Honour Mods during the three previous terms – and he was able to report to his father on 4 April that 'I did get a First after all', which served as sugar to the black draught of an imaginary 'walking tour in Somerset with a college friend' which would keep him from visiting Little Lea that vacation.

During the summer of 1920 Mrs Moore and her daughter Maureen moved permanently to Oxford, renting a small house in Headington towards which Lewis helped. He continued to live in college during term until the following June, when, after the custom of normal undergraduates, he moved out into lodgings – but in his case it was into what was largely his own rented house, shared with the Moores. Lewis described his 'usual life' to Greeves after the move: 'I walk and ride out into the country, sometimes with the family, sometimes alone. I work; I wash up and water the peas and beans in our little garden; I try to write; I meet my friends and go to lectures. In other words I combine the life of an Oxford undergraduate with that of a country householder – a feat which I imagine is seldom performed. Such energies as I have left for general reading go almost entirely on poetry – and little enough of that.'

'What had actually happened,' writes Warren Lewis, 'was that Jack had set up a joint establishment with Mrs Moore, an arrangement which bound him to her service for the next thirty years and ended only with her death in January 1951. How the arrangement came into being no one will ever know, for it was perhaps the only subject which Jack never mentioned to me; more than never mentioned, for on the only occasion when I hinted at my curiosity he silenced me with an abruptness which was sufficient warning never to re-open the topic.'

There were many drawbacks to this curious state of bondage to which Lewis had voluntarily submitted himself. To begin with, it made him miserably poor at a time when his academic and creative life seemed to demand complete freedom from financial worries. He had an adequate allowance for a bachelor undergraduate living in college or lodgings, but not for a householder with a 'mother' and adopted sister largely dependent on him. And he could not, of course, ask his father to increase his allowance as the whole 'set-up' with the Moores was kept a secret from him.

Mrs Moore seems to have been highly possessive and selfish – or thoughtless – to an astonishing degree. Lewis was expected to help with the housework and run errands for her, even when they were able to employ two resident maids, a daily and a handyman-gardener. 'I came to live with him after my retirement from the Army in 1932,' writes Warren Lewis, 'and in the vacation we shared a workroom. I do not think I ever saw Jack at his desk for more than half an hour without Mrs Moore calling for him. "Coming!" Jack would roar, down would go his pen, and he would be away perhaps five minutes, perhaps half an hour; and then return and calmly resume work on a half-finished sentence.'

The most immediate result of Lewis's double life when he

moved out of college was to prevent him from following up the lead given by even the relative success of *Spirits in Bondage* and his first tentative steps towards taking his place among the new, young poets of the twenties, or of entering into any kind of literary life outside the ordinary university round. A proposed anthology did not appear, and there were no more letters to Hartmann and Pasley about founding their own poetic movement. With his great mental ability and his developing powers of concentration, Lewis was just able to take a Double First in Literae Humaniores – Mods – in March 1920 and Greats in June 1922. He also competed for the Chancellor's English Essay Prize, the subject set being 'Optimism', and won it triumphantly on 24 May 1921.

Another interesting experience about this time was two meetings with W. B. Yeats, then living in Oxford, which he described fully to his brother in March 1921 (see *Letters*, pp. 56–8). Yeats seems to have made a considerable impression on Lewis, who modelled the physical appearance of his magician in *Dymer* (vi. 6–9) on him: 'If he were now alive I would ask his pardon with shame for having repaid his hospitality with such freedom,' he wrote in the preface to the new edition of 1950. 'It was not done in malice, and the likeness is not, I think, in itself, uncomplimentary.' And something of this grander Yeats may have helped to create Merlin in *That Hideous Strength*.

The visits to Yeats were among the more interesting highlights of the Oxford side of Lewis's double existence during the years before he graduated from the Junior to the Senior Common Room. It would be possible to follow him in considerable detail through these years with the aid of copious letters to his brother, the regular reports to his father, and from April 1922 a reasonably full diary which he continued, with occasional lapses, until March 1927 – but both letters and diaries are well represented, with long extracts, in the already published *Letters of C. S. Lewis*, edited by Warren Lewis in 1966. The diary, though of great interest from the more external point of view, tells little or nothing of Lewis's spiritual adventures: it was, indeed, almost a public document and was read out loud from time to time to Mrs Moore and her daughter, or handed over to Warren to peruse when on leave.

Already in 1921 Lewis had made up his mind that an academic career was what he most hankered after – and if possible an academic career in Oxford. But it seemed an almost impossible ambition.

However, on 18 May 1922 ideas for the future were taking more definite shape, and he was writing to his father that one of his tutors, to whom he went for a testimonial, 'instead of giving me one advised me very earnestly not to take any job in a hurry; he said that if there was nothing for me in Oxford immediately after Greats, he was sure there would be something later; that the college would almost certainly continue my scholarship for another year if I chose to stay up and take another school, and that "if I could possibly afford it" this was the course which he would like me to take.' And another tutor pointed out that 'the actual subjects of my own Greats school are a doubtful quantity at the moment: for no one quite knows what place Classics and Philosophy will hold in the educational world in a year's time. On the other hand, the prestige of the Greats school is still enormous: so that what is wanted everywhere is a man who combined the general qualification which Greats is supposed to give, with the special qualifications of any other subjects. And English Literature is a "rising" subject. Thus if I could take a First, or even a Second, in Greats, *and* a First next year in English Literature, I should be in a very strong position indeed . . . In such a course I should start knowing more of the subject than some do at the end: it should be a very easy proposition compared with Greats.'

Lewis went on to point out to his father that he could pretty certainly get a job at once as a schoolmaster, though his inability to play games might count against him – but that 'the point on which I naturally like to lean is that the pundits at Univ. apparently don't want me to leave Oxford.' To this Albert Lewis responded generously, and in the end continued his son's allowance until he obtained his fellowship at Magdalen in September 1925.

Meanwhile Lewis was awarded a First in Greats, which was announced on 4 August 1922, the day before he took his B.A. in company with E. F. Watling, L. R. Farnell, the Vice-Chancellor and Rector of Exeter College (author of *Cults of the Greek States*), performing the ceremony.

A typical extract from Lewis's diary may serve to round off the picture of that Summer Term of 1922: 'Wednesday, 24th [of May]. Very hot again. Worked on Greek History memorizing in the alleyway. D. [Mrs Moore] worried by shooting pains in her right arm. I left home at about 12.45 and bussed into Oxford, meeting Barfield outside the "Old Oak" . . . From here we walked to Wadham gardens and sat under the trees. We began with Christina Dreams: I condemned them – the love dream made a man incapable of real love, the hero dream made him a coward. He took the opposite view, and a stubborn argument followed. ["In those days the new psychology was just beginning to make itself felt in the circles I most frequented at Oxford," he wrote in the preface to the 1950 edition of *Dymer*. "This joined forces with the fact that we felt ourselves (as young men always do) to be escaping from the illusions of adolescence, and as a result we were much exercised about the problem of fantasy or wishful thinking. The 'Christina Dream', as we called it, after Christina Pontifex in Butler's novel [*The Way of All Flesh*, 1903], was the hidden enemy whom we were all determined to unmask and defeat."] We then turned to *Dymer* which he had brought back: to my surprise his verdict was even more favourable than Baker's. He said it was "by streets" the best thing I had done, and "could I keep it up?" . . . He said Harwood had "danced with joy" over it and had advised me to drop everything else and go on with it. From such a severe critic as Barfield the result was very encouraging . . . The conversation ranged over many topics and finally died because it was impossible to hold a court between two devil's advocates. The gardens were ripping – lilac and chestnut magnificent. I find Wadham gardens fit my image of Acrasia's island very well [the witch-maiden in Spenser's "Bower of Bliss" in *The Faerie Queene*]. I walked with him as far as Magdalen, took a turn in the cloisters, and then came home for tea. Went in again to Carritt at 5.45 and read him my paper. Interesting discussion: he was on his usual line of right unrelated to good, which is unanswerable: but so is the other side . . .'

We may note here that Lewis had begun seriously on *Dymer* on 2 April and finished Canto I, more or less as published, by 11 May. (See Note 1, p. 176, in *Narrative Poems*, edited by Walter Hooper (1969), for full table of dates.) The references to Christina Dreams and Acrasia's 'Bower of Bliss' in the diary tie up with the poem, as Lewis recorded in the preface to the 1950 reprint of *Dymer*. Here he points out how strong had been his 'romantic longing' for the 'Hesperian or Western Garden system' of imagery, and how 'by the time I wrote *Dymer* I had come under the influence of our common obsession about Christina Dreams, into a state of angry revolt against that spell . . . In all this, as I now believe, I was mistaken. Instead of repenting my idolatry I spat upon the images which only my own misunderstanding greed had ever made into idols.' Nevertheless, in 1945 he was warning Green against the subtler dangers of the Christina Dream as revealed in an early version of his fantasy story, *The Wood that Time Forgot*: 'Now for a matter which I would not mention if it were not that you and I (obviously) can converse with the freedom of patients in the same hospital. None of these faults is purely *literary*. The talent is certain: but you have a sickness in the soul. You are much too much *in* that enchanted wood yourself – and perhaps with no very powerful talisman round your neck. You are in love with your heroine – which is author's incest and always spoils a book. I know all about it because I've been in the wood too. It took me years to get out of it: and only after I'd done so did re-enchantment begin. If you try to stay there the wood will die on you – and so will you!'

Of the companions mentioned in the diary extracts, Lewis wrote in *Surprised by Joy*: 'The first lifelong friend I made at Oxford was A. K. Hamilton Jenkin, since known for his books on Cornwall. . . . My next was Owen Barfield. There is a sense in which Arthur and Barfield are the types of every man's First

Friend and Second Friend. The First is the *alter ego*, the man who first reveals to you that you are not alone in the world by turning out (beyond hope) to share all your most secret delights. . . . But the Second Friend is the man who disagrees with you about everything. He is not so much the *alter ego* as the anti-self. Of course he shares your interests; otherwise he would not become your friend at all. But he has approached them all at a different angle. . . . Closely linked with Barfield of Wadham was his friend (and soon mine) A. C. Harwood of The House, later a pillar of Michael Hall, the Steinerite school at Kidbrooke. He was different from either of us; a wholly imperturbable man.'

On the day before sitting for Greats, Lewis went for a long walk up Hinksey Hill, 'sat down in the patch of wood – all ferns and pines and the very driest sand and the landscape towards Wytham of an almost polished brightness. Got a whiff of the real Joy, but only momentary.' Schools over, he tried for a lectureship in Classics at Reading under E. R. Dodds, later Regius Professor of Greek at Oxford, but without success.

In August Lewis and the Moore establishment moved again, this time to Hillsboro, Western Road, Headington, and in mid-September he spent ten days with his father at Little Lea. Warren was also there, and the atmosphere seemed less strained. Arthur Greeves was at home, but Lewis noted that although they saw each other frequently, 'we found practically nothing to say to each other,' for, though he may not have realized it in set terms, Lewis's mind had outgrown Greeves's, and he needed the more stimulating friendship of men such as Jenkin and Barfield and Harwood, and others whom he was soon to meet, notably Coghill and Dyson and Tolkien.

Back in Oxford he was trying for a classical fellowship at Magdalen, having an interview with the President, Sir Herbert Warren, and sitting for the examination during the last week of September – but without success. Accordingly on 13 October 1922 he began his more formal work for the English School by visiting his new tutor, F. P. Wilson (1889–1963; later to be Merton Professor of English Literature, 1947–57), at that time attached to

Exeter College. 'Wilson was not there but I found him at his house in Manor Place. He tells me I shall have my work cut out to manage the work in time' (the English course normally took over two years, following Mods or Pass Mods). Next day he went to St Hugh's College in search of his language tutor, Miss E. E. Wardale, author of *An Old English Grammar* (1922); and soon Lewis was revelling in Old English under her skilled supervision: 'It is very curious that to read the words of King Alfred gives more sense of antiquity than to read those of Sophocles. Also, to be thus realizing a dream of learning Anglo-Saxon which dates from Bookham days.'

Now that he had to write essays on English literature, with the finest examples in the language daily before him, Lewis began to think about his own literary performance: 'My prose style is really abominable, and between poetry and work I suppose I shall never learn to improve it,' he confided sadly to his diary . . . In later life he was to achieve one of the finest and most lucid prose styles of any writer of his period.

The reading of medieval English literature caused Lewis to have a fresh look at and a deeper consideration of Christianity, and even the first reading of *Troilus and Criseyde* set him arguing on the subject with Jenkin. 'We talked of Troilus [on a walk on 18 October 1922] and this led us to the question of Chivalry. I thought the mere ideal, however unrealized, had been a great advance. He thought the whole thing had been pretty worthless. The various points which I advanced as good results of the Knightly standard he attributed to Christianity. After this Christianity became the main subject.'

There were many such rambles and talks with Jenkin at this time: on a beautiful November day, 'above the forest ground called Thessaly', he got 'the real Joy' again, between a discussion of *The Wanderer* and *The Seafarer*, and 'Jenkin's undisguised delight in the more elementary pleasure of a ramble.' On other such outings they were deciding that of Housman's *Last Poems* 'some are exquisite – some mere sentimental jingle', or that Saintsbury's *History of English Literature* was 'a very poor book:

his articles on Chaucer and Keats seem designed to prevent anyone reading them.'

The difficulty of finding enough time for reading, with so much whittled away by the exactions of Mrs Moore, led Lewis to develop the habit of reading as he walked. 'I find that one really sees more of the country with a book than without,' he decided, 'for you are always forced to look up every now and then and the scene into which you have blundered without knowing it comes upon you like something in a dream.'

After Christmas 1922 with his father at Little Lea, Lewis was back in Oxford revelling in lectures by Strickland Gibson on bibliography and C. T. Onions (soon to be a much revered friend at Magdalen) on Middle English, and enjoying his Anglo-Saxon studies which he found were much more extensive than he had expected. He was also reading Donne for the first time and finding 'The Second Anniversary' ' "a new planet": I never imagined or hoped for anything like it,' but 'The Soul's Progress' he dismissed as 'mostly bosh and won't scan.'

Meanwhile he had begun to attend the English classes organized by George Gordon who had just become Merton Professor of English Literature in succession to Walter A. Raleigh, a post which he held until 1928 when he became President of Magdalen and was succeeded by David Nichol Smith. The first meeting, on 26 January, did not impress him very much – 'Gordon was sensible rather than brilliant' – but the next, held on 2 February, brought Lewis a new friend: 'We were a much smaller gathering. This afternoon a good-looking fellow called Coghill from Exeter read a very good paper on "realism" – as defined in his own special sense – from *Goboduc* to *Lear*. He seems an enthusiastic, sensible man, without nonsense, and a gentleman, much more attractive than the majority. The discussion afterwards was better than last week's.'

The friendship with Coghill ripened fast, and they were soon going for long walks together, eagerly discussing both literature and life. On the first walk, by the Hinkseys and Thessaly, on 11 February, Lewis 'found to my relief that he still has an open mind on ultimate questions: he spoke contemptuously of the cheap happiness obtainable by people who shut themselves up in a system of belief' – but, as he recorded in *Surprised by Joy*, 'I soon had the shock of discovering that he – clearly the most intelligent and best-informed man in that class – was a Christian and a thoroughgoing supernaturalist.'

'We used to foregather in our rooms,' wrote Professor Coghill in 1965, 'or go off for country walks together in endless but excited talk about what we had been reading the week before – for Wilson [whom they both had as tutor] kept us pretty well in step with each other – and what we thought about it. So we would stride over Hinksey and Cumnor – we walked almost as fast as we talked – disputing and quoting, as we looked for the dark dingles and the tree-topped hills of Matthew Arnold. This kind of walk must be among the commonest, perhaps among the best, of undergraduates' experience. Lewis, with the gusto of a Chesterton or a Belloc, would suddenly roar out a passage of poetry that he had newly discovered and memorized, particularly if it were in Old English, a language novel and enchanting to us both for its heroic attitudes and crashing rhythms . . . his big voice boomed it out with all the pleasure of tasting a noble wine . . . His tastes were essentially for what had magnitude and a suggestion of myth: the heroic and romantic never failed to excite his imagination, and although at that time he was something of a professed atheist, the mystically supernatural things in ancient epic and saga always attracted him . . . We had, of course, thunderous disagreements and agreements, and none more thunderous or agreeing than over *Samson Agonistes*, which neither of us had read before and which we reached, both together, in the same week; we found we had chosen the same passages as our favourites, and for the same reasons – the epic scale of their emotions and their over-mastering rhythmical patterns . . . Yet when I tried to share with him my discovery of Restoration comedy he would have none of it. . . .'

The brief, concentrated English course drew to an end in June 1923. On 1 June Lewis attended Gordon's last class held in Nevill Coghill's rooms at Exeter, when they discussed tragedy:

'There was some good discussion. Later we drifted to talking of Masefield and then to War reminiscences. Coghill then produced some port to celebrate our last meeting, and we drank Gordon's health. I for one drank with great sincerity, for he is an honest, wise, kind man, more like a man and less like a don than any I have known. My opinion of him was rather low at first and has gone up steadily ever since.'

The actual examination took place from 14–19 June. 'The English School is come and gone,' Lewis wrote to his father on 1 July, 'though I still have my viva to face. I was of course rather hampered by the shortened time in which I took the School and it is in many ways so different from the other exams that I have done that I should be sorry to prophesy.'

The viva took place on 10 July, the external examiners being W. A. Craigie, the Icelandic scholar, and H. F. B. Brett-Smith, the editor of Peacock. 'Most of the vivas were long and discouraging,' wrote Lewis in his diary. 'My own lasted about two minutes. I came away much encouraged, and delighted to escape the language people.'

The results appeared on 16 July, Nevill Coghill and C. S. Lewis being among the six to obtain 'First Class Honours in the Honour School of English Language and Literature.'

III. THE YOUNG DON

It might be thought that C. S. Lewis, with a Double First in Classics and a First in English, to say nothing of the Chancellor's Prize and a published volume of verse, would have found a fellowship waiting for him in the autumn of 1923. But the post-war 'bulge' was at its worst, no college seemed to appreciate his outstanding merits as a tutor and lecturer – they were, of course, still represented only by his examination results – and he still had two years of struggle and anxiety before him.

F. P. Wilson suggested a post-graduate degree, B.Litt. or D.Phil., and Lewis was tempted by the idea. Just after the results of his finals came out, in mid-July 1923, he went to tea with Wilson. 'He asked me if I had a book in my head. I said at first "No – unless you mean an epic poem", but afterwards trotted out various schemes which have been more or less in my mind. He thought my idea of a study of the Romantic Epic from its beginnings down to Spenser, with a side glance at Ovid, a good one: but too long for a research degree . . .'

It seems that anxiety over the future and the need to earn money to keep his establishment at Headington going prevented Lewis from following up Wilson's suggestion. The book finally materialized as *The Allegory of Love* (1936), but no real start could be made on it until some time after he had achieved his fellowship at Magdalen. 'Domestic drudgery is excellent as an alternative to idleness or to hateful thoughts,' he wrote in his diary the following March, '– which is perhaps poor D.'s reason for piling it on at this time: as an alternative to work one is longing to do and able to do (*at this time* and Heaven knows when again) it is maddening. No one's fault: the curse of Adam . . . I managed to get in a good deal of writing in the intervals of jobbing in the kitchen and doing messages in Headington,' he added. 'I wrote the whole of the last canto [of *Dymer*] with considerable success, though the ending will not do. I also kept my temper nearly all the time.'

'Family life' produced even more trying distractions than the constant chores and the frequent removals from house to house. An experience which he mentions in *Surprised by Joy* and which had an effect on his spiritual development took place the term before he sat for his finals in English, and he wrote to Arthur Greeves in April 1923 describing it and his reactions to it: 'We have been through very deep waters. Mrs Moore's brother – "the Doc." – came here and had a sudden attack of war neurasthenia. He was here for nearly three weeks, and endured awful mental tortures. Anyone who didn't know would have mistaken it for lunacy.' After 'three weeks of Hell the Doc. was admitted to a pensions hospital at Richmond. [There] quite suddenly heart failure set in and he died – unconscious at the end, thank God . . . Isn't it a damned world – and we once thought we could be happy with books and music!'

Worry about the future was fairly intense in that autumn of 1923 when there was still no sign of a fellowship. 'D. and I had a conversation on the various troubles that have pursued us,' he wrote in his diary on 8 September: 'losses for the past, fears for the future, and for the present, all the humiliations, the hardships, and the waste of time that come from poverty. Poor D. feels keenly (what is always on my mind) how the creative years are slipping past me without a chance to get to my real work.' And out walking a couple of weeks later while suffering from depression and ill-health, 'I went through Mesopotamia and then to Marston where I had some beer and a packet of cigarettes – an extravagance of which I have not been guilty this many a day.'

After correcting Higher School Certificate examination papers to earn a little money, Lewis went off to Ireland at the end of September to visit his father. With great generosity and foresight Albert Lewis promised to continue his allowance. 'While Jacks was at home,' he wrote in his diary on 11 October, 'I repeated my promise to provide for him at Oxford if I possibly could, for a maximum of three years from this summer. I again pointed out to him the difficulties of getting anything to do at 28 if he had ultimately to leave Oxford.'

Back again at Univ. the following term, the new Master, Sir Michael Sadler, was offering to get Lewis some reviewing in London periodicals. He gave him a copy of the recently published *Wordsworth* by H. W. Garrod, the Professor of Poetry, and asked him for a specimen review. Lewis supplied this, but there is no evidence that it or any other reviews were published at this time.

Towards the end of November he had his first pupil, a young man of eighteen called Sandeman who was trying to win a scholarship to Oxford, whom Lewis was to coach 'in essay writing and English for the essay paper and general papers which these exams always include.'

The only other events for the rest of the year were visits to Harwood in London and Barfield in the country, and three weeks at Little Lea: 'My three weeks in Ireland, though improved by Warnie's presence, were as usual three weeks too long.'

On returning to Oxford, Lewis was trying for a fellowship at St John's, apparently in Philosophy since he submitted an essay on 'The Promethean Fallacy in Ethics' together with testimonials from Carritt and Wilson. Nothing came of this, and Nevill Coghill got the English fellowship at Exeter College in February. Lewis, still thinking that his future lay in philosophy, considered trying for a research fellowship at All Souls, and entering for a D.Phil. degree.

On 29 February he dined at High Table in Univ. as Carritt's guest, and his host told him of a fellowship in Philosophy that was to be awarded at Trinity, worth £500 a year, and advised him to try for it. Walking home late that night, Lewis recorded in his diary, 'looking at the details of the Trinity fellowship as I passed the lamps – for some reason the possibility of getting it and all that would follow if I did came before my mind with unusual vividness. I saw it would involve living in and what a break up of our present life that would mean, and also how the extra money would lift terrible loads off us all. I saw that it would mean pretty full work and that I might become submerged and poetry crushed out. With deep conviction I suddenly had an image of myself, God knows when or where, in the future looking back on these years since the War as the happiest or the only really valuable part of my life, in spite of all their disappointments and fears. Yet the longing for an income that would free us from anxiety was stronger than all these feelings. I was in a strange state of excitement – and all on the mere hundredth chance of getting it.'

So the first few months of 1924 dragged along through disappointments and much enjoyment of his leisure when writing and revising *Dymer*, which was nearing completion. In April Lewis had a poem, 'Joy', accepted by the *Beacon* – an attempt to capture in verse the experiences which he was again having from time to time: the first stanza (of six) deals most nearly with the moment of spiritual ecstasy:

> Today was all unlike another day.
> The long waves of my sleep near morning broke
> On happier beaches, tumbling lighted spray
> Of soft dreams filled with promise. As I woke,
> Like a huge bird, Joy with the feathery stroke
> Of strange wings brushed me over. Sweeter air
> Came never from dawn's heart. The misty smoke
> Cooled it upon the hills. It touched the lair
> Of each wild thing and woke the wet flowers everywhere.

Lewis was still hoping for the Trinity fellowship when he dined at High Table with the President on 4 May, and met many of the other Fellows there and in the Senior Common Room – doubtless that they might consider his suitability if there was any chance of his election.

Next day, however, Sir Michael Sadler offered him a temporary post at Univ. – to take over Carritt's work as Philosophy tutor during the coming academic year which Carritt was to spend in America. After being assured that the appointment would not stand in his way if he got the Trinity fellowship, and that the emolument would be at least £200, Lewis accepted gratefully.

Much of his time was now taken up preparing for this his first serious assault upon his chosen profession. But he found time for evenings of discussion with Coghill and other friends; for a week in London with Harwood when he paid his first visit to the Elgin Marbles – 'what impressed me most was the Artemis among the reliefs of the other gods – the only one I have ever seen that is virginal – but *not* in the way that appeals to a man's base love of virginity – and without being girlish and insignificant' – and saw Leo Baker playing First Lord in a very bad production of *As You Like It* by the Old Vic Company.

He also spent several weekends and odd days with Warren, who was now stationed near Colchester, and went on expeditions with him on his motor cycle. On a typical visit (8 July 1924) Lewis records that after a drink in the Mess 'we then motored back to town [Colchester] to a civilian club of which Warnie is a member, where he had provided a royal feast of the sort we both like: no nonsense about soup and pudding, but a sole each, cutlets with green peas, a *large* portion of strawberries and cream, and a tankard of the local beer which is very good. So we gorged like Roman Emperors in a room to ourselves and had good talk.'

In this way they explored a good deal of the country within reach of Oxford and later much of Wiltshire and the counties north of London. An expedition in July 1924 took them in search of Wynyard, at Warnie's suggestion. 'I assented eagerly,' wrote Lewis in his diary that day. 'I love to exult in my happiness at being for ever safe from at least one of the major ills of life – that of being a boy at school.'

Lewis was correcting local examination papers throughout July, and at the beginning of August press of work on these and on his lectures in philosophy for the coming term caused a break in his diary which finally widened to six months.

Lewis gave his first lecture on 14 October 1924 – to an audience of four, owing to a mistake in the lecture list and an important lecture by someone else at the same hour. However, he was able to report to his father that it 'went off all right . . . Otherwise everything goes well. All my new colleagues are kindness itself and everyone does his best to make me feel at home – especially dear old Poynton. I find the actual tutoring easy at the time (though I am curiously tired at the end of the day) and have already struck some quite good men among my pupils.'

One of these first pupils, H. D. Ziman, recorded 40 years later that he found him 'the most stimulating of my tutors.'

By February 1925 Lewis was well settled into his new duties, giving an average of four tutorials a day – three in the morning and one between tea and dinner – and lecturing twice a week, though sometimes the audience was so small that he took them to his college rooms for an informal discussion instead.

Though living at Headington, he often reached college in time for breakfast, returned home in the afternoon but was back for tutorial and Hall dinner, with often a meeting of a literary or philosophic society thereafter. He was most conscientious about attending such meetings, and seems to have got much enjoyment from them. For example, on 12 February after Hall, 'I went to Ware's rooms in Worcester Street for a meeting of the Philosophical Society. Ziman read his paper on causality. I, having heard it all from him in the morning, was rather bored. The discussion afterwards drifted off on to Touche's and Dawson's favourite position and I had an enjoyable argument. Home late.'

At this time Lewis lunched on most days of the week with F. H. Lawson, the law tutor at Univ. who later that year became a Fellow of Merton and in 1948 was elected Professor of Comparative Law at Brasenose; and D. L. Keir, the historian, whom he found a more entertaining companion than the erudite lawyer: 'The usual brisk but not really interesting conversation,' Lewis confided to his diary after one of these meals.

But he had very few other entertainments. To go to the theatre was a rare event indeed – and then also perhaps from a sense of duty, as for example the visit to the O.U.D.S. production of *Peer Gynt* on 10 February 1925 of which he records 'I was very disappointed in the play. The general idea of a history of the soul is all right, but Peer's soul hasn't enough in it to last for four hours: most of him is mere Nordic windbagism. No good making a story of Peer: you only want to kick his bottom and get on. The

Troll parts from the visual point of view were the best stage devilment I've ever seen.'

He and Warren had spent three weeks over Christmas in Belfast, and on their return toured on the motor cycle via Shrewsbury and Ludlow – 'an orgy of woods, hills, broad rivers, grey castles, Norman abbeys and towns that have always been asleep.' But almost as soon as he got back to Oxford he went down with 'flu: 'I am very much afraid my organism is acquiring the *habit* of getting this troublesome complaint every time it becomes prevalent,' he wrote to his father.

Diary writing lapsed again from March till August, most of the time being taken up between his tutorial duties and domestic life at Headington. He had a few days away on the motor cycle with Warren, visiting Salisbury, Wells and Stonehenge.

'This is my last term "in bond" at Univ.,' he wrote to his father after returning to Oxford, 'and there is still no word of the Fellowship. I begin to be afraid that it is not coming at all. A Fellowship in English is announced at Magdalen and of course I am applying for it, but without any serious hopes as I believe much senior people are in for it.'

The chances of getting the Magdalen fellowship seemed remote at first. Soon, however, he found himself left with only one serious rival, J. N. Bryson (later a Fellow of Balliol and a leading authority on the Pre-Raphaelites); but a satisfactory dinner to be 'looked-over' by the other Magdalen Fellows and several interviews with Sir Herbert Warren, the President, tipped the scales in his favour – doubtless aided by the good offices of Gordon; and on 20 May 1925 he was elected.

'The President and Fellows of Magdalen College have elected to an official Fellowship in the College as Tutor in English Language and Literature, for five years as from next June 25, Mr Clive Staples Lewis, M.A. (University College)', ran the gratifying announcement in *The Times* of 22 May, and the long prologue was over.[1]

[1] 'For five years' was a mere matter of form. Re-election was almost certain, provided the Fellow fulfilled his duties satisfactorily.

Lewis was not altogether sorry to leave Univ., feeling – rightly or wrongly – that the college might have done more to keep him, had it wanted him. But he kept up his connections with friends there, was later made an Hon. Fellow, and near the end of his life (though he may never have known) there was a suggestion, if not a firm proposal, that he should be elected Master. He also gave up philosophy for English with few regrets, feeling already that the former led nowhere: 'I have come to think that if I had the mind, I have not the brain and nerves for a life of pure philosophy,' he told his father. 'A continued search among the abstract roots of things, a perpetual questioning of all the things that plain men take for granted, a chewing the cud for fifty years over inevitable ignorance and a constant frontier watch on the little tidy lighted conventional world of science and daily life – is this the best life for temperaments such as ours? Is it the way of health or even of sanity?' But the philosophical training was not wasted. Its methods gave weight to his later theological writings, and it is particularly apparent in such a work as *The Abolition of Man*. And he was always ready to 'fill in' with a philosophy tutorial or lecture if required.

Lewis's first reaction on gaining the fellowship was to write to his father a moving letter of gratitude for the faith and the financial support which had made it possible for him to hold on at Oxford until he achieved his goal, while others less fortunate or less persevering had been forced to drop out of the lists. He then went on, with a gaiety that showed better than protestations his relief and happiness, to describe the 'admission' ceremony at Magdalen: 'English people have not the talent for graceful ceremonial. They go through it lumpishly and with a certain mixture of defiance and embarrassment as if everyone felt he was being rather silly and was at the same time ready to shoot the first man who said so. In a French or Italian University now, this might have gone off nobly.'

Lewis seems to have had a deep craving for ritual and pageantry all his life, a craving which finds expression in most of his works of fiction, notably the cosmic celebrations near the end of both

Perelandra and *That Hideous Strength*. But he fought shy of it, felt 'lumpish and embarrassed' when he came across it in actual experience – from university ceremonies to ritual in religious services – and avoided it whenever possible.

Before setting to work on the necessary preparation for his first term at Magdalen, Lewis spent a few days with the Barfields in London (as soon as he had finished the exam correcting for which he had already signed on) and then went with Mrs Moore and Maureen for three weeks' holiday at Oare on the borders of Exmoor. There he spent many days walking, usually alone, in the Doone country, reading for enjoyment, and only towards the end turning to works that he might be teaching the following term.

Apparently Lewis paid a visit to Belfast during this same Long Vacation when he discussed the furnishing of his rooms in Magdalen, for he was writing to his father on 21 October in dismay over the quantity of furniture he was expected to supply – far more than they had planned on transporting from Ireland. 'At one time I thought I should have to take pupils in my bedroom as the bed was the only thing to sit down on,' he remarked ruefully. But 'my external surroundings are beautiful beyond expectation and beyond hope. To live in the Bishop's Palace at Wells would be good but could hardly be better than this. My big sitting-room looks north and from it I see nothing, not even a gable or spire, to remind me that I am in a town. I look down on a stretch of grass which passes into a grove of immemorial forest trees, at present coloured with autumn red. Over this stray the deer. They are erratic in their habits. Some mornings when I look out there may be half a dozen chewing the cud just beneath me, and on others there will be none in sight – the one little stag (not much bigger than a calf and looking too slender for the weight of his own antlers) standing still and sending through the fog that queer little bark or hoot which is these beasts' "moo". It is a sound that will soon be as familiar to me as the cough of the cows in the field at home, for I hear it day and night. On my right hand as I look from these windows is "his favourite walk" [Addison's Walk, round Magdalen Meadow]. My smaller sitting-room and bedroom look out southward and across a broad lawn to the main buildings of Magdalen with the tower beyond it.'

Lewis occupied these rooms (New Buildings 3.4) for almost thirty years, and in some way he seems to be more closely associated with them than either with his subsequent rooms in Magdalene, Cambridge, or even with the Kilns, his home in Headington Quarry from 1930 until his death in 1963. To the New Buildings at Magdalen (it was built about 1740, which is 'new' in Oxford when one thinks of Chaucer reading in Merton library) came most of those who sought C. S. Lewis, from pupils and celebrity-hunters to the greatest writers and scholars of his age. There most of his famous books were written, from *The Allegory of Love* to *The Last Battle*; and there for a little while – a moment in Oxford's history – a group gathered to read and discuss their works, as similar groups had met and will meet again. A century earlier it was William Morris, Burne-Jones, R. W. Dixon and their friends in Cormell Price's rooms at B.N.C.; this time (in 1942) Tolkien was reading the half-written *Lord of the Rings*, Charles Williams *All Hallows' Eve*, and C. S. Lewis *Perelandra* . . .

But all this was still far in the utterly unexpected future when the new English don moved in early in October 1925 to meet his first pupils and begin preparing his first lectures.

The concentration on work at Magdalen took up most of his time and prevented diary writing until the following summer, and much in the way of letter writing too. The long screeds to Arthur Greeves had already grown fewer and become less intimate, and although Lewis continued to write to his earliest friend, we learn relatively little of his more personal feelings and experiences from them.

But indeed there was little to record of Lewis's first years at Magdalen. He worked hard and conscientiously at his profession, and his experiences in so doing differed only in detail from those of any other don. He did not suddenly become the best lecturer and (for the right pupil) the best tutor in the English School at Oxford: it was ten or fifteen years before such a description could be considered seriously.

Among Lewis's first pupils was John Betjeman: but there is no indication that either discerned the other's future greatness or felt that the experience was anything out of the ordinary. In fact, Lewis considered that he did not do anything like enough work, was particularly slack over Old English, and in a moment of exasperation described him as 'an idle prig'.

His first lectures caused him considerable trouble. Having announced as his theme 'Eighteenth-Century Precursors of the Romantic Movement', he discovered that F. P. Wilson was lecturing on 'English Poetry from Thomson to Cowper', and he wrote to his father on 4 December 1925, 'in fact it is the same subject under a different name. This means that, being neither able nor willing to rival Wilson, I am driven to concentrate on the prose people of whom at present I know very little. I have as hard a spell cut out for me between now and next term as I have ever had.'

However, even an attack of German measles at the beginning of the following year did not prevent the lectures from being prepared. 'Will you think me affected if I number a small illness among the minor pleasures of life?' he wrote to his father on 25 January 1926. 'The early stages are unpleasant but at least they bring you to a point when the mere giving up and going to bed is a relief. Then after twenty-four hours the really high temperature and the headache are gone: one is not well enough to get up, but one is ill enough not to want to get up. Best of all, work is impossible and one can read all day for mere pleasure with a clear conscience.'

(Lewis never changed his views, and as late as 1959 Green remembers finding him laid up with a heavy cold, and his positive delight when he was found to have a temperature and could look forward to a three-day 'holiday in bed', instead of getting up and going to Cambridge.)

'I have given my first lecture,' he went on later in the same letter to his father. 'I suppose my various friends in the English Schools have been telling their pupils to come to it: at any rate it was a pleasant change from talking to empty rooms in Greats. I modestly selected the smallest lecture room in college. As I approached, half wondering if anyone would turn up, I noticed a crowd of undergraduates coming into Magdalen, but it was no mock modesty to assume that they were coming to hear someone else. When however I actually reached my own room it was crowded out and I had to sally forth with the audience at my heels to find another. The porter directed me to one which we have in another building across the street. So we all surged over the High in a disorderly mass, suspending the traffic. It was a most exhilarating scene. Of course their coming to the first lecture, the men to see what *it* is like, the girls to see what *I* am like, really means nothing: curiosity is now satisfied – I have been weighed, with results as yet unknown – and next week I may have an audience of five or none.'

Besides his own pupils, Lewis took a class of seven girls at Lady Margaret Hall each week during the Hilary Term of 1926, and found several of them clever and stimulating, and 'very good at discussion'. Contrary to a rumour that persisted for many years, Lewis neither looked down on women undergraduates nor refused to tutor them: he made no distinction between them and his male pupils – and made no special allowances. His bluff manner, the lightning speed at which his mind worked, and the downright assertion or contradiction that often seemed like a snub though not so intended, was apt to alarm or antagonize the more sensitive of his male pupils: this treatment could have seemed to show a veiled contempt to some of his female pupils who were not accustomed to anything of the kind. This may have started the rumour, which would also have been encouraged by Lewis's preference for male society and dislike of social occasions that demanded small talk.

The hard work at the beginning of Lewis's career as lecturer and tutor at Magdalen cut down even the social events which he did enjoy. One, however, which he made a point of attending was a dinner with Nevill Coghill to meet Walter de la Mare and A. L. Rowse – the latter he continued to meet in Oxford, the former he does not seem to have met again. A much closer friend made at this time, and the earliest among his new Magdalen associates, was Colin Hardie the young classics tutor: being depressed over the outbreak of the General Strike in May 1926, they went to the cinema 'where I saw Felix (excellent) and Harold Lloyd for the first time in my life.'

'Nearly all my pupils went off during the Strike to unload boats or swing batons or drive engines,' he wrote to his father on 5 June. 'We of course had to stay on as long as any pupils were left, and it had just got to the point of us having to go when the thing ended. I don't mind telling you that I was in a funk about it. Docking was filled up and I would sooner have gone to the War again than have been a constable.'

Another acquaintance at this time who afterwards became a close friend – though the attraction was not immediate – was J. R. R. Tolkien, six years his senior, who had just been elected Rawlinson and Bosworth Professor of Anglo-Saxon at Oxford. They met at the English Faculty Meeting at Merton College on 11 May 1926. 'He is a smooth, pale, fluent little chap,' wrote Lewis in his diary, 'can't read Spenser because of the forms – thinks language is the real thing in the School – thinks all literature is written for the amusement of *men* between thirty and forty – we ought to vote ourselves out of existence if we were honest – still the sound changes and the gobbets are great fun for the dons. No harm in him: only needs a smack or two.'

Within a year or so, however, any initial antipathy was long forgotten, and they were meeting in each other's rooms and talking far into the night. 'Tolkien came back with me to college and sat discoursing of the gods and giants of Asgard for three hours,' is a typical note, from a letter to Arthur Greeves in December 1929.

During 1926 Lewis was still much concerned about poetry. *Dymer* was at last completed, and accepted by J. M. Dent and Sons in May, being published on 18 July. Before its appearance he was showing some concern over the definition of poetry, siding with Abercrombie and the 'Georgians' against Eliot and the 'Moderns'. Perhaps piqued at his failure to get any of his own poems accepted, he hatched the idea of a 'literary dragonade: a series of mock Eliotic poems to be sent up to the *Dial* and the *Criterion* until sooner or later one of these filthy editors falls into the trap'. Coghill and Hardie, and his pupil Yorke, joined in the scheme – but it does not seem to have gone very far. However it took Lewis many years to come to terms with 'modern' poetry – and though he never accepted it as equal in value to the best of the traditional variety, he came to recognize the greatness of some of its exponents and numbered Eliot and Auden among personal friends. However his favourite contemporary poets seem to have been Charles Williams, Roy Campbell and Kathleen Raine – perhaps he inclined to be over-partial to the poetry when he liked the poet. He never lost his respect for Masefield and the best of the Georgians, whom he would quote, praise and defend when occasion called – though he would allow few virtues to Noyes, perhaps on account of his own dislike for 'elfin' poetry, even if written by Herrick or Drayton.

He was reading the proofs of *Dymer* at this time and feeling an author's usual sensation of failure and disappointment when it is too late to rewrite or revise. 'I never liked it less,' he confessed, 'I felt that no mortal could get any notion of what the devil it was all about. I am afraid this sort of stuff is very much hit or miss, yet I think it is my only real line.'

That it was a miss was not, however, the opinion of the more discerning reviewers. 'Mr Clive Hamilton's long allegorical poem *Dymer* is executed with a consistent craftsmanship which excites admiration even where criticism is readiest to speak,' wrote Dilys Powell in the *Sunday Times* on 19 September. And after picking out several 'felicitous phrases' assured the reader that 'the tedious-ness which is so often the chief feature of allegorical poetry is absent'. But, prophetically, she concluded, 'Mr Hamilton has mistaken his opportunity. The idea was not one for treatment in verse. The exigences of the poetic line prevent such an easy sequence as the allegory demands: but as a prose tale how splen-didly it would have flowed!'

And A. T. Quiller-Couch wrote to Guy Pocock, the editor at Dent's, who passed it on to Lewis, '*Dymer* is a fine piece of work:

fine in conception and full of brilliant lines and images. Can you
convey my thanks to the author of the best new thing I have read
for many a long day? He has that gift of metaphor too, which
Aristotle was cunning enough to spot as the one quality of style
which cannot be taught or imparted because it is genius, and its
happy owner is born with it.'

After Christmas with his father and Warren (the last Christmas
they were all to spend together, for Warren was posted to the Far
East the following April), Lewis began on his next poem, *The
King of Drum*, still feeling that his literary future lay in the direction of epic. The full history of this, perhaps his most successful
work of this kind, is given by Walter Hooper in the introduction
to *Narrative Poems* (1969) where it was first published. Lewis
worked eagerly on the poem for a time, but seems to have given
it up as *Dymer* proved more and more obviously to be a failure
from the financial point of view. By 1938, when he consulted John
Masefield on its merits, he had rewritten it as *The Queen of Drum*,
with a certain amount of Christian symbolism worked into it.
Masefield urged publication, and other friends read and enjoyed
it from time to time – but somehow it never won into print,
though he was still considering publication twenty years after this.

The burst of poetic creativity in January 1927 coincided with
the first definite evidence for the spiritual worries and struggles
that were to lead Lewis back to Christianity four years later.
During a solitary walk on 18 January he 'was thinking about
imagination and intellect and the unholy muddle I am in about
them at present: undigested scraps of Anthroposophy and psycho-
analysis jostling with orthodox idealism over a background of good
old Kirkian rationalism. Lord, what a mess! And all the time
(with me) there's the danger of falling back into most childish
superstitions, or of running into dogmatic materialism to escape
them. I hoped *The King of Drum* might write itself so as to clear
things up – the way *Dymer* cleared up the Christina Dream
business.' But he was still attacking religion – with, perhaps, some
of the over-shrill contempt of the man who does not want to believe
rather than of one who simply does not believe. 'A pest on all this

nonsense which has half spoiled so much beauty and wonder for me, degraded pure imagination into pretentious lying, and truths of the spirit into mere matters of *fact*, slimed everything over with the trail of its infernal mumbo-jumbo,' he wrote in his diary on 8 February 1927, after re-reading the myth of Atlantis from Plato, and realizing how Steiner had interpreted it from the point of view of Anthroposophy. 'How I would have enjoyed this myth once: now behind Plato's delightful *civilized* imagination I always have the picture of dark old tradition picked up from mumbling medicine men, professing to be "private information" about facts. To bed and had a much worse night than I have had for a long time.'

But Lewis's spiritual biography of the next few years will be dealt with fully in a later chapter: in 1927 he was still trying to 'live by philosophy' – like A. C. Bradley in *The Masque of Balliol* he was still seeking refuge 'in the blessed Absolute'. His diary writing was, however, growing more and more sporadic, and some time during the following year must have come his acceptance of theism which 'cured me of the time-wasting and foolish practice of keeping a diary.'

Meanwhile his outer life at Oxford continued much on the lines of any other don. Though still superior and contemptuous of the average philistine undergraduates – 'a drinking, guffawing cry of barbarians with hardly any taste among them' – he was performing what seemed his duties to them with conscientious thoroughness. Evenings were given up to reading and debating societies; he attended parties given by his pupils – one of these by John Betjeman on 24 January 1927 in his rooms in St Aldates – 'a very beautiful panelled room looking across to the side of the House,' he recorded. 'I found myself pitchforked into a galaxy of super-undergraduates, including Sparrow of the Nonesuch Press and an absolutely silent and astonishingly ugly person called McNiece, of whom Betjeman said afterwards, "He doesn't say much, but he's a great poet". It reminded me of the man in Boswell "who was always thinking of Locke and Newton". The conversation was chiefly about lace curtains, arts and crafts (which they all dislike), china ornaments, silver versus earthen teapots, architecture, and the strange habits of "hearties". The best thing was Betjeman's very curious collection of books. Came away with him and back to college to pull him along through Wulfstan until dinner time.' Certainly Lewis did not find himself at home among the brittle young world of what he was later to describe as 'The Empty Twenties' – but there was some truth in a moment of self-recognition recorded the previous year: 'Was led somehow into a train of thought in which I made the unpleasant discovery that I am becoming a prig – righteous indignation against certain modern affectations has its dangers, yet I don't know how to avoid it either.'

On the family side of things, Warren set off for Shanghai in April 1927, after a night at Oxford to say goodbye to his brother in a rather nostalgic mood – 'the bus [from Oxford] did not start at once, and I watched Jack in his mac and old cloth hat stride along until he was out of sight.' He had visited Ireland briefly the week before to see his father – for the last time as it turned out.

Lewis stopped regular diary writing at this time, but continued to some extent in the form of an occasional journal to Warren. For part at least of the following year Lewis kept a diary in Anglo-Saxon, none of which seems to have survived except a literal translation of the account of the election of George Gordon to succeed Sir Herbert Warren as President of Magdalen in 1928.

In the first of the diary-letters to his brother, Lewis described a walking tour with Owen Barfield to Marlborough and Salisbury Plain: this was always his favourite form of holiday and he continued to take them until his mid-fifties when failing health put an end to them – his most frequent companion in later years being his brother and their most usual site the north of Ireland during the Long Vacation. (See the *Letters of C. S. Lewis* for full account of this typical tour.)

Apart from longer or shorter walks and thoughts on the books he was reading, Lewis had little news to impart either to his father or to his brother at this time. Albert Lewis's health was beginning to cause anxiety, and Lewis exerted himself to be entertaining in his letters, quoting amusing schoolboy howlers from the examination papers he was again correcting that summer, and telling anecdotes of the more eccentric dons with whom he came in contact. There is an occasional illuminating remark about himself: 'like all us Celts I am a born rhetorician, one who finds pleasure in the expression of forcible emotions independently of their grounds and even to the extent to which they are felt at any time save the moment of speaking.' And the same letter concludes, 'I am going bald at a prodigious rate and in a few years time you will have a better head of hair than either of your sons.'

In September Lewis was on holiday with Mrs Moore and Maureen at Perranporth in Cornwall and wrote an ecstatic account of the surf-bathing to Warren. He tore himself away from the delights of the seaside for a visit to his father. 'Jack arrived, bright and cheerful and amusing as usual,' recorded Albert Lewis in his diary. But the Cornish trip 'was not official and should not be referred to in letters' to their father, he instructed Warren.

This year Lewis began learning the language of the sagas – 'it is an exciting experience when I remember my first passion for things Norse' – and to Arthur Greeves he wrote, 'I am realizing a number of very old dreams in the way of books – reading Sir Gawain in the original [Middle English] and, above all, learning Old Icelandic. We have a little Icelandic Club in Oxford called the "Kolbitar": which means (literally) "Coal-biters", i.e. an Icelandic word for old cronies who sit round the fire so close that they look as if they were biting the coals. We have so far read the younger Edda and the Volsung Saga: next term we shall read the Laxdale Saga. *You* will be able to imagine what a delight this is to me, and how, even in turning over the pages of my Icelandic Dictionary, the mere name of god or giant catching my eye will sometimes throw me back fifteen years into a wild dream of northern skies and Valkyrie music: only they are now even more beautiful seen through a haze of memory.'

He spent four weeks with his father towards the end of the Long Vacation. 'Jacks sets me a very good example of industry,' wrote Albert Lewis to Warren on 26 September 1927. 'I leave him at breakfast when I go out and immediately he has finished it he goes up to the end room and works steadily till lunch. In the afternoon he goes out for a walk. I am glad to say that he is in good health and great spirits and has many funny "wheezes" about the older dons at Oxford.'

Not all Lewis's 'work', however, was of a very academic nature, as he seems to have spent much of the month at Little Lea compiling an *Encyclopaedia Boxoniana* of all his and Warren's early stories. At about this time also he began his only attempt at a modern novel, which did not get much beyond the first 7,000 words. The fragment that remains among the *Lewis Papers* (vol. IX, pp. 291–300) takes the narrator, Dr Easley, from Liverpool to Belfast on a first visit to his Irish relations, with a good deal of amusing dialogue with a loquacious Irishman whom he meets on the voyage – typical of the voyages which Lewis had made and was still to make so many times.

At Oxford there was little time for writing during term. Most of each day was taken up with tutorials and lectures, with a walk in the afternoon if not captured for chores by Mrs Moore. The evenings were mostly filled also, as he explained to Warren when excusing the brevity of letters written to him in term time: 'My evenings for the fortnight in term run thus: *Mon:* Play-reading with undergraduates (till midnight). *Tue:* Mermaid Club [literary discussion]. *Wed:* Anglo-Saxon with undergraduates. *Thurs, Fri, Sat, Sun:* Common Room till late. *Mon:* Play-reading. *Tues:* Icelandic Society. *Wed:* Anglo-Saxon. *Thurs:* Philosophical Supper. *Fri, Sat, Sun.* As you will see this gives at the very best only three free evenings in the even weeks and two in the odd. And into these two everything in the way of casual entertaining, correspondence, and what we used to call "A-h-h-h!" has to be crammed.'

That Christmas he spent with his father in Belfast. As Albert Lewis aged, he became more and more difficult and demanding, but Lewis himself was learning ever greater patience and charity – though still occasionally letting off steam to Warren in letters packed with examples of their father's exigent behaviour. This

Christmas, besides walks with Arthur Greeves, he managed to get out for one evening to give him and John Bryson dinner at a Belfast hotel – 'to be seated in a hotel, eating an ordinary dinner and drinking your wine, indulging in ordinary chat, and then to reflect that Belfast is outside the window, is a marvellous sensation. I discovered to my surprise that Bryson (whom I always regarded as an imposing junior Don) was in just the same state at home as Arthur and myself,' he wrote to Warren in the current diary-letter.

Albert Lewis finally retired on a pension from the Petty Sessions in May 1928, his health growing more precarious. This made visits home even more of a penance, since his father was in the house all the time; but Lewis managed to stay for part of each vacation, and continued with long and cheerful letters.

Early in 1928 he was working on the idea of a book about sixteenth-century letters, sparked off by reading the letters of Erasmus, which necessitated long, quiet days in the Bodleian which he described in glowing terms to his father. But very soon he found himself immersed and fascinated by medieval French poetry, of which he was transcribing and translating scraps in letters to Warren, apologizing that 'my reading contains less and less that I can share with my non-professional friends,' but delighting in his new discovery of the world of courtly love and allegory. 'Don't you think this is rather jolly?' he wrote to Warren in April 1928. 'In one of those gardens in a dream, which medieval love poetry is full of, we find the tomb of a knight, dead for love, covered with flowers. Then [he quotes the Old French and goes on] it can be very roughly Englished:

> And birds that for the soul of that signor
> Who lay beneath, songs of true love did pour:
> Being hungered, each from off the flowers bore
> A kiss, and felt that day no hunger more.

The odd thing is that one would expect the same rhyme going all through to be monotonous and ugly: but to my ear it produces a beautiful lulling like the sound of the sea.'

This letter is the first indication that Lewis's mind was turning seriously in the direction of his most famous volume of literary scholarship, *The Allegory of Love*, and by July of the same year he was writing the first draft. 'I have actually begun the first chapter of my book,' he told his father on the 10th. 'The actual book is going to be about medieval love poetry and the medieval idea of love, which is a very paradoxical business indeed when you go into it.'

Little else happened in 1928 of which Lewis took much note. Besides the usual visits to Belfast, Arthur Greeves stayed with him at Magdalen in the early autumn. After a great deal of 'College politics', inner rings and cliques functioning in full force, George Gordon was elected President of Magdalen in November, to the general satisfaction of Lewis himself, and indeed the majority of the Fellows.

Lewis spent Christmas 1928 with his father – the last, though he had no idea that such a thing was likely – and was able to present him with his two earliest reviews, both in the *Oxford Magazine*, of Evelyn Waugh's *Rossetti* (25 Oct.) and Hugh Kingsmill's *Matthew Arnold* (15 Nov.) – the first laudatory and the second condemnatory in the extreme, one of the earliest examples of his witheringly logical approach, the *delenda est Carthago* in which he became so adept in later years. (Yet he developed no animus against the author since, as Chad Walsh records, he was quoting 'Kingsmill's' brilliant parody of A. E. Housman with much glee and commendation a dozen years later.)

A 'flu-ish cold, with temperature and sore throat, confined Lewis to bed and prevented him from visiting his father in April 1929, his only holiday from Oxford being a four-day walking tour with Barfield and several other friends from Salisbury to Lyme Regis.

In July, as usual, Lewis began on the correction of examination papers, telling his father, 'I am still undecided (it depends largely on when I finish Chapter II of the book) whether August 12th or something like August 25th would be best for me,' and urging him to take a holiday with him away from Little Lea. He crossed to Ireland on the earlier date and was writing to Warren on the

25th: 'This is a line to let you know that P. is rather seriously ill.' Albert Lewis's health deteriorated rapidly, with Clive in day and night attendance – and writing bulletins to Warren in Shanghai, who could not possibly receive them for a month or six weeks. On 3 September an operation was deemed necessary. This was performed a few days later, and seemed successful. 'The operation, in spite of what they prophesied, discovered cancer,' wrote Clive to Warren on 29 September. 'They said he might live a few years. I remained at home, visiting him in the Nursing Home for ten days . . . By this time I had been at home since Aug. 11th, and my work for next term was getting really desperate and, as [the doctor] said I might easily wait for several weeks more and still be in the same position . . . I crossed to Oxford on Saturday, Sept. 22. On Tuesday 24 I got a wire saying that he was worse, caught the train an hour later, and arrived to find that he had died on Tuesday afternoon.'

Both Warren and Clive felt Albert Lewis's death far more than they had thought possible; and the wrench of leaving Little Lea, their home for most of their lives, whatever their later reactions to it, was also acute. The letters for the next six months are taken up mainly with the business of sorting and selling or keeping the contents of the house; employing a caretaker while the house was put up for sale, and generally winding up the Lewis affairs in Belfast.

In November the letters show Lewis living a normal Oxford life again – sitting up late talking of Norse mythology with Tolkien; learning Textual Criticism so as to be able to teach it the following term to B.Litt. students; reading Anglo-Saxon poetry with a congenial and promising pupil, Neil Ker (afterwards Reader in Palaeography) – 'immensely fine . . . Ker shares my enthusiasm for the saga world and we had a pleasant evening – with the wind roaring outside'; attending meetings of the Icelandic Society, the Linguistic Society, the Michaelmas Club, and so on.

As soon as term ended he was off to Ireland, staying with Arthur and setting to work at Little Lea each day. On his return journey to Oxford on 21 December he was reading Bunyan's *Grace*

Abounding: 'I should like to know in general what you think of all the darker side of religion as we find it in old books. Formerly I regarded it as mere devil-worship based on horrible superstitions. Now that I have found and am still finding more and more the element of truth in the old beliefs, I feel I cannot dismiss even their dreadful side so cavalierly. There must be something in it: only what?'

He was present at the Christmas Eve celebrations in Magdalen for the first time that year, and found them most impressive. He still did not attend church, even on Christmas Day, but was finding more and more of a religious experience during his long walks in the country – 'the utter homeliness, the Englishness, the Christendom of it' – so different from Co. Antrim a week or so earlier, and yet that too was but 'another instance . . . [of] the "broad-mindedness" of the infinite . . . Perhaps it is less strange that the Absolute should make both than that we should be able to love both.'

Looking back in 1935 to his long friendship with Greeves, Lewis summed up their relationship and what he owed to the friend who always remained steadfast to the Christian faith however much he bombarded him with the 'thin artillery' of the rationalist. 'He remains victor in that debate. It is I who have come round. The thing is symbolical of much in our joint history. He was not a clever boy, he was even a dull boy; I was a scholar. He had no "ideas". I bubbled over with them. It might seem that I had much to give him and that he had nothing to give me. But this is not the truth. I could give concepts, logic, facts, arguments, but he had feelings to offer, feelings which most mysteriously – for he was always very inarticulate – he taught me to share. Hence, in our commerce, I dealt in superficies, but he in solids. I learned charity from him but failed, for all my efforts, to teach him arrogance in return.'

Meanwhile plans for the future were going ahead. Warren was to join the Lewis-Moore set-up, but a bigger house must be found, and now there might be sufficient money to purchase a definite home of their own, if Little Lea sold well enough.

Warren's service abroad ended in March, and he reached England on 16 April 1930 and went straight to London where his brother met him, took him back to Oxford and then down to Bournemouth where the family holiday was in progress.

Later in the month they went over to Belfast to continue sorting out the accumulation of years at Little Lea, selecting what books and furniture to keep, and arranging for the sale of the rest. They had already decided what to do with all the toys which had been the foundation and background to the world of Boxen and its literature, and Clive had written to Warren in January: 'I should not like to make an exception even in favour of Benjamin. After all, these characters (like all others) can, in the long run, live only in "the literature of the period", and I fancy that when we look at the actual *toys* again (a process from which I anticipate no pleasure at all) we shall find the discrepancy between the symbol and the character rather acute. No, Brother. The toys in the trunk are quite plainly corpses. We will resolve them into their elements, as nature will do to us.' Like the children at the end of *Dream Days*, 'we took turn about in digging a hole in the vegetable garden in which to put our toys,' recorded Warren in his diary on 23 April 1930, 'and then carried the old attic trunk down and buried them. What struck me most was the scantiness of the material out of which that remarkable imaginary world was constructed. By tacit mutual consent the boxes of characters were buried unopened.'

Warren was posted to Bulford on Salisbury Plain in mid-May, but was able to get leave early in June to superintend the final sale of Little Lea, which he left for the last time on 3 June.

But little more than a fortnight later their combined house-hunting on the outskirts of Oxford led them to the Kilns, Headington Quarry, which was to be their home for the rest of their lives – by the end, 33 years later, much dearer to C. S. Lewis who was to know there his greatest happiness and his greatest sorrow near the end of his life.

On 7 July 1930 Warren wrote in his diary that on the previous morning 'Jack and I went out and saw the place, and I instantly caught the infection. We did not go inside the house, but the eight-acre garden is such stuff as dreams are made on. I never imagined that for us any such garden would ever come within the sphere of discussion. The house (which has two more rooms than Hillsboro) stands at the entrance to its own grounds at the northern foot of Shotover at the end of a narrow lane, which in turn opens off a very bad and little-used road, giving as great privacy as can be reasonably looked for near a large town. To the left of the house are the two brick kilns from which it takes its name – in front, a lawn and hard tennis court – then a large bathing pool, beautifully wooded, and with a delightful circular brick seat overlooking it. After that a steep wilderness broken with ravines and nooks of all kinds runs up to a little cliff topped by a thistly meadow, and then the property ends in a thick belt of fir trees, almost a wood. The view from the cliff over the dim blue distance is simply glorious.' The pool or 'lake' in the woods they soon discovered 'has quite distinguished literary associations, being known locally as "Shelley's Pool", and there is a tradition that Shelley used to meditate there.'

This ideal little estate was duly purchased that July for £3,300, and £200 more set aside for building on two additional rooms – one of which became the new 'little end room'. Shortage of money unfortunately prevented them from buying the adjoining field for £300, and a few years later an unsightly row of small houses was built on it. The rest of the Kilns environment, however, remained in almost unspoilt beauty until after C. S. Lewis's death, though by then the area at the end of their lane, in a square from the bypass to the London road, was a solid block of development, joining on to the suburbs of Oxford. The land to the south up the 'cliff' to Shotover still remains as Green Belt.

The remainder of the lease of Hillsboro was sold fairly satisfactorily in August, and the Lewis brothers, with Mrs Moore and Maureen, and 'Mr Papworth' the dog, moved into the Kilns during the second week in October 1930.

IV. CONVERSION

After all his anxiety over finding a suitable home, it is ironic that Lewis now had a far more pressing matter on his mind than moving into the Kilns. He had been fighting for years to keep God at bay and the purchase of the Kilns almost coincided with the end of this struggle. The fullest account of how this was resolved he was later to tell in *Surprised by Joy* but, to fit it into perspective, we must move back a few years.

It was shortly after he had taken his finals in the English School that Lewis arrived at what he called his 'New Look' which involved the belief that 'the Christian myth' – as he called it – conveyed as much truth as most minds are able to grasp. The pleasant thing about this belief was that there was nothing to fear and – better yet – nothing to obey. Then, in 1924, while he was deputizing for E. F. Carritt at Univ., a number of things began to unsettle this comfortable 'New Look'. A re-reading of Euripides' *Hippolytus*, with its world's end imagery, threw him again into the state of intense longing. Shortly afterwards he read Samuel Alexander's *Space, Time and Deity* (1920) and found there a distinction between 'enjoyment' and 'contemplation' which was thereafter to play a very important part in his intellectual make-up.

According to Alexander, you 'enjoy' the act of thinking and 'contemplate' whatever it is you are thinking about. Applying this distinction, Lewis discovered that the essential property of, say, love is attention to the beloved. To think about not the beloved but loving *itself* is to enjoy your own thoughts and to cease attending to the object of those thoughts. Thus, if we try to look 'inside ourselves' and watch what is going on, nearly everything that was going on before we looked is stopped. There broke upon Lewis the realization that his watching for Joy to come along had been an unconscious attempt to 'contemplate the enjoyed'. Even Joy, he now saw, was not an end in itself, but a reminder or pointer to something else – something far more desirable than the sensations and images which accompany Joy.

From here he went on to see that, in experiencing Joy, we yearn for that *Absolute* – his name for God – beside which we are mere 'appearances'. This interest in the Absolute began to tie in with the philosophy he was now teaching at Univ. One difficulty he found from teaching such philosophical idealists as Hegel and F. H. Bradley is that their 'Absolute' could not be made clear enough to satisfy Lewis. He found the theistic idealism of George Berkeley more persuasive because it was easier to get some notion of what Berkeley's 'God' is. Nevertheless, for Lewis this 'God' did not enter into personal relations: we could no more 'meet' him than Hamlet could meet Shakespeare.

Not long afterwards Lewis read Chesterton's *The Everlasting Man* and was surprised to find the whole Christian outline of history making sense. An even stronger blow at his efforts to keep God at bay came in 1926 when he was entertaining the hardest-boiled atheist he knew. He was shattered when the atheist, remarking on what good evidence there was for the historicity of the Gospels, said, 'Rum thing. All that stuff of Frazer's about the Dying God. Rum thing. It almost looks as if it had really happened once' (*Surprised by Joy*, p. 211).

Some time after this Lewis was going up Headington Hill on top of a bus when he was aware of being offered a completely free choice: either accept or reject God. He could open the door or keep it shut. In a situation such as this, when it is almost perfectly clear what one *ought* to do, he saw that freedom and necessity come very close to being the same thing. In so far as the choice lay with him, he chose to open the door. When this happened, Christian friends such as Barfield, Tolkien and Hugo Dyson joined in making it nearly impossible for him to do otherwise.

There had for some time been an ethic attached to his idealism and Lewis believed that only by attempting complete virtue could he see beyond his own selfish perspective and understand 'universal Spirit'. Though still a long way from believing in Christianity, he nevertheless felt he ought to *act* as though he believed. This attempt at virtue no doubt contributed to the belief he expressed in all his theological books, and most succinctly in *The Abolition of Man* where he says: 'Only those who are practising the Tao [moral law] will understand it.'

In his attempt to bring his acts, thoughts and desires into harmony with 'universal Spirit' he discovered how all but impossible it is for an atheist to attempt to do the will of God without, sooner or later, coming, as St John says (7:17), 'to know of the doctrine'. This was a horrible revelation to him at the time and he felt that, in his case, it was as ridiculous to speak of his 'search' for God as it is to speak of the mouse's search for the cat.

He was still hoping that he might not be interfered with and be allowed to retain his freedom when God closed in on him. In what is perhaps the most moving passage in his autobiography he tells in *Surprised by Joy* how it happened: 'You must picture me alone in that room in Magdalen, night after night, feeling, whenever my mind lifted even for a second from my work, the steady, unrelenting approach of Him whom I so earnestly desired not to meet. That which I greatly feared had at last come upon me. In the Trinity Term of 1929 I gave in, and admitted that God was God, and knelt and prayed: perhaps, that night, the most dejected and reluctant convert in all England. I did not then see what is now the most shining and obvious thing; the Divine humility which will accept a convert even on such terms. The Prodigal Son at least walked home on his own feet. But who can duly adore that Love which will open the high gates to a prodigal who is brought in kicking, struggling, resentful, and darting his eyes in every direction for a chance of escape? The words *compelle intrare*, compel them to come in, have been so abused by wicked men that we shudder at them; but, properly understood, they plumb the depth of the Divine mercy. The hardness of God is kinder than the softness of men, and His compulsion is our liberation.'

This conversion was, however, to theism pure and simple, and not to Christianity. He knew nothing about the Incarnation at this stage. Oddly enough, the transition from theism to Christianity was one which, despite its importance, Lewis claimed to remember very little about. Because it is so lightly sketched in *Surprised by Joy*, it seems the most appropriate subject for the remainder of this chapter.

One practical result of Lewis's becoming a theist is that he began attending his college chapel on weekdays and his parish church on Sundays – and this despite his distaste for the 'public' aspect of church-going and his more intense dislike of organ music which he once described to Walter Hooper as 'one long roar'. He also began reading St John's Gospel in Greek – thus initiating a practice he was to continue for the rest of his life: to read some portion of the Bible almost every day. From St John he got a more rounded picture of Christ than that he had had in 1916 when he described Christianity as one among many mythologies and the Divine Son as a 'Hebrew philosopher'. Indeed, his views were so radically altered that he wrote to Arthur Greeves on 9 January 1930 complaining that 'In spite of all my recent changes of view, I am . . . inclined to think that you can only get what *you* call "Christ" out of the Gospels by picking and choosing, and slurring over a great deal.' Though still uncertain as to what the Gospels *meant*, Lewis had already begun his defence of a full and undiluted Christian faith.

Lewis discontinued his diary in 1929 but, fortunately for his biographers, he and Arthur Greeves had returned, after a lapse of several years, to the practice of writing every week. The latter had held out for years against Lewis's atheism and it is, perhaps, natural that Lewis should now regard him as his Father Confessor. One of the most striking changes in Lewis's letters is a sense of personal well-being and happiness. More than ever he delighted in his afternoon walks, conversations and books. As the frail securities of his recent atheism crumbled, they made way for a deep and genuine humility. He even admitted to *liking* the Christianity in the works of John Bunyan and George MacDonald and felt as though his youth had been given back to him.

On 5 January 1930 he wrote to Greeves about a new discovery:

'In the evening I started to read the Everyman volume of *Jacob Boehme* . . . The Dialogue at the end, called the Supersensual Life, was fairly easy going, and I should advise you to get and read it at once. Then I turned back and began the longer work, the *Signatura Rerum* . . . it has been about the biggest shaking up I've got from a book since I first read *Phantastes* . . . No fooling about for me: and I keep one hand firmly gripped round the homely and simple things. But it is a real book: i.e. it's not like a book at all, but like a thunderclap. Heaven defend us – what things there are knocking about the world!' Lewis was, at the same time, finding books by MacDonald which he had not previously read – one of which was *The Diary of an Old Soul*. Writing to Arthur Greeves about it on 26 January 1930, he spoke of the beauty of finding himself 'on the main road with all humanity . . . It is emphatically coming home, as Chaucer says "Returneth *home* from worldly vanitee".'

The afternoon walks from Magdalen to Headington, Lewis regarded as periods of 'meditation' – times which he now set aside for the specific purpose of self-examination. Burrowing into his past, he was appalled at what he found. On 30 January 1930 he told Greeves that, though he was being supported in respect to chastity and anger, his main cause of alarm was pride which he recognized as his besetting sin. 'I have found out ludicrous and terrible things about my own character. Sitting by, watching the rising thoughts to break their necks as they pop up, one learns to know the sort of thoughts that do come. And, will you believe it, one out of every three is a thought of self-admiration: when everything else fails, having had its neck broken, up comes the thought "What an admirable fellow I am to have broken their neck!" I catch myself posturing before the mirror, so to speak, all day long. I pretend I am carefully thinking out what to say to the next pupil (for *his* good, of course) and then suddenly realize I am really thinking how frightfully clever I'm going to be and how he will admire me . . . when you force yourself to stop it, you admire yourself for doing *that*. It's like fighting the hydra . . . There seems to be no end to it. Depth under depth of self-love and self-admiration . . . *Pride* . . . is the mother of *all* sins, and the original sin of Lucifer – so you are rather better off than I am. You at your worst are an instrument unstrung: I am an instrument strung but preferring to play itself because it thinks it knows the tune better than the Musician.'

Lewis continued to accord to pride the fear it deserved and even devoted a whole chapter to it in his first BBC broadcasts, (later included and revised in *Mere Christianity*). Years later when Walter Hooper asked if he set much store by his growing fame, Lewis answered, 'One cannot be too careful *not* to think of it!'

Though he continued to argue Christian doctrine with friends such as Barfield and Tolkien, Lewis said very little about the change he was going through to friends of his undergraduate days. An exception, however, was A. K. Hamilton Jenkin. Writing to him on 21 March 1930, Lewis confessed that his outlook had changed considerably since they were fellow-Martlets at Univ.: 'It is not precisely Christianity, though it may turn out that way in the end. I can't express the change better than by saying that whereas once I would have said "Shall I adopt Christianity?", I now wait to see whether it will adopt me: i.e. I now know there is another Party in the affair – that I'm playing poker, not Patience, as I once supposed.'

In the summer of 1930 when Lewis and Mrs Moore were negotiating the purchase of the Kilns, the question arose as to who the heirs of the property would be. This had the incidental effect of causing Lewis to consider the question of whether or not he would ever marry. He was forced into deeper consideration by the reading of Coventry Patmore's long poem, *The Angel in the House*. Writing to Arthur Greeves about it on 7 June 1930, he said that though he liked individual lines in it, he was troubled by Patmore's theory of marriage as a mystical image of, and approach to, God: 'He is extremely down on people who take the ascetic view. They will be shut without the fold as "too good" for God. The whole poem has raised a lot of difficulties in my mind. Even if it were true that marriage is what he says, what help does this give as regards the sexual problem for the innumerable people who can't marry? Surely for them asceticism remains the only path? And if, as he suggests, marriage and romantic love is the real ascent to Spirit, how are we to account for a world in which it is inaccessible to so many, and are we to regard the old saints as simply deluded in thinking it specially denied to them?'

This raises the question as to why Lewis included himself – which he did – among those who cannot marry. He probably felt that marriage was ruled out because of his promise to Paddy Moore that, in the event of Paddy's death, he would look after his mother and sister. Despite this promise, the present domestic arrangement – for which all had worked so hard, and for which Lewis had years before suffered a partial estrangement from his father – would almost certainly have terminated had he taken a wife. There is, besides this, good reason for believing that Lewis liked the arrangement he had come to with Mrs Moore. Even without the Moores, he might still have preferred to remain single, and he once told Walter Hooper that he had 'always been a bachelor at heart'.

Shortly after reading *The Angel in the House*, Lewis exchanged his Bombay edition of Kipling for the complete works of Morris. He had regarded the eroticism in some of Morris's romances as dangerous and apt to lead to sensuality but, after reading Morris's *Love is Enough*, he regarded the poet in a new light: 'You know,' he wrote to Greeves on 30 June 1930, 'I always thought Morris the most essentially *pagan* of all poets . . . Now in *Love is Enough* he raises himself right out of his own world. He suddenly shows that he is at bottom aware of the real symbolical import of all the longing and even of earthly life itself. In the speeches of Love (who is the most important character) there is clear statement of eternal value (coupled with a refusal to offer you crudely personal immortality) and also, best of all, a full understanding that there is something beyond pleasure and pain. For the first (and last?) time the light of *holiness* shines through Morris's romanticism, not destroying but perfecting it. Reading this has been a great experience to me: and coming on top of the *Angel in the House* has shown me that in my fear of the sensual cheat which lurked at the back of my old romantic days (see *Dymer* VII) I have aimed at too much austerity and even dishonoured love altogether. I have become a dry prig. I do hope I am not being mocked – that this is not merely the masked vanguard of a new sensuality. But I verily believe not. In this light I shall come back to Morris and all that world. I have the key now and perhaps can stand the sweetness safely.'

Greeves was, frankly, confused by this and, in replying to Lewis's letter, assumed that Lewis, in his return from 'austerity', *now* believed that chastity in an unmarried man was not so important as he had once thought. Lewis wrote to him on 8 July 1930 making it quite clear that 'absolute chastity' was his goal but that he now saw that he had gone about it the wrong way. He had aimed at it by means of repression and a contemptuous distrust of emotional and imaginative experiences which border on the voluptuous. The right way, he maintained, was 'to keep always alive in one's soul a certain tenderness and luxuriousness always reaching out to *that of which* (in my view) sex must be the copy. In other words, whether, while I was right in seeing that a copy must be different from an original, I ought . . . to have remembered that it must also be *like* it else how would it be a copy? . . . the whole thing has made me feel that I have never given half enough importance to love in the sense of the *affections*.'

Lewis went on in the same letter to say that he and Barfield had been bathing in the River Thames. 'Picture us lounging naked under the pollards on a flat field: mowers in the next field: and tiny young dragon flies – too small to be frightful yet – darting among the lilies. Here I learned to dive which is a great change in my life and has important (religious) connections.' Writing about this first dive in one of his notebooks sometime later, he explained the religious connections: 'Nothing is simpler than this art. You do not need to do anything, you need only to stop doing something – to abstain from all attempt at self-preservation – to obey the command which Saint Augustine heard in a different context, *Securus te projice*.'

Lewis had been seriously trying to obey the will of God when, on re-reading *The Princess and the Goblin* and *The Princess and Curdie* during the spring of 1930, he was jolted into seeing how difficult this is. MacDonald's fairy stories helped him to realize that imaginative people, such as himself, are likely to confuse the mere *thinking* about a duty with the actual doing it. This was specially borne home to him by the passage in *The Princess and the Goblin* where Curdie dreams that he has waked and then, upon really waking up, finds that he is still in bed. 'It is so fatally easy,' he wrote to Greeves on 15 June 1930, 'to confuse an aesthetic appreciation of the spiritual life with the life itself – to dream that you have waked, washed, and dressed and then to find yourself still in bed.'

Lewis considered it one of his greatest mercies that he was permitted to know God for some months before he had any belief in a future life. A preoccupation with immortality can, he believed, corrupt our thoughts about Heaven and Hell – meaningless apart from the presence or absence of God – and corrupt *us* whenever we treat mere 'survival' as an end in itself. As we have seen, he became a theist in 1929, but it is not until the summer of 1930 that his letters show that he had given any thought to the possibility of there being an after-life. What may have set him thinking was an article on 'Death' which Barfield had written and which Lewis particularly admired because of its similarity to MacDonald's treatment of this subject. In a letter to Arthur Greeves on 29 July 1930, Lewis, reflecting on the 'full understanding' that he and Greeves enjoyed and which he hoped would never be lost, went on to say: 'It is an interesting and rather grim enquiry – how much of our present selves we could hope to take with us if there were another life. I take it that whatever is *merely* intellectual, *mere* theory, must go, since we probably hold it only by memory habit, which may depend on the matter of the brain. Only what has gone far deeper, what has been incorporated into the unconscious depths, can hope to survive. This often comes over me when I think of religion: and it is a shock to realize that the mere *thinking* it may be nothing, and that only the tiny bit which we really practise is likely to be ours in any sense of which death cannot make hay.'

It is interesting to note how, more and more, Lewis saw problems from a Christian perspective. After a friend in Belfast discouraged Arthur Greeves from going on with a novel he was writing and hoping to publish, Greeves turned to Lewis for advice, trusting that the author of *Spirits in Bondage* and *Dymer* could show him how he, too, could break into the publishing world. It is not clear whether Lewis had read Greeves's manuscript – though he had long been after him to write – but his answer was intended, not as help in getting a manuscript accepted, but as a warning against staking one's happiness on literary success. 'I am *still* as disappointed an author as you,' he wrote on 18 August 1930. 'From the age of sixteen onwards I had one single ambition, from which I never wavered, in the prosecution of which I spent every ounce I could, on which I really and deliberately staked my whole contentment: and I recognize myself as having unmistakably failed in it . . . The side of me which longs, not to write, for no one can stop us doing that, but to be approved as a writer, is not the side of us that is really worth much. And depend upon it, unless God has abandoned us, he will find means to cauterise that side somehow or other. If we can take the pain well and truly now and by it *forever* get over the wish to be distinguished beyond our fellows, well: if not we shall get it again in some other form. And honestly, the being cured, with all the pain, has pleasure too: one creeps home, tired and bruised, into a state of mind that is really restful, when all one's ambitions have been given up. Then one can really for the first time say "Thy Kingdom come": for in that Kingdom there will be no pre-eminences and a man must have reached the stage of not caring two straws about his own status before he can enter it. Think how difficult that would be if one *succeeded* as a writer: how bitter this necessary purgation, at the age of sixty, when literary success had made your whole life and you had *then* got to begin to go through the stage of seeing it all as dust and ashes . . . Better take it now: better learn the trick that makes you free for the future.'

Though Lewis had no desire to publish anything at this point, he still felt he must write. On 1 June 1930 he sent Greeves the first instalment of a novel entitled *The Moving Image*. He hoped that by writing four pages each week he would eventually finish it. His heavy schedule of tutorials, lectures and college business appears to have forestalled him for he abandoned it soon afterwards. Not one page of the novel has been found, and he last mentioned it to Greeves on 22 June of the same year: 'By the way, about the "Moving Image" I should warn you that there is going to be a great deal of conversation: in fact it is to be almost a Platonic dialogue in a fantastic setting with story intermixed. If you take *The Symposium*, *Phantastes*, *Tristram Shandy* and stir them all up together you will about have the recipe.'

One of the main reasons why *The Moving Image* was never completed may have been because, though Lewis had given up hopes of being a successful poet, he was far more interested in writing verse. Two of the long poems which were published after his death in the collection *Narrative Poems* (1969) were, quite clearly, being written and/or revised at this time: *The Nameless Isle* which bears the date 'Aug. 1930' and *The Queen of Drum* which he began years previously but was still rewriting.

Lewis seems, however, to have been far more pleased with some short religious lyrics he was composing in his spare time. Writing to Greeves about them on 28 August 1930, he said: 'I have found myself impelled to take infinitely more pains, less ready to be contented with the fairly good and more determined to reach the best attainable, than ever I was in the days when I never wrote without the ardent hope of successful publication.'

The religious lyrics which he is referring to are those that eventually found their way into *The Pilgrim's Regress* and were later reprinted in *Poems* (1964). It was not, however, to Arthur Greeves that Lewis turned for criticism of his verse, but to Owen Barfield who was himself writing a good deal of poetry at this time. Indeed, there are probably very few of Lewis's poems that were not offered to him for criticism. The manuscript of *The Nameless Isle* contains numerous marginal notes in Barfield's hand and the short religious poems were sent to him, one by one, as they were written, with the question, 'Is this any good?'

As Lewis rarely dated even letters before 1930, it is impossible to say in what order the poems were written; nevertheless, they quite clearly represent a kind of spiritual odyssey and are, perhaps, the richest and best of all the religious poems he wrote. A good many versions of these early poems have survived in Lewis's notebooks. That he put, not only considerable effort, but a large part of himself into them is perhaps illustrated by the fact that in the summer of 1930 Lewis copied nine of them into a little booklet which he sent to Barfield. The cover of the booklet bears the title *Half Hours with Hamilton, or Quiet Moments* and – for Barfield's amusement – the following preface: 'It is hoped that this little selection from my works, from which all objectionable matter has been carefully excluded, will be found specially suitable for Sunday and family reading, and also to the higher forms of secondary schools.' Of this selection, the following – which is exactly as it appears in *Half Hours* – seems to have gone through the most revisions and best illustrates how Lewis felt about God's invasion of his life.

> You rest upon me all my days
> One never changing eye
> Dreadful and undivided as the blaze
> Of some Arabian sky,
>
> Where dead still in the stifling tent
> Pale travellers crouch, and bright
> About them noon's long drawn astonishment
> Hammers the hills with light.
>
> Oh for but one cool breath in seven,
> One wind from northern climes,
> The shifting and the castle-clouded heaven
> Of my old Pagan times!
>
> But you have seized all in your rage
> Of Oneness. Round about,
> Beating my wings, all ways, within your cage,
> I flutter, but not out.

Lewis had another project in hand which probably no one

knew about until it was discovered after his death. Shortly after his conversion to theism, he wrote what might be described as an early version of *Surprised by Joy* except that it is even less 'personal' than *Surprised by Joy*. Though he had not been converted to Christianity when he finished it, his purpose was very nearly the same in both books: to explain how the experience of Joy led him to become a theist. This early manuscript (now in the possession of Walter Hooper) fills 62 pages of a notebook and ten loose sheets and begins with a statement of what it is about: 'In this book I propose to describe the process by which I came back, like so many of my generation, from materialism to a belief in God. If that process had been a purely intellectual one, and if I were therefore simply giving a narrative form to a work of apologetic, there would be no place for my book. The defence of Theism lies in abler hands than mine. What makes me bold to contribute my own story is the fact that I arrived where now I am, not by reflection alone, but by reflection on a particular recurrent experience. I am an empirical Theist. I have arrived at God by induction.'

Probably the simplest explanation of why Lewis did not try publishing his 'autobiography' is that he still could not understand what part *Christ* played in Christianity. Till he understood this he no doubt felt it best to keep quiet and continue his search for the answer. Meanwhile he found a fellow-traveller in his brother who was home from the Army and living in the Kilns. On 10 January 1931 Lewis told Greeves that Warren 'has been with us all the month here . . . He and I even went together to Church twice: and – will you believe it – he said to me in conversation that he was beginning to think the religious view of things was after all true. Mind you (like me, at first), he didn't *want* it to be, nor like it: but his intellect is beginning to revolt from the semi-scientific assumptions we all grew up in, and the other explanation of the world seems to him daily more probable.'

Shortly after this Lewis was writing to Greeves about his most recent MacDonald acquisition, *What's Mine's Mine*. Before he became interested in Christianity, Lewis's criticism of Morris,

MacDonald and other favourites had been primarily about literary values. Now that he was examining his own heart with unmerciful frankness, his letters were characterized by what has been wryly referred to as the 'expository demon' in him: his penetrating observations about moral values in, or suggested by, the books he was reading. In a letter dated 17 January 1931 he says about *What's Mine's Mine* and other novels by MacDonald: 'I wonder did he indulge (day-dreamily) an otherwise repressed fund of indignation by putting up in his novels bogeys to whom his heroes could make the stunning retorts and deliver the stunning blows which he himself neither could nor would deliver in real life. I am certain that this is morally as well as artistically dangerous and I'll tell you why. The *pleasure* of anger – the gnawing attraction which makes one return again and again to its theme – lies, I believe, in the fact that one feels entirely righteous oneself only when one is angry. *Then* the other person is pure black, and you are pure white. But in real life sanity always returns to break the dream. In fiction you can put absolutely *all* the right, with no snags or reservations, on the side of the hero (with whom you identify yourself) and all the wrong on the side of the villain. You thus revel in unearned self-righteousness which would be vicious even if it were earned. Haven't you noticed how people with a fixed hatred, say, of Germans or Bolshevists, *resent* anything which is pleaded in extenuation, however small, of their supposed crimes. The enemy must be unredeemed black. While all the time one *does* nothing and enjoys the feeling of perfect superiority over the faults one is never tempted to commit.'

Lewis appears to have got the kind of spiritual sustenance he most needed from writers such as Morris and MacDonald, but he felt he ought to be reading some specifically theological works. On clearing out his father's home, he came across a copy of Brother Lawrence's *Practice of the Presence of God* which he found very disappointing. 'It is full of truth', he wrote to Greeves on 1 June 1930, 'but somehow I didn't like it: it seemed to me a little unctuous. That sort of stuff, when it is not splendid beyond words, is terribly repulsive.' Some weeks later (8 July) he wrote to

Greeves about Thomas Traherne's *Centuries of Meditation* which he complained suffered from the author's shirking the problem of evil. In June 1931 he came across William Inge's *Personal Religion and the Life of Devotion* which he considered one of the best books of its kind that he had struck.

The truth is that Lewis never got on well with purely devotional books. What he infinitely preferred were solid works of theology that he had to work at to understand. His attitude towards the two kinds of books is summed up in a preface he wrote some years later for a translation of St Athanasius's *The Incarnation of the Word of God*: 'For my own part, I tend to find the doctrinal books often more helpful in devotion than the devotional books, and I rather suspect that the same experience may await others. I believe that many who find that "nothing happens" when they sit down, or kneel down, to a book of devotion, would find that the heart sings unbidden while they are working their way through a tough bit of theology with a pipe in their teeth and a pencil in their hand.' He must have said as much to Greeves because, when Lewis was on holiday in Ulster during August 1931, he was presented with the works of the sixteenth- and seventeenth-century Anglican divines, Richard Hooker and Jeremy Taylor.

Though Shakespeare had never been one of the indispensable poets of his youth, Lewis was now making a serious study of his plays for tutorial purposes. Shortly after his return from Ireland he read *The Winter's Tale* and was fired with excitement over Act V, Scene iii, in which Hermione is introduced as a statue and then comes to life. 'Hitherto', he wrote to Greeves on 5 September 1931, 'I had thought it rather silly: this time, seeing that the absurdity of the plot doesn't matter, and is merely the scaffolding whereby Shakespeare (probably unconsciously) is able to give us an image of resurrection, I was simply overwhelmed. You will say that I am here doing to Shakespeare just what I did to Mac-Donald over *Wilfred Cumbermede*. Perhaps I am. I must confess that more and more the value of plays and novels becomes for me dependent on the moments when, by whatever artifice, they succeed in expressing the great *myths*.'

Lewis was still thinking about myth and resurrection when, on Saturday evening (19 September 1931), he invited Tolkien and Hugo Dyson to dine with him in Magdalen. Probably none of them had any idea what a momentous impact this night's conversation was to have on Lewis who was finally to see how his beliefs about myth, paganism and Christianity cohere. After dinner the three friends strolled up Addison's Walk discussing myth and metaphor till a wind storm tore through the trees and drove them inside. In Lewis's rooms they talked about Christianity till 3.00 a.m. when Tolkien left to go home. After seeing him through the little postern door that opens on to Magdalen Bridge, Lewis and Dyson continued the discussion for another hour, walking up and down the cloister of New Buildings.

On Monday, 28 September, Lewis and Warren took a picnic lunch to Whipsnade Zoo, Warren driving his motor cycle and his brother riding in the side-car. That evening Warren recorded in his diary that, while watching an enclosure of bears, they were attracted by a 'delightful brown plethoric one which sat up and saluted for buns. Jack is full of the dream of adding a pet bear to our private menagerie, which he intends to christen "Bultitude".' This, no doubt, is the original 'Mr Bultitude' who later found his way into *That Hideous Strength*. But something of far greater importance happened to Lewis on the *way* to Whipsnade for, as he says in *Surprised by Joy*: 'When we set out I did not believe that Jesus Christ is the Son of God, and when we reached the zoo I did. Yet I had not exactly spent the journey in thought. Nor in great emotion. "Emotional" is perhaps the last word we can apply to some of the most important events. It was more like when a man, after long sleep, still lying motionless in bed, becomes aware that he is now awake.'

A few days later (1 October) Lewis wound up a long letter to Arthur Greeves with the news: 'I have just passed on from believing in God to definitely believing in Christ – in Christianity. I will try to explain this another time. My long night talk with Dyson and Tolkien had a good deal to do with it.'

Greeves was, quite naturally, elated by this turn of events and begged to know how it happened. Lewis was uncertain whether his belief in Christ was clear enough in his own mind to explain to another. Nevertheless, at Greeves's insistence, he wrote on 11 October a brief summary of how it had come about. As Lewis's conversion to Christianity coloured everything that happened afterwards, it is only proper that Lewis should tell his own story.

'What has been holding me back (at any rate for the last year or so) has not been so much a difficulty in believing as a difficulty in knowing what the doctrine *meant*: you can't believe a thing while you are ignorant *what* the thing is. My puzzle was the whole doctrine of Redemption: in what sense the life and death of Christ "saved" or "opened salvation to" the world. I could see how miraculous salvation might be necessary: one could see from ordinary experience how sin (e.g. the case of a drunkard) could get a man to such a point that he was bound to reach Hell (i.e. complete degradation and misery) in this life unless something quite beyond mere natural help or effort stepped in. And I could well imagine a whole world being in the same state and similarly in need of miracle. What I couldn't see was how the life and death of Someone Else (whoever he was) 2000 years ago could help us here and now – except in so far as his *example* helped us. And the example business, tho' true and important, is not Christianity: right in the centre of Christianity, in the Gospels and St Paul, you keep on getting something quite different and very mysterious, expressed in those phrases I have so often ridiculed ("propitiation" – "sacrifice" – "the blood of the Lamb") – expressions which I could only interpret in senses that seemed to me either silly or shocking.

'Now what Dyson and Tolkien showed me', he went on to say, 'was this: that if I met the idea of sacrifice in a Pagan story I didn't mind it at all: again, that if I met the idea of a god sacrificing himself to himself (cf. the quotation opposite the title page of *Dymer*) I liked it very much and was mysteriously moved by it: again, that the idea of the dying and reviving god (Balder, Adonis, Bacchus) similarly moved me provided I met it anywhere *except* in the Gospels. The reason was that in Pagan stories I was prepared to feel the myth as profound and suggestive of meanings beyond my grasp even tho' I could not say in cold prose "what it meant". Now the story of Christ is simply a true myth: a myth working on us in the same way as the others, but with this tremendous difference that *it really happened*: and one must be content to accept it in the same way, remembering that it is God's myth where the other are men's myths: i.e. the Pagan stories are God expressing Himself through the minds of poets, using such images as He found there, while Christianity is God expressing Himself through what we call "real things". Therefore it is *true*, not in the sense of being a "description" of God (that no finite mind would take in) but in the sense of being the way in which God chooses to (or can) appear to our faculties. The "doctrines" we get *out of* the true myth are of course *less* true: they are translations into our *concepts* and *ideas* of that which God has already expressed in a language more adequate, namely the actual incarnation, crucifixion, and resurrection.'

V. CHRISTIAN SCHOLAR
AND ALLEGORIST

At the dissolution of the family home in Belfast an enormous mass of diaries, letters and other papers relating to the Lewis and Hamilton families came to light. Albert Lewis rarely threw anything away and, though the papers were not arranged into any semblance of order, Warren saw in them the kernel of a family history and, shortly after his temporary retirement from the Army in December 1930, he set about arranging and editing them. He spent, all told, several years typing the 3,563 pages that make up the eleven volumes of *Lewis Papers* and which cover the years 1850–1930.

By the middle of September 1931, Warren had got as far with the family memoirs as 1915. Lewis then asked Arthur Greeves if he might borrow the letters he had written to him, promising that his brother should not see those that dealt with 'It' – the name he and Greeves gave to Joy – and those which touched on the topic of sex.

While vetting the 160 letters he had written to Arthur Greeves for inclusion in the family *Papers*, Lewis came, as it were, face to face with his past. He was surprised to discover what a large percentage of the letters were about the pleasure 'It' had given him and – now that he was a Christian – with what assiduity he had followed the wrong track in searching for its source. The benefits he gained from this review of his life were summarized in a letter to Arthur Greeves on 1 October 1931. 'To me, as I re-read them, the most striking thing is their egotism: sometimes in the form of priggery, intellectual and even social: often in the form of downright affectation (I seem to be posturing and showing off in every letter) . . . How ironical that the very things which I was proud of in my letters then should make the reading of them a humiliation to me now! Don't suppose from this that I have not enjoyed the other aspects of them – the glorious memories they call up. I think I have got over *wishing* for the past back again. I look at it this way. The delights of those days were given to lure us into the world of the Spirit, as sexual rapture is there to lead to offspring and family life. They were nuptial ardours. To ask that they should return, or should remain, is like wishing to prolong the honeymoon at an age when a man should rather be interested in the careers of his growing sons. They have done their work, those days and led on to better things.'

One thing which puzzled Arthur Greeves about Lewis's conversion was that the *spontaneous* appeal of the Christian story continued to be so much less to him than that of paganism. He asked if this might be due, in the main, to Lewis's upbringing in non-Roman Ulster and man's basic imperfection. Lewis agreed that these might have something to do with it, but felt that the chief cause lay elsewhere, possibly in the fact that paganism had furnished him with the initial 'sweetness' which he had needed to start him on the spiritual life.

Though his grandfather Hamilton had been an evangelical churchman who never tired of deprecating the Church of Rome from his pulpit, Lewis does not appear to have shared these sentiments except during his two years at Wynyard School when he affected disgust at the High Church practices of St John's Church in Watford. Indeed, from the time of his conversion to the end of his life, Lewis achieved the rare and seldom-attempted feat of avoiding any show of partisanship. At the same time, however, he distrusted the various manifestations of liberalism (or 'Christianity-and-water' as he came to call it) and any attempt to forge an intellectual or political party out of Christianity.

Later, when his theological works began to appear, many of his critics confused his strong emphasis on 'salvationism' with modern Puritanism. But Lewis had long been aware of the negative and joyless elements in Puritanism – had indeed seen how they affected his friend Arthur Greeves – and in a letter to Greeves dated 6 December 1931 he explained why he distrusted the Ulster brand of Christianity: 'I feel that I can say with absolute certainty . . . that if you ever feel that the *whole spirit and system* in which you were brought up was, after all, right and good, then you may be quite sure that that feeling is a mistake. . . . My reasons for this are 1. That the system denied pleasures *to others* as well as to the votaries themselves: whatever the merits of *self*-denial, this is unpardonable interference. 2. It inconsistently kept *some* worldly pleasures, and always selected the worst ones – gluttony, avarice, etc. 3. It was ignorant. It could give no "*reason* for the faith that was in it". Your relations have been found very ill grounded in the Bible itself and as ignorant as savages of the historical and theological reading needed to make the Bible more than a superstition. 4. "By their fruits ye shall know them." Have they the *marks* of peace, love, wisdom and humility on their faces or in their conversation? Really, you need not *bother* about that kind of Puritanism. It is simply the form which the *memory* of Christianity takes just before it finally dies away altogether in a commercial community: just as extreme emotional ritualism is the form it takes on just before it dies in a fashionable community.'

Shortly after their memorable visit to Whipsnade in September 1931, Warren re-enlisted for a tour of duty in China. Lewis felt very acutely the loss of his company, not only at the Kilns, but in Magdalen as well. Since his temporary retirement in December 1930, Lewis had shared his college rooms with his brother and whenever he was not engaged in tutorials or other work they were usually to be found together and enjoying the same circle of friends.

Though Lewis spent all his weekends and vacations at the Kilns, he stayed most nights in Magdalen during term. This meant that he and Mrs Moore saw each other less frequently than in the old days. Besides this, his literary and theological interests took him more and more into the company of friends such as Tolkien, Barfield, Coghill and Dyson whom it was generally more convenient to meet in college. As the old tradition of having friends home for tea began to disappear, Mrs Moore – now in her fifty-eighth year – saw little, if anything, of those friends Lewis had made since they moved to the Kilns.

Fortunately for her, Mrs Moore had much else to occupy her. Besides eight acres of land, a large part of which was under cultivation, she had to superintend the cooking and the running of a ten-room house. Wages were, of course, much lower then than now and she had a succession of maids to help her.

Shortly after their move to the Kilns, a gardener and general factotum had been found to care for the vegetable garden, the greenhouse and the several acres of apple orchard that lay in front of the house. This was Fred Paxford, who was the same age as Lewis and who lived in a small wooden bungalow on the other side of the old brick-kilns. Paxford was a countryman of immense integrity and surely one of the most unorthodox gardeners in the world. He was a great favourite with Mrs Moore and, unless she made him do otherwise, slept till mid-morning and went to bed long after the rest of the household was asleep.

Though an optimist at heart, Paxford was given to gloomy prognostications and hymn-singing which, quite unaware to him, was sometimes so loud that it could be heard by those who lived near the Kilns. Once when Mrs Moore was confined to bed for some weeks, she called Paxford to her bedside and taught him the rudiments of cooking. Thereafter, he was able to prepare a very tolerable meal though, as Walter Hooper observed when he lived there, the dinners cooked by Paxford were always served up to the accompaniment of 'Abide with me' uttered with so much feeling that every dish on the table rattled.

This unusual gardener was also entrusted with the daily shopping. Though generous to a fault with his own money, he was intent on cutting the Kilns' household expenses to a minimum by a most uncomfortable and misguided brand of economy. He absolutely refused to buy tea or sugar till he had searched the larder and was convinced that the last spoonful had been used. The greenhouse was considered Paxford's private domain and few people, excepting Mrs Moore, were allowed inside. There he raised some beautiful fruits and vegetables, few of which reached the table as they were allowed to reach such perfection that most eventually rotted where they grew. Perhaps the most distinctive of Paxford's attributes was his ability to 'hold things together with a nail and a piece of string'. Once when a pane of glass in Warren's study was broken, he replaced it with one he could find no other use for: it is opaque and remains there as an eye-sore to this day. Though Paxford was almost fanatically attached to Mrs Moore, his second loyalty was to Lewis – or 'Mr Jack' as he called him – whom he served as a devoted friend and servant till the latter's death. Those who would know more about him will find his 'portrait' in *The Silver Chair* where, as Lewis told Hooper, he served as the model for Puddleglum the Marshwiggle.

As Mrs Moore was very kind to animals, the Kilns became a fashionable retreat for stray dogs and cats. Chief among her pets was the dog Mr Papworth, who was somewhat mixed in breed, but predominately a terrier. Though he never made an elaborate fuss over them, Lewis liked dogs too and Mr Papworth accompanied the family on all their holidays. Mr Papworth, who died in 1937, became a bit queer in his old age – his chief oddity being that he would not eat if he were watched. Eventually the only way discovered for getting food inside him was by what might be called the Orpheus-Eurydice method. This required that Lewis walk down the village street with a bowl of food, followed by Mr Papworth who would eat whatever Lewis threw over his shoulder. What made this method 'Orphean' was that, should Lewis look round to *see* what happened, Mr Papworth would give him a fierce look and ignore the food. Barfield once followed behind the dog and watched, as did many amused villagers, Lewis feed Mr Papworth his peripatetic dinner.

During term, when Lewis spent the nights in college, he was called (with tea) at 7.15. After a bath and shave he usually had time for a few paces in Addison's Walk before he went to Matins in Magdalen chapel at 8 o'clock. From 8.15 to 8.25 he breakfasted in Common Room, after which he answered letters until his first pupil arrived at 9 o'clock. His morning tutorials usually lasted from 9 till 1 o'clock which, he complained, was too long a time for a man to act the gramophone in. At 1 o'clock Maureen collected him in the 'family car' and drove him home for lunch. The car had been acquired shortly after the move to the Kilns and, though it was usually driven by Maureen or Paxford, Lewis did at one time learn to manipulate the gears and get it moving. What stopped him was not a crash but, as he told Hooper, the universal agreement that he should not be allowed behind the wheel. Still, he did not mind this and was always delighted to be a passenger when someone else was driving.

Lewis was one of those rare people who enjoy almost every kind of weather which, as he says in *That Hideous Strength*, is 'a useful taste if one lives in England'. On most afternoons he took a long walk and, now that he lived at the Kilns, he could stretch his legs and potter about in his own wood. After tea he was driven back to college where he had pupils from 5.00 till 7.00. After dinner, which was at 7.15, he usually attended the undergraduate societies described in Chapter III. Tuesday was an especially busy day as it included 'Beer and Beowulf' evenings when those pupils reading Anglo-Saxon came to his rooms for instructions and drinks.

The only exceptions to this rigorous programme were Saturdays when he had no pupils after tea and Mondays when he had none. He nevertheless went into college on Mondays as it had become a regular custom for Tolkien to drop in about mid-morning. From Lewis's rooms they usually went to the Eastgate Hotel (just across the High Street from Magdalen) or to a nearby pub for a pint of beer. Writing to his brother about these sessions, Lewis said: 'We talk English School politics; sometimes we criticize one another's poems; other days we drift into theology or "the state of the nation"; rarely we fly no higher than bawdy or puns.'

By 'bawdy' Lewis did not mean what are commonly called 'dirty stories'. He disliked stories containing smut or which bordered on the blasphemous, and when told in his presence he did not disguise his annoyance. By his own definition, bawdy ought to be outrageous and extravagant but it must not have anything cruel or pornographic about it. One example of Lewis's taste in bawdy is a story he once told Kingsley Amis and Brian

Aldiss about a Bishop of Exeter who was giving prizes at a girls' school. 'They did a performance', said Lewis, 'of *A Midsummer Night's Dream*, and the poor man stood up afterwards and made a speech and said (piping voice): "I was very interested in your delightful performance, and among other things I was very interested in seeing for the first time in my life a female Bottom." '

Excepting perhaps Hugo Dyson, Lewis was unrivalled at punning, and one of his students has recorded one of his most brilliant ones. The occasion was a dinner-party at which one of the courses was a haggis, the national dish of Scotland, consisting of the blood and guts of sheep. Seated next to Lewis was a Portuguese dignitary who, while eating the haggis, remarked that he felt like a 'gastronomic Columbus'. 'The comparison is wayward in your case,' replied Lewis. 'Why not a vascular da Gama?'

Since *Dymer* appeared in 1926, Lewis had published four book reviews in the *Oxford Magazine* and two letters in literary journals. Though *The Allegory of Love* was still being written, Lewis was anxious to air some of his literary views in print. On 3 March 1930 he read a paper to the Martlets on 'The Personal Heresy in Poetics' in which he attacked the notion that poetry is the 'expression of personality' and is useful for putting us into contact with the 'poet's soul': in short, that a poet's 'Life' and 'Works' are two diverse expressions of a single quiddity.

Two writers whom he accused of being specially guilty of the 'personal heresy' were E. M. W. Tillyard in his book on *Milton*, and T. S. Eliot in his essay on 'Dante'. Lewis was confident that he could get the essay published in some orthodox literary journal but he wanted it to be seen by the 'heretics' themselves, to take a swipe at them on their own home-ground. He offered it to T. S. Eliot for publication in the *Criterion*.

Oddly enough, Eliot did not trouble to acknowledge it and, after six months' waiting, Lewis wrote to him on 19 April 1931 suggesting that, as he believed Eliot 'had some sympathy with' his 'formal proof' that poetry 'never was nor could be the "expression of personality" save *per accidens*', he might at least get round to accepting or rejecting the paper. 'I do not', he added, 'wish by any pressure on you to reduce my own chances of reaching a public on a subject about which current views exasperate me beyond bearing.'

It is regrettable that Lewis very rarely saved letters addressed to him. Even those few which missed the waste-paper basket survived because they were useful as book-markers. Our ignorance, then, of what was in Eliot's letters is entirely owing to Lewis's habit of eternally 'tidying up' his desk rather than any ill-will he may have felt towards the writer.

Eliot, apparently, asked if he were writing other essays of a similar nature for Lewis said in a letter of 2 June 1931: 'The essay does, as you have divined, form the first of a series of which I have all the materials to hand. The others would be 2. Objective Standards of Literary Merit. 3. Literature and Virtue (This is not a stylistic variant of "Art and Morality": that is my whole point). 4. Literature and Knowledge. 5. Metaphor and Truth. The whole, when completed, would form a frontal attack on Crocean aesthetics and state a neo-Aristotelian theory of literature (not of Art, about which I say nothing) which *inter alia* will re-affirm the romantic doctrine of imagination as a truth-bearing faculty, though not quite as the romantics understood it.'

The 'Personal Heresy' essay got no further with Eliot than did Lewis's 'Eliotic' poems of 1925 and was eventually returned. Having failed, then, to get into the columns of the *Criterion*, Lewis threw his energies into the more scholarly works he had in hand: *The Allegory of Love* and – an off-shoot of it – an essay on 'What Chaucer Really Did to *Il Filostrato*' which appeared in *Essays and Studies* for 1932. The autumn of 1931 and the winter of 1932 turned out to be profitable months because, in writing the papers he mentioned to Eliot, Lewis found an opportunity for formulating and clarifying his ideas about literary criticism.

Still, the thing Lewis *most* wanted to say for the benefit of others continued to be left unsaid – the story of the 'wanting and having' experience of Joy that led to his conversion. Until 1929 Joy had no conscious connection with God but he had tried to put as much as he understood of it into an autobiographical poem written in 1922–23, a portion of which is quoted in Chapter I. The ecstatic aspect of Joy he managed to convey in a short poem 'Joy' published in the *Beacon* in 1924. His third attempt followed on the heels of his conversion to theism when he wrote the first draft of a prose autobiography – or 'the prose *It*' as he called it – which was discussed in the last chapter.

In the spring of 1932 he had another go at writing the story of Joy leading on to conversion. This, like the first attempt, was to be in the form of a long narrative poem. Only 34 lines of it have survived in a letter written to Owen Barfield on 6 May 1932 in which he says, 'I am not satisfied with any part I have yet written and the design is ludicrously ambitious. But I feel it will be several years anyway before I give it up.' As Lewis had read most of Chesterton's theological books by this time it does not seem fanciful to suppose that Lewis's idea of a spiritual 'voyage' was based on an idea suggested by Chesterton in his book on *Orthodoxy*. 'I have often', wrote Chesterton, 'had a fancy for writing a romance about an English yachtsman who slightly miscalculated his course and discovered England under the impression that it was a new island in the South Seas . . . His mistake was really a most enviable mistake . . . What could be more delightful than to have in the same few minutes all the fascinating terrors of going abroad combined with all the humane security of coming home again.'

This new verse autobiography begins with an idea of his Chestertonian 'voyage':

I will write down the portion that I understand
Of twenty years wherein I went from land to land.
At many bays and harbours I put in with joy
Hoping that there I should have built my second Troy
And stayed. But either stealing harpies drove me thence,
Or the trees bled, or oracles, whole airy sense
I could not understand, yet must obey, once more
Sent me to sea to follow the retreating shore
Of this land which I call at last my home, where most
I feared to come; attempting not to find whose coast
I ranged half round the world, with fain design to shun
The last fear whence the last security is won.

Lewis wrote another 100 lines of this new autobiography before he went on his annual spring walking tour with Barfield and Dom Bede Griffiths shortly after Easter of 1932. After this his tight schedule did not afford a break till 16 May when he and Barfield went to hear Wagner's *Siegfried* at Covent Garden. After this he was overwhelmed with work till the end of July. As soon as he was free, he wrote – exhausted – to Arthur Greeves asking if he might be his house-guest in Belfast from 15–29 August.

After so many attempts to tell the story of his conversion, it sounds incredible to say that Lewis wrote his first full-length prose work, *The Pilgrim's Regress,* during his fortnight's holiday in Ireland. Nevertheless, we have it in his own words that he did. On 25 March 1933 he told Arthur Greeves that he wished to dedicate the book to him because, as he said, 'It is yours by every right – written in your house, read to you as it was written.' After sending the manuscript to Barfield for criticism, Lewis wrote to him on 29 October 1932 saying that, because of his 'long prepara-tion by failure in the prose "It" and the autobiographical poem' (the last one), the book 'spurted out so suddenly' that he had very little objective judgement of it.

In turning from a 'voyage' by sea to a journey by road, Lewis is of course imitating Bunyan. In casting his story into the form of an allegory, he is not only following Bunyan but using a medieval technique which his years of work on *The Allegory of Love* had eminently qualified him for. Though he never used allegory in any of his later books, he found, as did Bunyan, that it provided a sudden release for what he wanted to say. In the verses attached to the first part of *The Pilgrim's Progress*, Bunyan says that while working on quite a different book, he 'Fell suddenly into an Allegory' and that once he had his 'Method by the end; Still as I pull'd, *it came.*'

Not only did Lewis's allegory 'come' as unimpeded as Bunyan's, but he found it the perfect receptacle for describing his progress from 'popular realism' to Christianity and the particular part which Joy had played in it. He was, at the same time, spared from putting himself into the limelight as it is his pilgrim, John, who undergoes the journey.

Before the book was vetted by Barfield, Lewis asked Arthur Greeves for his criticisms and he suggested that the shower of Greek and Latin quotations either be translated or omitted. This Lewis was not prepared to do for, as he said, 'one of the contentions of the book is that the decay of our old classical learning is a contributory cause of atheism'. Greeves would also have had him aim at greater simplicity of meaning. Lewis argued that, though the *spirit* of man must 'become humble and trustful like a child and, like a child, *simple in motive*', Christ did not mean that the 'processes of thought by which people become Christians must be childish processes. At any rate', he went on to say, 'the *intellectual* side of my conversion was *not* simple and I can describe only what I know.'

Greeves criticized as well Lewis's style, urging him to be more 'correct, classical and elaborate'. Lewis's answer to this is something of a landmark for it shows that his intention was, from the first, to write simply and clearly. His later books are more readable, but even in *The Pilgrim's Regress* it is obvious that he had a natural sensibility for idiom and the cadences of popular speech. 'I aim', he wrote to Greeves on 4 December 1932, 'chiefly at being idiomatic and racy, basing myself on Malory, Bunyan, and Morris, tho' without archaisms: and would usually prefer to use ten words, provided they are honest native words and idiomatically ordered, than one "literary word". To put the thing in a nutshell you want "The man of whom I told you" and I want "The man I told you of".'

By Christmas 1932 Lewis had finished revising the manuscript, drawn a map to go on the end leaves and sent it to J. M. Dent and Sons. They accepted it on condition that it be shortened and the title altered. At the last moment they wanted to illustrate it – an idea that Lewis was successful in resisting. The title which appeared on the proof copy was *The Pilgrim's Regress, or Pseudo-Bunyan's Periplus: An Allegorical Apology for Christianity, Reason and Romanticism*. Dents knew that some people would not understand the meaning of 'Periplus' (circumnavigation) and Lewis was prevailed upon to omit 'or Pseudo-Bunyan's Periplus' before the book was published in May 1933.

The book had some favourable reviews but was not a commercial success as Dents sold only 680 of the 1,000 copies they printed. It was noticed by Sheed and Ward, the Roman Catholic publishers, and Dents printed a further 1,500 copies and passed them all over to this firm who brought out their edition in 1935.

The Regress put many backs up because of the broadsides Lewis launched at the High Anglicans (Neo-Angular) and Broad Churchmen. Lewis's Irish friend, Canon Claude Chavasse, was one of those who criticized him for hasty generalizations. Admitting that his book was over-bitter and uncharitable, Lewis said, 'What I am attacking in Neo-Angular is a set of people who seem to me . . . to be trying to make of Christianity itself one more high-brow, Chelsea, bourgeois-baiting fad' and 'T. S. Eliot is the single man who sums up the thing I am fighting against.' The Broad Church, he went on to say, suffers from a 'confusion between mere natural goodness and Grace which is non-Christian' and is 'what I most hate and fear in the world.'

Most critics supposed Lewis to be more Catholic than he believed himself to be probably because he appeared to give more importance to 'Mother Kirk' than to faith. He was furious when he discovered that Sheed and Ward had, in a blurb on the jacket of their edition, written 'This story begins in Puritania (Mr Lewis was brought up in Ulster) . . .' – thus implying that the book was an attack on his country and the Anglican Church.

Quite apart from the richness of its ideas, *The Pilgrim's Regress* – specially because it is an allegory – was found to be too complicated for those who come to the Faith by simpler routes. Lewis realized this and wrote an explanatory preface and running headlines for the edition Geoffrey Bles brought out in 1943.

One thing which more than compensated for Lewis's belief that he had failed with his new book, was that his brother had retired from the Army and arrived at the Kilns during Christmas 1932.

'He has become a permanent member of our household', Lewis wrote to Greeves on 4 February 1933, 'and I hope we shall pass the rest of our lives together . . . We both have a feeling that "the wheel has come full circuit", that the period of wanderings is over, and that everything which has happened between 1914 and 1932 was an interruption.'

Another thing which brightened up the winter of 1932 was a children's story which Tolkien had just written. Lewis found *The Hobbit* – as it later came to be called – uncannily good, another door into the world of faerie he had first discovered in *Phantastes*. At the same time, he had mixed feelings about supervising a thesis on George MacDonald. He found it difficult to approach as *work* something so old and intimate, and felt that the American girl who was writing on 'The Fairy Tales and Fantasies of George MacDonald' quite unworthy of her subject. Nevertheless, he persevered and the girl, Miss M. M. McEldowney, was awarded the B.Litt. in 1934.

In celebration of Warren's retirement, the Lewis brothers decided to combine a holiday at sea with a visit to their uncles in Scotland. On 28 July 1933 they took a train to Arrochar where they stayed the night. The next day they spent walking on the shores of Loch Long and Loch Lomond and across the mountains between them. Lewis, who wilted in very hot weather and claimed to have the constitution of a polar bear, was delighted on discovering a pool tucked away in the mountains near Loch Lomond. There they stripped and lay in the pool under a little waterfall. This glorious day was followed by a week's visit to their uncles Bill and Dick (Albert's brothers) at Helensburgh. Uncle Bill, whom they had nicknamed 'Limpopo', bore a strong resemblance to their father, and in a letter to Arthur Greeves on 17 August Lewis said, 'It was uncannily like being at home again – specially when Uncle Bill announced on the Sunday evening "I won't be going into town to-morrow" and we with well-feigned enthusiasm replied "Good!" '

The next day, Monday, 7 August, they sailed from Glasgow in a Clyde Shipping Company boat down the River Clyde, crossed the Irish Sea, and docked in Belfast the following morning. After walking about Campbell College and Little Lea, they visited their old parish church, St Mark's, so that Warren could see for the first time the stained-glass window they had erected there in memory of their parents. They sailed again at 1 o'clock the same day from Waterford and arrived in Plymouth on 10 August. En route to Oxford they visited Romsey Abbey (14 August). Lewis, on learning that one of the twelfth-century abbesses had rejoiced in the name of Joan Jack, observed to his brother that she '*must* have been a comfortable, easy-going kind of person'.

Back in Oxford, Lewis was taken to the cinema (17 August) to see *Cavalcade*. He expected it to be interesting historically but came out feeling he had been at a debauch. He was, nevertheless, lured back a few weeks later to see *King Kong* which he liked because of its rather Rider Haggardish atmosphere. Still, he never cared for this kind of amusement. Once, when Hooper suggested that they see a film, Lewis summed up his attitude to the cinema: 'I like *some* science-fiction, *some* romances of high adventure, but I can't take' – (holding his nose) – '*dram – a*!'

Almost immediately after *King Kong* Lewis settled down to work. He had been one of the public examiners in the Honours School of English from 1931–33 and, once free of this obligation, he disappeared into the Duke Humphrey Library of the Bodleian to finish his book on medieval love poetry. The only substantial break he took before the book was completed was a week's walking tour with Warren in January 1935 during which they toyed with the delightful notion of devising a 'beer map' of England in which each area would be depicted with a different colour to indicate which Beer Baron controlled it.

Finally, after eight years of research and writing, Lewis wrote to R. W. Chapman of the Oxford University Press on 18 September 1935 saying, 'I have now finished my book *The Allegorical Love Poem* and am in search of a publisher.' After outlining the chapters, he went on to say: 'The book as a whole has two themes: 1. The birth of allegory and its growth from what it is in Prudentius to what it is in Spenser. 2. The birth of the romantic conception of love and the long struggle between its earlier form (the romance of adultery) and its later form (the romance of marriage).'

Kenneth Sisam was asked to look after the book and he wrote to Lewis on 20 September to say that the Delegates of the Oxford University Press wished to consider it at their first meeting in Michaelmas Term. He also thanked Lewis for consenting to write the volume on *English Literature in the Sixteenth Century* for the Oxford History of English Literature – a promise which Lewis's former tutor, Professor F. P. Wilson, had extracted from him a few months earlier.

On 29 October the Delegates announced that they definitely wished to publish *The Allegorical Love Poem* and thereafter things began to move with unusual speed. Dom André Wilmart, the Patristics scholar, was asked to read and comment on the first two chapters, after which the book went to press and Lewis received the first batch of proofs before Christmas 1935. But Lewis, as will be seen, was not the only one to read them, and that other proof-reader must now be introduced.

Some years before Dr R. W. Chambers had asked Lewis if he had read the 'spiritual shockers' of Charles Williams. Lewis made a mental note to try one but had not bothered till, in February 1936, when visiting Nevill Coghill in Exeter College, he heard his host praising Williams's novel *The Place of the Lion*. That night he took Coghill's copy home and read it. It seems a pity to contradict the story Lewis told in the preface to *Essays Presented to Charles Williams* (1947) about how he wrote a fan letter to Williams twenty-four hours later, but it does not appear to be entirely accurate. What did happen was that he wrote to Arthur Greeves on 26 February saying: 'I have just read what I think a really great book, *The Place of the Lion* by Charles Williams. It is based on the Platonic theory of the other world in which the archetypes of all earthly qualities exist: and in the novel . . . these archetypes start sucking our world back. The lion of strength appears in the world and the strength starts going out of houses and things into him. The archetypal butterfly . . . appears and all the butterflies of the world fly back into him. But man contains and ought to be able to rule all these forces: and there is one man in the book who does, and the story ends with him as a second Adam "naming the beasts" and establishing dominion over them. It is not only a most exciting fantasy, but a deeply religious and (unobtrusively) a profoundly learned book. The reading of it has been a good preparation for Lent as far as I am concerned: for it shows me (through the heroine) the special sin of abuse of intellect to which all my profession are liable, more clearly than I ever saw it before. I have learned more than I ever knew yet about humility. . . . Do get it, and don't mind if you don't understand everything the first time. . . . It isn't often now-a-days you get a Christian fantasy.' Then, so captivated was he by the novel, he sent Coghill's copy to Cecil Harwood and a note to Barfield urging him to read it next. He also mentioned the book to Sir Humphrey Milford, the head of the Oxford University Press.

On 11 March 1936 Lewis wrote to Charles Williams praising *The Place of the Lion* and suggesting that they meet. Williams, who was on the editorial staff of the Oxford University Press, answered by return of post.

12 March 1936

My dear Mr Lewis,

If you had delayed writing another 24 hours our letters would have crossed. It has never before happened to me to be admiring an author of a book while he at the same time was admiring me. My admiration for the staff work of the Omnipotence rises every day.

To be exact, I finished on Saturday looking – too hastily – at proofs of your *Allegorical Love Poem*. I had been asked to write something about it for travellers and booksellers and people so I read it first. I permit myself to enclose a copy of what I said, because I wrote this on Monday and yesterday our Sir Humphrey told me in the afternoon that he understood you had been reading my *Lion*. So if ever I was drawn to anyone – imagine! I admit that I fell for the *Allegorical Love Poem* so heavily because it is an aspect of the subject with which my mind has always been playing . . . I regard your book as practically the only one that I have ever come across, since Dante, that shows the slightest understanding of what this very peculiar identity of love and religion means . . . As to your letter, what can I say? The public for all these novels has been so severely limited (though I admit in some cases passionate) that it gives me very high pleasure to feel that you liked the *Lion* . . . I do think it was extremely good of you to write and extraordinarily kind of the Omnipotence to arrange the coincidence. You must be in London sometimes. Do let me know and come and have lunch or dinner . . . I am here practically every day for all the day, and if you will send me a post card first I will see that I am . . . Do forgive this too long letter, but after all to write about your *Love Poem* and my *Lion* and both our Romantic Theology in one letter takes some paragraphs.

> Very gratefully yours,
> Charles Williams

During the latter part of March, when Lewis was compiling an index for his book, the publishers suggested that the title be altered as the word 'allegorical' – though not 'allegory' – tended to put people off. Among the list of next titles which Lewis thought of using was *The House of Busirane*. The publishers felt, however, that this made it sound too much like a novel and several of the staff, including Charles Williams, felt that *The Allegory of Love* might give a better idea of what the book is about. Lewis was persuaded to agree and the book was published on 21 May 1936 as *The Allegory of Love: A Study in Medieval Tradition*.

Up to this time Lewis was hardly known outside Oxford. With *The Allegory of Love* he firmly established himself as a first-rate scholar and a writer of exceptional imaginative power. The reviewer for *The Times Literary Supplement*, adding one bouquet to another, said that in his chapter on Chaucer's *Troilus and Criseyde* 'Mr Lewis reaches his full stature as a critic. His . . . appreciation of Chaucer's marvellous poem [is] of the very highest quality . . . the proof, if the reader of his book needs any, that the historical method, in the hands of one who can keep imaginative control of the facts, adds depth to appreciation while taking nothing from its immediacy.' Since its publication *The Allegory of Love* has, over and over again, been classed as one of those rare books, such as Bradley's *Shakespearean Tragedy*, Ker's *Epic and Romance*, and John Livingston Lowes's *Road to Xanadu*, which not only shed fresh light on literature but which are truly 'unputdownable'.

It would be misleading to talk about what the critics *said* about Lewis's book as it goes on being praised by many – as well as

debunked by a few who believe the author made too little use of
the Patristic Fathers or that he was wrong in suggesting that
romantic love was an invention of the Middle Ages. Nevertheless,
to give some idea of how immediately successful *The Allegory of
Love* was with the most eminent scholars of the 1930s, Professor
R. W. Chambers wrote to Lewis on 28 January 1938 saying that
'on second reading it seems to me quite the greatest thing done in
England for medieval studies since Ker's *Epic and Romance*.' In
1937, when Lewis and Dr E. M. W. Tillyard were midway
through their controversy over the 'Personal Heresy' in the pages
of *Essays and Studies*, Tillyard broke off to congratulate his
opponent: 'May I', he wrote, 'be allowed to say what lively
pleasure and admiration I experienced in reading the *Allegory of
Love*? Not only have I learnt a very great deal but I got that rare
joy – the sense of much matter marshalled, digested into a *book*.
At last, I exclaim, a medievalist who is also a critic. And I found
the preliminary matter quite as thrilling as the rest: the account of
how allegory arose was something that I had long been wanting.
And your plea for accepting allegory and your putting of that
acceptance to critical use does seem to me to matter enormously.
It casts light on what should not be but undoubtedly is a disgrace-
fully dark place . . . I see you are whacking back at me in the next
volume of *Essays and Studies*; and I look forward to the article
provided the mincemeat you reduce me to is not too small.'

Since he first put pen to paper Lewis had a natural itch to
write. With the publication of *Spirits in Bondage*, however, his
desire for fame began seriously to inhibit his ability to write
easily. Then came his conversion which, though it helped him
accept the fact that he might never be a successful poet, led him
to question the value of cultural activities. Was he – or, for that
matter, was *anyone* – justified in spending so much time on
literature? Was it not very like fiddling while Rome burned? By
the time *The Allegory of Love* was published he had come a long
way towards answering this question.

The conclusions he reached are found in two important but
neglected essays written in the late thirties. In the first, 'Christian-

ity and Literature', Lewis maintained that though the recipe for writing Christian and secular literature is the same (good diction and the like), a Christian approach to literary theory and criticism ought not to be like that of most secular writers. The latter describe great authors as always 'breaking fetters', 'bursting bonds' and generally 'being themselves'. Though the New Testament has nothing to say of literature, the metaphors it most often uses are those of 'imitation', 'reflection' and 'assimilation'. In St John's Gospel, Christ 'copies' the operation of the Father. Thus, while secular critics aim at being 'original' and 'creative', 'originality', Lewis believed, is plainly the prerogative of God alone.

The Christian approach to literature, Lewis concludes, ought to be very like Phemius's claim to be a poet (in *Odyssey* xxii, 347): 'I am self-taught; a god has inspired me with all manner of songs.' 'The unbeliever', says Lewis, 'may take his own temperament and experience, just as they happen to stand, and consider them worth communicating simply because they are facts, or, worse still, because they are his. To the Christian his own temperament and experience, as mere fact, and as merely his, are of no value or importance whatsoever: he will deal with them, if at all, only because they are the medium through which, or the position from which, something universally profitable appeared to him.'

The second essay has a story attached to it. Shortly after its publication *The Pilgrim's Regress* won the attention of the Reverend Dr Alec Vidler who became the editor of the monthly journal *Theology* in 1938. Dr Vidler, hoping to develop some literary interest in the journal, invited Lewis to become a 'literary collaborator', thereby introducing him into the world of professional theologians. Lewis was quick to accept, explaining to Dr Vidler in a letter of 23 March 1939 that 'open lists and "the rigours of the game" ' was what he wanted and liked. His fighting instincts were immediately roused when he read an article by Brother George Every on 'The Necessity of *Scrutiny*' (a literary magazine made famous by its editor, F. R. Leavis) in the columns of *Theology* (March 1939) in which Brother Every suggested that theological students should be 'tested' on their ability to read a new piece of writing on a secular subject, thus hinting that 'culture' and 'good taste' were on a par with Christianity.

Though Lewis sometimes overstated his opinions in conversation, he never rushed them into print. After much deliberation he answered Brother Every in a carefully reasoned article entitled 'Christianity and Culture' (*Theology*, March 1940). In this miniature *apologia* he argues the claims both for and against culture, arriving at the following conclusions: (1) The safest and shortest way towards salvation is devotion to the person of Christ. (2) Most men glorify God by doing to his glory things which, though not *per se* acts of glorification, become so by being offered to him. (3) Though culture in itself will save no man, it sometimes has a distinct part to play in bringing souls to Christ – is sometimes a road *into* Jerusalem, and sometimes *out*. (4) People such as himself, who are not fit for any other kind of work, are justified in making their living by teaching and writing.

It was this last point which set free Lewis's own genius – as we shall see from the chapter that follows.

VI. INKLINGS AND OTHERS

In the days when Lewis kept a diary and his father filed away both his and Warren's incoming letters, it was easy to follow him chronologically. But from 1931 onwards not only was the continuity broken, but Lewis was tending more and more to divide his life into compartments that occasionally could only be described accurately as watertight. His home life became more and more separated from his life in Magdalen, until his move to Cambridge: one could be a constant visitor to him in college without ever having been to the Kilns. And it is a perpetual surprise to some of his closest friends to discover other friends of his as close of whom he had never even spoken – or speaking hinted that he knew them.

To pupils and younger friends Lewis was simply a bachelor don living in college rooms. Pupils would be invited in twos or threes to stimulating – some found it 'overwhelming' – talk in his rooms after Hall of an evening, where they would be regaled with port, beer and the inevitable pot of strong tea.

Even when he was known only as a tutor, and as the author of *The Allegory of Love*, Lewis was so good a lecturer that undergraduates who usually avoided as many as possible attended his, made sure of completing the course (which usually meant two lectures a week for six weeks) – and sometimes came again when Lewis repeated the same series.

Lewis lectured almost entirely from a written text; but he would add to this, both during the lectures with additional examples or explanations, and in the basic text before delivering the course again where further research or later criticism made this desirable. There were also the lighter moments: good laughs which he timed with all an actor's skill, and knew from previous experience when to expect so that he could build up to them. Thus in the 'Prolegomena to Medieval Studies' (the basis of his last book, *The Discarded Image*), in describing the various types of men born under the different planetary influences, when he came to Jupiter: 'the Jovial character is cheerful, festive; those born under Jupiter are apt to be loud-voiced and red-faced – it is obvious under which planet *I* was born!' always produced its laugh.

On one occasion during the war, when the audience at his lectures came to consist predominantly of women, and these tended more and more to come without their academic gowns (which were still statutory wear at lectures), Lewis strode into the Hall at his usual speed, but did not begin to lecture when he had deposited his notes on the lectern. Instead, he gazed slowly up and down the crowded tables with a blank stare until, like Mr Puff, he had produced 'a proper expectation in the audience'; then, with his usual perfect timing, he exclaimed, 'Oh! I must apologize for wearing a *gown*!' At the next lecture gowns were in fashion again.

Whether one had read any of his works or not, the first sight of C. S. Lewis was always a surprise. One undergraduate just initiated to lecturers as varied as Tolkien, Edmund Blunden and Lascelles Abercrombie, remembers the shock as he sat for the first time in the Hall at Magdalen in October 1938 and there strode in a big man with a large red face and shabby clothes, looking like nothing so much as a prosperous butcher, who began addressing his audience in a loud, booming voice and with tremendous gusto.

Of course one soon got over this first impression when Lewis began lecturing. It was obvious even in such utilitarian lectures as his two 'Prolegomena' series (to 'Medieval' and 'Renaissance Literature') that one was listening not merely to a scholar of immense erudition, but to a lover of literature who had read every text he mentioned, had enjoyed most of them, and was eager to share both his knowledge and his enthusiasm with anyone whom he could persuade to do so.

Lewis was popularly supposed to regard both lectures and

tutorials as a complete waste of his valuable time, and to hold undergraduates in the uttermost contempt. But even if these assumptions had been correct, no one could deny that he gave more fully and conscientiously than most tutors of the very best that he could give.

Perhaps the impression of not wasting more time than was absolutely necessary was given by the fact that Lewis did indeed seek to exemplify Kipling's dictum about filling 'the unforgiving minute with sixty seconds' worth of distance run'. He lectured for precisely three-quarters of an hour, and he never waited to answer questions. Two minutes before the end of the lecture he would quietly gather his notes together, return the watch which at one time he was in the habit of borrowing from the nearest member of his audience, and prepare to leave – lecturing all the time. Then, as he finished his last sentence, he would step off the dais and stride down the hall at top speed. If he was at all late in arriving at the lecture, he would begin it even before he entered the hall: several times the great voice came booming up the steps outside the hall door and Lewis would enter in haste, lecturing vigorously.

Later on he had a watch of his own; but in the Michaelmas Term of 1938 at least he was forced to borrow one. The nearest undergraduate chanced to be Roger Lancelyn Green, who sat almost at his feet and sported an obvious pocket watch and chain – and only he would know, as the watch was returned to him, that the lecture was ending. But not by the wildest stretch of imagination could Green have dreamt that 25 years later the book built out of those lectures to which he was listening with such interest would be dedicated to him.

Lewis's knowledge certainly seemed prodigious. Every quotation that was not originally in English was given in the correct language, followed by a translation: Norse, Old and Middle English, Latin, Greek, French, German, Italian – even Old Welsh, though that was probably the only one of these languages which he would not have been able to read unseen with ease. His interest was in the written rather than the spoken word, and on the way to Greece in 1960 when the plane was forced down at Naples by bad weather, he made no attempt to talk Italian, beyond the few bare words needed to procure a bottle of Chianti; and in Greece itself he made no attempt to learn even the odd phrase in Modern Greek, though during an enforced wait he picked up a local paper and was soon eagerly translating as much as his knowledge of the ancient language enabled him to do – and was earnestly working out how the meanings of words had changed ('*nerō* for water, instead of *hudor*: ah, of course! *nēro* from the Nereids!'), and what certain new or obscure words could mean.

Another undergraduate who became Lewis's pupil remembers his interview for a demyship at Magdalen in March 1941, and 'the plump, cheerful man, with a large red countryman's face, and a loud voice, who rolled his r's, and who asked most of the questions.' And when Derek Brewer had been accepted by the college and written to ask his future tutor what he should read before coming up in October, Lewis had replied with a long letter of good advice: certain relevant Latin works (to be read in the Loeb Edition with the English on the opposite page); 'a fairly sound Biblical background is assumed by most of the older English writers: if you lack this, acquire it'; and concluded: 'Chaucer, Shakespeare, Milton are certainties whatever shortened course or ordinary course you take. Next to these in importance come Malory, Spenser, Donne, Browne, Dryden, Pope, Swift, Johnson, Wordsworth. After that it becomes more a matter of taste. The great thing is to be always reading but not to get bored – treat it not like work, more as a vice! Your book bill ought to be your biggest extravagance.'

Mr Brewer came into residence for a year in Michaelmas Term 1941 – and found Oxford still itself as far as English literature was concerned. Lewis rarely suggested 'any critical books, and in those days there were indeed few that were much good. Neither he nor anyone else ever mentioned to me such names as I. A. Richards or F. R. Leavis. Nor did Lewis ever mention his own work' – though the days of decline were even then at hand when freshers on coming up would inquire who their examiners were to be, and then make a point of reading and digesting anything they had written. For Lewis, true to the great tradition of English scholarship, concentrated always 'on actual texts and their historical meaning, rather than on modern critical books,' and was never fully convinced that any Oxford tutor could fall so low as to teach the tenets of cultural disintegration which he sought to discredit in *The Abolition of Man*.

In 1947 Mr Brewer returned to take up his interrupted course, and records that 'in those crowded days just after the War Lewis gave tutorials from 10 to 1 and 5 to 7, (apart from one or two lectures) from Monday to Friday. A heavy load . . . He had a set of rooms in the middle of the handsome eighteenth-century New Buildings at Magdalen. The high-ceilinged principal room faced north over the deer-park, and we met there in groups for Old English translation and occasionally for individual tutorials. A door led off to a bedroom, and another to a small inner room, with windows looking south to the rest of the College, where Lewis kept his books, and we often had tutorials. All the furniture was very shabby. A large table filled the middle of the main room, where he wrote, with wooden chairs around, and there were a couple of battered armchairs by the marble fireplace in which we sat opposite each other for tutorials. There was always a smell of pipe-tobacco. My most vivid memory of Lewis in this room is during the great freeze-up in the winter of 1947, when there was no heating [on account of power-cuts decreed by the Socialist Government], and he sat in his armchair fully clothed, with a dressing-gown on top, and on top of that a blanket which came up over his head like a cowl. It was rather like medieval castles, he said, where you put on extra clothes when you came inside, as Gawain did in the great Middle English poem of *Sir Gawain and the Green Knight*.

'The general form of the tutorial was simple. First, after two or three minutes of general conversation, one read the essay. The reading of this, and the effort of composition were, if done seriously, the major part of a full week's work that included preparation of translation and attendance at lectures. Reading the essay usually took me about ten minutes. Lewis listened with extreme intentness, not, I am all too sure, because of the fascination of my words, but because it was his duty. Once, in the middle of an essay, the 'phone rang. I stopped and he answered it in the other room. When he returned after a five-minute interruption he repeated *verbatim* my last sentence as far as it had got. He had an astonishing verbatim memory, and could repeat chunks of prose to illustrate a point arising in discussion. Given any line in *Paradise Lost* he could usually continue with the next line.'

Warren Lewis comments also on his brother's amazing memory, which he put down to 'the long years of grinding self-inflicted poverty which had made it second nature to him never to buy a book if he could master its contents without doing so.' Even in later years when his own works were bringing in large royalties, Lewis seldom bought books, and had completely lost his early love of fine editions, hand-made paper and the other desiderata of the true bibliophile. On one occasion Green tried to give him a copy of George MacDonald's first book – a first edition inscribed by MacDonald to his wife's sister: but Lewis refused it, saying that he already had *Within and Without* in the cheap reprint of MacDonald's *Collected Poems*, and took no interest in first editions or association copies. This even went so far as his own manuscripts were concerned – which he used as scrap-paper as soon as typescripts had been made for the publisher. Green found that notes about one of his own books were written on the backs of two odd pages of an early version of *Miracles*: had he realized in time that Lewis treated even his completed manuscripts in this way, he would have tried to save one from the general destruction!

Apart from necessary work books and essential texts, Lewis's meagerly populated shelves looked as if they had been stocked entirely from 'the Fourpenny Box' – and in fact many of the sets: the 'Border' Scott, the 'Gadshill' Dickens, the 'Swanston' Stevenson, and so on, the titles almost illegible on their faded spines, probably came from his father's store of books at Little Lea. To these he was always pleased to add cheap volumes of fiction or copies of his friends' books: while refusing gifts of first editions as such from Green, he was delighted with spare copies of books new to him by such mutual favourites as Rider Haggard, F. Anstey and E. Nesbit – and was blissfully unaware when a really rare volume that he happened to want slipped in amongst them.

But to return to Derek Brewer's recollections of tutorials with Lewis: 'As I read the essay, he made notes. Many of these were minute points of verbal structure, rhythm, clarity, precision. In general Lewis had a Johnsonian literalism. He always claimed to be baffled by the phrase, too often applied to Chaucer, "with tongue in cheek", and would put it to comic visual effect. Such literalism, both on this small scale, and more generally in his whole outlook, was a very important part of his criticism, his religion, and the Socratic *faux-naiveté* that he often used in argument. To return to the essay, if he started to doodle I knew I was being boring. When the essay was finished he first gave a general word or two of judgement. One week I surpassed myself on Shakespeare's tragedies, and rejoiced in high praise. Next I thought I had produced something equally stunning, a judicious condemnation of the late romances. "Well," he began, "I couldn't disagree more." He was a "romance critic", not (as most modern critics are) a "tragedy critic". After a general comment or two he usually pointed out the small-scale deficiencies of the essay, not at all in a captious way. Then we discussed the principal points made, and any other things to be said about the texts. This was almost always delightfully interesting. He had a vivid response to the most various texts, a ready penetrating comment and wit. One of his most notable characteristics as a man as well as a tutor was his generous acceptance of variety and difference, sure of his own standards but tolerant of others, and of failings. Add to this an almost inexhaustible interest in literature and ideas.'

It would be easy to continue with recollections of Lewis as a tutor, for he had so many articulate pupils, from John Betjeman to Kenneth Tynan and John Wain, and so many now high in the ranks of English studies – John Lawlor, R. T. Davies, Derek Brewer and many more – that one must stand for all in the present case, though several of them have already published excellent descriptions and assessments.

But, as John Lawlor has pointed out (in *Light on C. S. Lewis*), 'the plain fact is that he hated teaching.' In his earlier years as a tutor Lewis was disappointed and frustrated by the poor numbers of students reading English, which made it necessary for him to continue for some time giving tutorials in philosophy and even political science; too few even of his English pupils rose above the mediocre (to one of his outstanding powers), and, 'Where he could not strike fire, he tended to accept with ironic resignation; but it did not endear teaching to him. Thirdly – and I have, I believe, kept the true order of importance – Lewis valued time as few men I have met, before or since, have done. After an early breakfast and a walk, nine o'clock in Term time would see him seated at his writing-table, wooden penholder and steel nib moving steadily over the page until the ten o'clock pupil knocked on his door. "The hungry generations tread thee down" was a witticism he ruefully acknowledged. No man was better equipped for silent industry, hour upon hour . . . To Lewis, tutorial work was a school of patience; and if one was ever disappointed that one's best things had gone unregarded, one was also conscious that one's best wasn't good enough to feed and sustain his most remarkable mind. The effect of this was that a good many of Lewis's pupils, including the very best of them, were reduced to silence or, worse, incoherence when dealing with him. . . .'

Lewis had something of this numbing effect on others besides pupils. Apart from the odd word at lectures, Green met him for the first time in November 1939 when he was asked to coffee and port one evening. There were several others present, probably Lewis's brighter pupils, and the talk was so scintillating and rarefied that Green sat a mute and over-awed spectator – and was never asked again. In March 1944, having been Lewis's pupil at a series of B.Litt. classes on textual criticism, and met him once or twice under other circumstances, Green called on him early one evening to show him a letter from Gordon Bottomley about the recently published *Preface to 'Paradise Lost'*. Under the circumstances Lewis cannot have resented having his time broken into, and he talked in friendly fashion for half an hour. But as his visitor was leaving, he suddenly boomed out: 'Green! How old are you now?' 'Twenty-five, sir.' 'Ah! A sad age to reach! You will never again be able to read one of the great epics of the world for the first time!' Green left hurriedly lest his opinion should be asked on Ariosto or Camoëns . . .

But Lewis was famous – or notorious – for such devastating remarks, which were too often reported maliciously as examples of his contempt for young people and his delight in scoring off them. In fact they were made in absolute good faith: Lewis simply found it impossible to realize or to remember that most of his hearers were infinitely less well read than he was, or to follow the workings of the average second-class mind. At a mixed dinner-party he had been heard to fire a sudden, petrifying question at one of the youngest ladies present – and then, as it were, to remember, and turn whatever answer she managed to stammer out into the gambit for a scintillating discourse – of which he was able skilfully to suggest that she was the originator.

He learnt what might be called mental charity more slowly than any other virtue – and it became most notable in his later years and particularly after his marriage. But he never outgrew the teachings of 'the Great Knock'. As he says of him in *Surprised by Joy*, 'the most casual remark was taken as a summons to disputation,' and so it was with Lewis himself. If a friend made a thoughtless remark or a loose generality in conversation, Lewis would boom out, 'I challenge that!' and the foils of logic would be clashing in a moment – thrust, parry and riposte, his eyes positively sparkling at the skilful play of words until one could almost hear the click and slide of pliant steel upon steel – and indeed the final thrust, given or very occasionally received, would often be accompanied by a joyous '*Touché!*'

Naturally Lewis's relations with his fellow members of Magdalen Senior Common Room varied over the 30 years of his residence in college. In *Surprised by Joy* he pays particular tribute to 'five great Magdalen men who enlarged my very idea of what a learned life should be – P. V. M. Benecke, C. C. J. Webb, J. A. Smith, F. E. Brightman and C. T. Onions. . . . In my earlier years at Magdalen I inhabited a world where hardly anything I wanted to know needed to be found out by my own unaided efforts. One or other of these could always give you a clue. . . . I found as always that the ripest are kindest to the raw and the most studious have most time to spare.'

But as early as 10 July 1928 he was writing to his father: 'I am almost ashamed to tell you – I am beginning to be rather disillusioned about my colleagues. There is a good deal more intrigue and mutual back-scratching and even direct lying than I ever supposed possible . . . Of course it may simply be that, being rather an innocent in practical matters myself, and having been deceived once or twice, I have rushed too hastily to conclusions. But the bad thing is that the decent men seem to me to be all the old ones (who will die) and the rotters seem to be all the young ones (who will last my time).'

However mistaken he may have been in the main, this rather jaundiced view of college politics, 'the Magdalen junta' and other 'inner rings' gave Lewis a good background for what might happen in a Senior Common Room where 'the rotters' really did gain control, as vividly imagined and described in the first chapter of *That Hideous Strength* (1945). In actual fact, although during his earlier years as a Fellow Lewis undoubtedly got on better with his seniors, he was also to make lasting friendships among the younger Fellows, notably with Colin Hardie the classics scholar. Nonetheless he continued to pay that deference to the old which, he maintained, was growing more and more out of fashion in the modern world. One noticed, for example, the gentleness and patience he showed to Professor Arthur Lee Dixon (1867–1955) whose mind was beginning to wander in his very last year, and with what tact and skill he would draw him out to talk of the days when Lewis Carroll employed him as temporary mathematics tutor at Christ Church, or when in the 1890s as a Fellow of Merton he was visited unexpectedly by Andrew Lang who had previously occupied the same rooms.

Canon Adam Fox, who became a Fellow of Magdalen about 1928, recollected forming a breakfast quartet with Lewis, Benecke and J. A. Smith: 'If my recollection is correct he never read the newspaper in Common Room himself.' (Lewis, in fact, never read the paper at all: he would skim the headlines of *The Times* and sometimes do the crossword.) 'I seem to think that in the earlier years, when he was struggling out of atheism into the Church, he rarely came to breakfast at all. But from about 1933 he attended Chapel regularly, and came in from it with Benecke and myself about 8.15 to join J.A. On Fridays our Chapel Service consisted of the Litany, which contains three substantial suffrages for the Sovereign and another for his family. As we came into Common Room one Friday Lewis commented: "That Litany makes one feel as if the Royal Family were not pulling their weight." There was a touch of haste without hurry about his attitude to breakfast, and he was always the first to leave us, being anxious to get back to his work and have a little time at something congenial before the pupils arrived.' Later, when fame began to swell his correspondence, Lewis always employed the hour or so between breakfast and his first pupil in concentrated letter writing; he also found time for a walk, usually before chapel, or perhaps sometimes in lieu of it, round 'Addison's Walk', the Magdalen meadow actually within the college bounds.

But, with Adam Fox, 'we must come back to him at breakfast in Common Room. I think he had a great respect for Benecke, but he had a real reverence for J.A., though both respect and reverence were mingled with some amusement. He had not many interests in common with Benecke, nothing to give or to receive about the College or about Music or about ancient history, in which Benecke had been tutor for many years in the past; and Benecke was in any case too modest to sustain a lively debate. But Lewis was a philosopher as well as a man of letters, and as such able to bring out J.A. much better, and make him show his paces. He asked him enticing questions and chaffed him not a little in an affectionate way. In me Lewis found someone much devoted to poetry as a reader but not as a student. I looked to him for information and opinion, but I must often have asked the wrong question. He sometimes surprised me, as when he named Dante as the best example of "pure poetry". He did not often quote poetry, at any rate so early in the morning.'

Canon Fox was struck by the way in which Lewis 'was notably detached from this world and yet made so great an impact on it. His innocence and ignorance were unlimited. He took a very slight interest in what was going on round about him in our little academic world. Some current discussion about College or University affairs which had been in everybody's mind and on everybody else's lips passed him by, though when at last he heard of it, he often made a very sound observation slightly tinged with petulance. About some proposed changes in the tutorial system which tended to exalt the Faculties at the expense of the Colleges he remarked "We shall soon be just the Staff" – an anticipation not far from the truth.'

Lewis had very definite ideas about university education and the proper relation between tutor and student. 'The student is, or ought to be, a young man who is already beginning to follow learning for its own sake, and who attaches himself to an older student, not precisely to be taught, but to pick up what he can,' he wrote in *Rehabilitations* (1939); and 'if education is beaten by training, civilization dies.' And by civilization he meant 'humanity', 'by which I do not mean kindness so much as the realization of the human idea. Human life means to me the life of beings for whom the leisured activities of thought, art, literature, conversation are the end, and the preservation and propagation of life merely the means. That is why education seems to me so important: it actualizes that potentiality for leisure, if you like for amateurishness, which is man's prerogative.'

'Perhaps one of the most significant of his contributions to the study of English Literature at Oxford was the part he played with his friend Professor J. R. R. Tolkien in establishing a syllabus for the Final Honour School which embodied his belief in the value of medieval (especially Old English) literature, his conviction that a proper study of modern literature required the linguistic training that the study of earlier literature gave, and his sense of the continuity of English literature,' said Helen Gardner in her obituary lecture to the British Academy, 'and the syllabus, which remained in force for over twenty years, was in many ways an admirable one.'

'The tap-root, Anglo-Saxon, can never be abandoned,' wrote Lewis. 'The man who does not know it remains all his life a child among real English students. There we find the speech-rhythms that we use every day made the basis of metre; there we find the origins of that romanticism for which the ignorant invent such odd explanations. This is our own stuff and its life is in every branch of the tree to the remotest twigs. That we cannot abandon.'

The only drawback to the English syllabus that Lewis created was the failure to find space for the literature of the Victorian age, '1830–1900' being added merely as an optional paper – which only about five per cent of candidates took, and for which they received little help either from tutors or lecturers. 'This meant,' concluded Helen Gardner, 'that in the period when Victorian Literature was coming into the domain of scholarship, Oxford made virtually no contribution to the development of techniques of dealing with the problems presented by this vast, untidy period of genius.'

Lewis had, of course, no bias against post-1830 literature, indeed the period included authors whom he considered among the 'very great' such as Morris and Kipling. Authors whom he did not admire such as James and Lawrence, he would dismiss as 'not for us' in conversation with literary friends – but he had read some at least of their works, which he could quote or refer to knowledgeably on occasion. Lewis did not enjoy the Restoration dramatists either, and Nevill Coghill has recorded that he never heard him quote from any of them. But on one occasion at least he quoted Congreve very appositely to Green, and he certainly discussed Dryden's plays with him, though he did not cross Magdalen Grove to see the Oxford University Dramatic Society perform *Marriage-à-la-Mode* there. But this was in accordance with his lack of interest in the theatre itself, and his surprising assertion that to see *A Midsummer Night's Dream* (acted under his windows in Magdalen Grove in 1942) performed in the open air would spoil it for him: if he was to see it all, it would have more magic for him in a theatre. But, like Hazlitt, he preferred to read Shakespeare's plays rather than see them acted.

He did, of course, visit the theatre occasionally; and he certainly made a pilgrimage to Covent Garden to see the complete cycle of *The Ring* – though how it fitted into his earlier conceptions of 'Northernness' fostered on William Morris and the actual Icelandic sagas, he did not say. His complete silence on the subject might be taken to suggest that he found the performance of opera singers as disillusioning as Morris had done; but for Wagner's music he never lost his admiration.

Although literature of the previous hundred years was not taught in Oxford in Lewis's day, he was as keenly interested in it as any modern student, and more widely read than most. Though not an enthusiastic reader of the more psychological type of novel, and expressing almost as little interest in Fielding and Smollett as in the dramatists of their period, he was an enthusiastic reader of Jane Austen, whose novels he re-read again and again. He read Scott with equal enthusiasm, but was more temperate in his admiration for Dickens, and cared much less for Thackeray and George Eliot; Hardy and Henry James he admired but did not enjoy, and had even less use for Lawrence and Joyce. He proclaimed Kipling to be the greatest prose writer of their generation – though with the reservations detailed in his lecture on 'Kipling's World'. Nevertheless he was greatly impressed by the Russians, and thought *War and Peace* the greatest novel ever written.

He seemed to know all the greater poets of the nineteenth century well – and probably knew the majority of minor poets to some extent. A chance conversation proved, for example, that he had read and could often quote from most of the Lang-Henley-Dobson group, and that he was well versed in the 'Georgians' – among whom, indeed, 'Clive Hamilton' should probably be classed. Perhaps on account of this affinity he ranked Yeats, Bridges and Masefield among the major poets, and spoke in praise of de la Mare. But he never came to terms with 'modern' poetry, though he was on friendly personal relations with W. H. Auden and T. S. Eliot towards the end of his life, and admired some of Roy Campbell's work. Most 'modern poetry' was a 'cult engineered by cranks with money, via *Horizon*', he remarked in 1949 at a lunch party where his guests included Ruth Pitter and Owen Barfield, and he went on to maintain that 'they could engineer a "Romantic Revival" themselves – if they had the money to start and run a paper.'

Lewis had been approached three years earlier by Laurence Whistler who, in association with Andrew Young, was hoping to found a periodical to challenge *Horizon*, and already had Ruth Pitter and Richard Church in favour of the scheme, with T. S. Eliot 'sitting on the fence, metaphorically'. Lewis was enthusiastic over the idea. 'I am pleased, to the point of being excited, by your suggestion,' he wrote to Mr Whistler on 9 January 1947. 'I have said again and again that what we very badly need is a new, frankly high-brow periodical *not* in the hands of the Left. I have usually added "If only we could find a right-minded capitalist." Money, I take it, is the first essential. I entirely agree that it should not be specifically Christian, much less Anglican: the Tao (in that sense) is to be the ring fence. In almost all existing periodicals one knows in advance how a certain book will be reviewed: the personal and political bias is no longer even disguised. That is what must be avoided.'

Lewis was not able to be present at the inaugural meeting that April, but sent a 'memorandum', the most relevant section of which reads:

'I think the Periodical ought to come before the public with *no* explicitly religious pretensions at all; its offer should be simply an offer of good poems, good stories, good articles, and good reviews. On the other hand, those who run it should in fact all be Christians. The standard they actually apply in admitting or rejecting contributions should *not* be that of agreement or disagreement with the Christian Faith, but that of agreement or disagreement with what may be called the "good Pagan" range of rationality and virtue. Thus while many, perhaps most, contributors would be explicitly

Christian, we would freely admit good work which was not, and might even admit work opposed to the Faith provided the opposition was based on appeal to reason and ethics. What would be definitely and always excluded (a) Total Scepticism: i.e. attacks on reason and natural morality. (b) Pornography, however highbrow. (c) Cynicism and Sadism however well disguised as "Realism". Thus, if they were all now alive, we should admit Aristotle (but not Heraclitus), Lucretius (but not Petronius), Voltaire (but not Anatole France), Hardy (but not Oscar Wilde) . . .'

'Nothing came of the idea,' writes Mr Whistler, 'probably because there was no general agreement; certainly because there was no money; and I suspect because it was thought, despite our disclaimers, that Young and I really did want to run it. C. S. Lewis believed us, I think, or he would not have been enthusiastic, but I doubt if some of the others did.' And so *Portico* never opened.

Indeed Lewis, with his loathing and distrust of 'inner rings', could never have been comfortable for long in what must have developed to some extent into a clique, however open a ring fence was designed for it. His interests were too wide and his tastes too individual – and he was essentially too modest a man – to set himself up as the head of any kind of literary 'school', or even to gather one about him. John Wain's description of the informal gatherings of certain of Lewis's friends known as the 'Inklings' errs in this direction, even if Mr Wain was not conscious of creating a wrong impression in his rather patronizing account of Lewis's Thursday evenings in *Sprightly Running*. About this passage Lewis wrote in *Encounter* (January 1963): 'The whole picture of myself as one forming a cabinet, or cell, or coven, is erroneous. Mr Wain has mistaken purely personal relationships for alliances. He was surprised that these friends were "so different from one another." But were they more different from one another than he is from all of them? Aren't we always surprised at our friend's other friendships? As at all his tastes?'

Lewis in fact refers to the Inklings as 'our own club', but it had no constitution or committee, or was indeed anything but a group of friends who met whenever possible on a Thursday evening after Hall in Lewis's rooms to discuss literary matters and read for criticism the latest instalments of work which they happened to have in progress: 'membership' was solely a matter of invitation.

According to Professor Tolkien, the Inklings developed from an actual literary society founded in University College in the mid-Thirties by an undergraduate called Tangye Lean who wished to have a few senior members and was able to interest both Lewis and Tolkien. Meetings took place in Tangye Lean's rooms in college, and 'its procedure was that at each meeting members should read aloud unpublished compositions. These were supposed to be open to immediate criticism.' The name Inkling was a kind of pun: the usual meaning of having a distant notion of something doubling with some such recollection of a scribbler and his works as the 'paper pellets of inky boys' in *Stalky & Co*. It was probably intended to be a modern version of the famous Scriblerus Club of very similar constitution whose original members were Pope, Swift, Gay, Arbuthnot and Parnell.

'The Club soon died,' continues Tolkien of the Inklings, 'but C.S.L. and I at least survived. Its name was then transferred (by C.S.L.) to the undetermined and unelected circle of friends who gathered about C.S.L., and met in his rooms in Magdalen. Although our habit was to read aloud compositions of various kinds (and lengths!), this association and its habit would in fact have come into being at this time, whether the original short-lived club had ever existed or not. C.S.L. had a passion for hearing things read aloud, a power of memory for things received in that way, and also a facility in extempore criticism, none of which were shared (especially not the last) in anything like the same degree by his friends.' (Letter dated 11 September 1967, in W. L. White's *The Image of Man in C. S. Lewis* (1970), pp. 221–2.)

The Inklings were in full swing by the time their most important recruit, Charles Williams, joined them in September 1939: the regular members at that time being Lewis (and his brother, who was, however, recalled to the Army at the outbreak of war), Tolkien, Coghill, Dyson, Barfield, Adam Fox and Dr 'Humphrey'

Havard. Ten years later (apart from Williams who died in 1945 and Adam Fox who had left Oxford) the members were the same, with the addition of Gervase Mathew, Colin Hardie, Christopher Tolkien and John Wain – with Lord David Cecil, Roy Campbell and C. E. 'Tom' Stevens (a Fellow of Magdalen) as less frequent visitors, and occasionally an ex-pupil of Lewis's, such as George Sayer, a master at Malvern, at Oxford on a visit, and others who might rank as guests rather than members.

'I can see that room so clearly now,' wrote John Wain of the last years of the Inklings' great decade, 'the electric fire pumping heat into the dank air, the faded screen that broke some of the keener draughts, the enamel beerjug on the table, the well-worn sofa and armchairs, and the men drifting in (those from distant colleges would be later), leaving overcoats and hats in any corner and coming over to warm their hands before finding a chair. There was no fixed etiquette, but the rudimentary honours would be done partly by Lewis and partly by his brother, W. H. Lewis, a man who stays in my memory as the most courteous I have ever met – not with mere politeness, but with a genial, self-forgetting considerateness that was as instinctive to him as breathing. Sometimes, when the less vital members of the circle were in a big majority, the evening would fall flat; but the best of them were as good as anything I shall live to see. This was the bleak period following a ruinous war, when every comfort (and some necessities) seemed to have vanished for ever; Lewis had American admirers who sent him parcels, and whenever one of these parcels had arrived the evening would begin with a distribution.'

It is impossible to catch the flavour, or the multiplicity of subjects bandied and discussed so brilliantly; but out of many, three from Warren Lewis's diary preserve at least an echo of the later meetings when discussion had largely taken the place of mutual criticism:

'*28 March 1946*. Present Jack and I, Christopher, Humphrey, Colin Hardie, Gervase Mathew. Interesting discussion on the possibility of dogs having souls.

'*27 September 1947*. Present Jack, Sayer, Colin Hardie, Christopher, Hugo and myself. Some enjoyable talk arising out of T. S. Eliot, one of whose poems Jack read superbly, but broke off in the middle declaring it to be bilge: Hugo defended it, Jack and Sayer attacked. I thought that though unintelligible, it did convey a feeling of frustration and despair. Jack thought it had nothing to say worth saying in any case. The conversation drifted to whether poets create or reflect the mood of their time.

'*22 January 1948*. A very pleasant little Inklings, present Colin, Tom Stevens, Christopher, Jack and I. We drank wine and finished a noble "old style Kentucky brandied cake" which some-one had sent Jack from America. Much talk of Public Schools and Sherlock Holmes stories.'

Lewis records of Charles Williams that from September 1939 'until his death we met one another about twice a week, sometimes more: nearly always on Thursday evenings in my rooms and on Tuesday mornings in the best of all public-houses for draught cider.' The second rendezvous of the Inklings was the back parlour of the Eagle and Child in St Giles's, Oxford, commonly known as the 'Bird and Baby' – though the inn-sign over the door shows Ganymede as quite a 'lusty juvenile'. Here Lewis was usually to be found from 11.30 to 1.00 on most Tuesdays: the day was changed to Monday after his appointment to the Cambridge Chair in 1954, as it was his custom to return to his new university on that day, by the afternoon train, after spending the weekend at the Kilns.

The Inklings' evenings in Magdalen grew fewer and ceased altogether shortly after 1950; but the Inkling meetings at the 'B. and B.' flourished exceedingly and continued until the last week of Lewis's life. The 'inner parlour' was never booked for the occasion, nor shut to the public in any way; but the Inklings nearly always had it to themselves. Only in 1962 when it was joined on to the main bar and the door removed did Lewis migrate regretfully across to the Lamb and Flag on the other side of the Giler – where a secluded corner at least was always obtainable.

On other days, if he was working in the Bodleian and it was vacation time – this was particularly true during the years when he was working on his volume for the *Oxford History of English Literature* (the O.H.E.L. – 'the O Hell!' as he called it) – Lewis would slip out to the King's Arms at the corner of Holywell about noon; and fledgling Inklings usually made their first appearance there. Green, for example, recorded in his diary on 26 September 1947, 'Worked hard in Bodleian. Met C. S. Lewis there, who asked me out for a drink and talk at "The King's Arms"; Christopher [Tolkien] joining us.' These meetings usually took place during the Long Vacation and, being summer, Lewis and his friends would settle themselves in the yard behind the pub for loud and merry discourse and argument. At the many gatherings which Green attended in 1948 and 1949 Hugo Dyson was usually there also, Professor Tolkien or his son Christopher frequently, Colin Hardie occasionally, and from time to time there was an additional visitor, usually someone whom Lewis had met by chance in the Bodleian.

The regular Tuesdays at the 'B. and B.' went on uninterrupted by the extra meetings at the King's Arms. There, in time, the most constant Inklings, besides Lewis himself, became R. B. McCallum (Master of Pembroke College), Colin Hardie, Humphrey Havard and Gervase Mathew; but one might be just as likely to find Tolkien or Coghill, Lord David Cecil or W. H. Auden; or American scholars such as Chad Walsh in 1948 or Walter Hooper in 1963.

Once again a few diary entries (this time Green's) will give a pale reflection of these meetings:

'*13 February 1951.* To "Eagle and Child" to meet C.S.L.: a grand gathering – Tolkien, McCallum, Major Lewis, Wrenn, Hardie, Gervase Mathew, John Wain, and others whose names I didn't catch. Discussion on C. Day Lewis (who was elected Professor of Poetry last week, beating C.S.L. by 19 votes): Lewis praised his *Georgics* but considered his critical work negligible.

'*9 November 1954.* To "B. and B." to meet Lewis; his brother, McCallum, Tolkien, Gervase M. there as well. Very good talk, about Tolkien's book [*The Lord of the Rings*], horror comics, who is the most influential and important man in various countries:

decided Burke for Ireland, Scott for Scotland, Shakespeare for England – but there difficulties arose, Pitt and Wellington also being put forward.

'*17 June 1963*. To "Lamb and Flag" about 12, there joined Jack. Several others – Gervase Mathew, Humphrey Havard, Colin Hardie, and a young American, Walter Hooper, who is writing some sort of book or thesis about Jack . . .'

'Only in retrospect did I realize how much intellectual ground was covered in these seemingly casual meetings,' wrote Chad Walsh (*C. S. Lewis: Apostle to the Skeptics* (1949), pp. 16–17). 'At the time the constant bustle of Lewis racing his friends to refill empty mugs or pausing to light another cigarette (occasionally a pipe) camouflaged the steady flow of ideas. The flow, I might add, is not a one-way traffic. Lewis is as good a listener as talker, and has alert curiosity about almost anything conceivable.'

VII. INTO THE FIELD OF ARBOL

From the beginning of his academic career Lewis specialized – if he, who was so omnivorous, specialized in anything – in English literature (omitting drama) from Middle English to Milton. *The Allegory of Love* (1936), his most famous and enduring work of scholarship, which won him the Israel Gollancz Award, set him on the path which he was to follow most successfully, and made natural and obvious the series of lectures, the 'Prolegomena' to 'Medieval and Renaissance Literature', distilled at the end of his life into *The Discarded Image*.

Although he wrote most of his fiction almost straight off with scarcely a correction and only occasional rewriting, Lewis worked over his academic books in several versions. Most were given first as lectures, and then, after they had been polished and refined by repetition, they were rewritten as books. Even published lectures were often tried out at Oxford before being given to a wider audience, as in the case of 'Hamlet, the Prince or the Poem?' which was delivered in the Schools at Oxford on 14 October 1938, before becoming the Annual Shakespeare Lecture to the British Academy on 22 April 1942 and being published in August of that year. (The original lecture was one of a weekly series on various aspects of Shakespeare given throughout the Michaelmas Term 1938, the other lecturers being Hugo Dyson, Ethel Seaton, Nevill Coghill, L. Rice-Oxley and J. N. Bryson: Lascelles Abercrombie, due to lecture on 28 October, died suddenly the previous night.)

A Preface to 'Paradise Lost' also originated in a series of eleven lectures given at Oxford during Michaelmas Term 1939, before being delivered as the Ballard Matthews Lectures at University College, North Wales, in 1941 and published 'Revised and Enlarged' in 1942. The earlier part of this book, dealing with Primary and Secondary Epic in general, and giving Lewis's own theory and conception of poetry, is one of his finest achievements as a literary critic. The high place which the book as a whole will always hold in Milton studies has often been acknowledged (though, of course, with violent disagreement from certain readers – usually for non-literary reasons); but a hitherto unpublished estimate from one of the greater Georgian poets, 25 years Lewis's senior, will set the book more clearly in its literary, as contrasted with its scholarly, place. Deeply impressed on first reading – as on numerous subsequent readings – Green sent a copy to Gordon Bottomley, who replied (2 March 1944):

'This book of C. S. Lewis on *Paradise Lost* has given me more and deeper pleasure than any book I have read for a very long time. Partly on account of his true vision of Milton; but not all. Greatly also for his luminous exposition of the nature of poetry: nothing has been written since Shelley (at least) which so exhibits the nature of poetry as the first half of this book does, and so disentangles the errors in the contemporary confusion about it. If the book could be bound up with Bridges' *Milton's Prosody*, the whole would be the best handbook to put into the hands of young poets that anyone could conceive. . . .

'And perhaps most of all I admire Lewis's diagnosis of the disease of originality, and the way in which he shows that all our generations have the same fundamentals and need to recognize them. O, a joy and a jewel of a book.'

Bottomley goes on to put his finger on one of Lewis's few outstanding critical blind-spots: his inability to appreciate spoken poetry (dramatic or otherwise): 'Throughout the book I only disagreed once – about the distinction he draws between the poetry that is to be seen, and the poetry that is to be heard – i.e. that which is read in the study, and that which is spoken. I believe this to be an unreal distinction; for (as I have often said) the sound of poetry is part of its meaning. This was borne out, and made clear to everyone present, at Masefield's "Oxford Recitations", where we explored the possibilities thoroughly, and were surprised ourselves when the speaking of pieces by Donne in his most corrugated moments suddenly clarified both meaning and intention, and turned to beauty. Another astonishment was the beauty of sound in Hopkins' "Golden and Leaden Echo".'

When Lewis began to write fiction, much of the inspiration was set moving by the academic studies on which he was engaged or which were still fresh in his mind. *Perelandra* was obviously the result of his concentration on *Paradise Lost* between 1939 and 1942; the spark that set *Out of the Silent Planet* on its course into the 'Field of Arbol' is less certain, but a probable clue is to be found in *The Allegory of Love*, published in 1936 and followed by a second edition 'with corrections' in 1938, the year in which *Out of the Silent Planet* was published.

When distinguishing the two meanings given to the conception of a 'Genius' in medieval thought, Lewis gives a quotation from Bernardus Sylvestris (*c.* 1140 AD), the relevant part of which runs: '*Illic Oyarses quidem erat et genius in artem et officium pictoris et figurantis addictus . . . Oyarses igitur . . . formas rebus omnibus et associat et ascribit.*' And he comments: 'This is the fullest description I have yet quoted of Genius A [the universal god of generation] . . . The name Oyarses, as Professor C. C. J. Webb has pointed out to me, must be a corruption of οὐσιάρχης ["ruling essence"]; and he has kindly drawn my attention to Pseudo-Apuleius *Asclepius* (XIX) where the Ousiarch of the fixed stars is certainly Genius A.' This passage is echoed on p. 250 of *Out of the Silent Planet*. And in the background of both is the medieval conception of the planets as containing or embodying some reflection of the Classical deities – or tutelary spirits – the mythological-cum-astrological personifications of Saturn and Jupiter, of Mars and Venus and Mercury about which Lewis was lecturing in his 'Prolegomena to the Study of Medieval Literature', and who were to appear with such magnificent effect in *Perelandra* and *That Hideous Strength*.

There is no further record of how Lewis came to write *Out of the Silent Planet*. He had always been interested in science fiction, had enjoyed Jules Verne and H. G. Wells as a boy, had sampled Edgar Rice Burroughs, but apparently been bored by what he read and not ventured far into Barsoom, and more recently had turned back to the ancient and medieval journeys into other worlds. He, of course, knew his Lucian, but was more influenced by the *Somnium Scipionis* and by the celestial journeys of Kepler and Kircher, and in certain ways by the more numinous travels of Dante and even the merely marvellous in *Orlando Furioso*.

But what seems to have moved Lewis to embark into the realms of inter-planetary fiction is best described in a card he wrote to Green (then unknown to him except as the undergraduate who lent him his watch at lectures) in answer to a 'fan' letter following a first delighted reading of *Out of the Silent Planet*:

'What immediately spurred me to write was Olaf Stapledon's *Last and First Men* [1931] and an essay in J. B. S. Haldane's *Possible Worlds* [1927], both of which seemed to take the idea of such travel seriously and to have the desperately immoral outlook which I try to pillory in Weston. I like the whole inter-planetary idea as a *mythology* and simply wished to conquer for my own (Christian) point of view what has always hitherto been used by the opposite side. I think Wells's *First Men in the Moon* the best of the sort I have read. I once tried a Burroughs in a magazine and disliked it . . . I guessed who you were as soon as you mentioned the lecture. I did mention in it, I think, Kircher's *Iter Celeste*, but there is no translation, and it is not very interesting. There is also Voltaire's *Micromégas* but purely satiric' (28 December 1938).

As he explained in the prefatory note to *Out of the Silent Planet*, Lewis spoke slightingly of Wells only 'for dramatic purposes' and was indeed always ready to defend *The First Men in the Moon*. When thanking Green for a copy of his *Into Other Worlds: Space-Flight in Fiction from Lucian to Lewis* (1957), he wrote: 'What a lot there is in it, and how much I didn't know! The Lunar Hoax interested me especially, not primarily as a hoax, though that is good fun too, but because some of it is really the best invention and description of extra-terrestrial *landscape* (the animals are less good), before *The First Men in the Moon*. I think you are hard on Wells. Obviously he touches off something in you which he didn't in me. I still think that a very good book indeed and don't dislike the Selenites themselves as much as you do' (17 November 1957).

After which it is almost unnecessary to deny a completely unfounded statement made recently that Wells 'served as a model' for Jules in *That Hideous Strength*: Lewis never met Wells, nor corresponded with him, nor knew him in any way except by his books – and he only cared for the early scientific romances written before Wells 'sold his birthright for a pot of message'.

'The real father of my planet books is David Lindsay's *Voyage to Arcturus*,' he wrote to Charles A. Brady on 23 October 1944 (see *Letters*, p. 205). 'I had grown up on Wells's stories of that kind; it was Lindsay who first gave me the idea that the "scientific-tion" appeal could be combined with the "supernatural" appeal.' And of Lindsay's masterpiece he wrote in the essay 'On Stories' (*Essays Presented to Charles Williams*, 1947, p. 98): 'His Tormance is a region of the spirit. He is the first writer to discover what "other planets" are really good for in fiction. No merely physical strangeness or merely spatial distance will realize that idea of otherness which is what we are always trying to grasp in a story about voyaging through space: you must go into another dimension. To construct plausible and moving "other worlds" you must draw on the only real "other world" we know, that of the spirit.'

And to another correspondent he wrote on 9 July 1939 (*Letters*, pp. 166–7), 'the danger of "Westonism" I meant to be real. What set me about writing the book was the discovery that a pupil of mine took all that dream of interplanetary colonization quite seriously, and the realization that thousands of people in one way and another depend on some hope of perpetuating and improving the human race for the whole meaning of the universe – that a "scientific" hope of defeating death is a real rival to Christianity. . . . You will be both grieved and amused to hear that out of about 60 reviews only 2 showed any knowledge that my idea of the fall of the Bent One was anything but an invention of my own. . . . any amount of theology can now be smuggled into people's minds under cover of romance without their knowing it.'

Certainly some readers of *Out of the Silent Planet* enjoyed it in spite of its Christian background, some because of it – and many without realizing it at all. But perhaps those who enjoyed it most did so in a way described by Dorothy Sayers writing to Lewis on 21 December 1953 about a young friend of hers: 'He told me how, in his undergraduate days, he read *Out of the Silent Planet* with great enjoyment, accepting it quite simply as a space-travel story until quite suddenly near the end (not, I think, until Ransom had got to Meldilorn) some phrase clicked in his mind and he exclaimed: "Why, this is a story about Christianity. Maleldil is Christ, and the Eldila are the angels!" He said it was a most wonderful experience, as though two entirely different worlds had suddenly come into focus together, like a stereoscope, and it's a thing he can never forget.'

Another undergraduate reader who had precisely the same experience was Roger Lancelyn Green who remembers vividly the thrill of excitement – the sudden moment of Joy – when Oyarsa was telling Ransom of Thulcandra, the silent planet – 'We think that Maleldil would not give it up utterly to the Bent One, and there are stories among us that He has taken strange counsel and dared terrible things, wrestling with the Bent One in Thulcandra' – and he realized in a blinding flash to what Oyarsa was referring. Until then it seemed no more than one of the best stories of its kind he had read, and one of the most exciting and convincing: thereafter it was like stepping into a new dimension – one that he was to find again more fully explored in *Perelandra*, but which could never again come with the thrill of revelation of that first reading.

'*Out of the Silent Planet*', wrote Marjorie Nicolson at the end of her great study of ancient *Voyages to the Moon* (1948, pp. 251–5), 'is to me the most beautiful of all cosmic voyages and in some ways the most moving . . . As C. S. Lewis, the Christian apologist, has added something to the long tradition, so C. S. Lewis, the scholar-poet, has achieved an effect in *Out of the Silent Planet* different from anything in the past. Earlier writers have created new worlds from legend, from mythology, from fairy tale. Mr

Lewis has created *myth* itself, myth woven of desires and aspirations deep-seated in some, at least, of the human race . . . As I journey with him into worlds at once familiar and strange, I experience, as did Ransom, "a sensation not of following an adventure but of enacting a myth." '

The book was well received by reviewers but did not have any spectacular sales until the publication of *The Screwtape Letters* in 1942 and his broadcast talks on the wireless during that and the following year made C. S. Lewis suddenly famous. But he seems to have had ideas of a sequel even before the publication of the book – though it is doubtful what he originally intended to write.

The end of *Out of the Silent Planet* hints at the 'force or forces' behind Weston which 'will play a very important part in the events of the next few centuries, and, unless we can prevent them, a very disastrous one'; and 'the dangers to be feared are not planetary but cosmic, or at least solar, and they are not temporal but eternal.' This might well seem a prelude to *Perelandra*; but what about the final words of the book? 'Now that Weston has shut the door, the way to the planets lies through the past; if there is to be any more space-travelling, it will have to be time-travelling as well . . . !'

Apparently Lewis had a tale of time-travel in his mind as the sequel and, before discarding it, even wrote at least 64 pages – all that survives of it: a tantalizing fragment found among his papers, of which no one seems to have known anything, and about which he wrote to nobody at the time of composition.

It begins as a direct sequel to the last sentence just quoted of *Out of the Silent Planet*:

' "Of course," said Orfieu, "the sort of time-travelling you read about in books – time-travelling in the body – is absolutely impossible."

'There were four of us in Orfieu's study. Scudamour, the youngest of the party, was there because he was Orfieu's assistant. MacPhee had been asked down from Manchester because he was known to us all as an inveterate sceptic, and Orfieu thought that if once he were convinced the learned world in general would have no excuse for incredulity. Ransom, the pale man with the green shade over his distressed-looking eyes, was there for the opposite reason – because he had been the hero, or victim, of one of the strangest adventures that had ever befallen a mortal man. I had been mixed up with that affair – the story is told in another book – and it was to Ransom I owed my presence in Orfieu's party . . .'

After discussing the possibilities of time-travel, and deciding that it is impossible in the Wellsian sense of a bodily movement through time, Orfieu introduces his guests to the 'Chronoscope' – an instrument like a cinema projector which catches an apparently arbitrary time-sequence either past or future, we are not told which, and reflects it on a screen where it seems absolutely real and three-dimensional as if on a stage or through a window in time – but quite silent. (Subconsciously, Lewis may have got the idea from chapter 16 of Rider Haggard's *When the World Shook* (1919) where Yva is able to catch the light-rays and reflect them back from remote space to show Arbuthnot a similarly vivid picture of events happening 250,000 years ago.)

The picture which Orfieu and Scudamour show Ransom, Lewis and MacPhee is of a Dark Tower of which they are presently able to see the interior where a man sits like a graven image, filling them with horror, partly by his very unhumanness, but mainly by a poisoned sting like a miniature unicorn's horn which sticks out from his forehead and with which he stabs or inoculates in the spine a series of normal human victims who come in one by one as into the presence of a god and submit themselves to this agonizing process, which apparently dehumanizes them: 'they entered the room as men, or (more rarely) women; they left it automata.'

For a long time the watchers do not know whether they are looking into the past or the future; but at length they decide that it is the future, and that the Dark Tower is in fact a copy of the university library made by a later civilization – as we might model a modern building on the Parthenon. But presently they recognize Scudamour's exact double among the people whom they see most constantly through the Chronoscope; they see him become a Stinging-man with the unicorn horn – and then in a dramatic moment he and they see his fiancée Camilla, or her exact double, brought to be stabbed and made an automaton by him – and in a sudden unreasoning moment of passion Scudamour flings himself at the Chronoscope and breaks it.

But in doing so he breaks the time barrier and his soul and that of his double in the Othertime change bodies (rather as the Professor and his pupil do in Conan Doyle's story 'The Great Keinplatz Experiment'). 'You remember what Orfieu said the first evening about time-travel being impossible because you'd have no body in the other time when you got there?' says Ransom. 'Well, isn't it obvious that if you got two times that had replicas that difficulty would be overcome. In other words, I think that the Double we saw on the screen had a body not merely like poor Scudamour's but the same: I mean, that the very same matter which made up Scudamour's body in 1938 made up the brute's body in Othertimes. Now if that were so – and if you then, by any contrivance, brought the two times into contact, so to speak – you see?' 'You mean they might – might jump across?' 'Yes, in a sense. Scudamour, under the influence of a strong emotion, makes what you might call a psychological leap or lunge at the Othertime . . . The Othertime occupant of that body is caught off his guard – simply pushed out of his body – but since that identical body is waiting for him in 1938, he inevitably slips into it and finds himself in Cambridge.'

The Othertime man occupying Scudamour's 1938 body escapes from the college and we last see him walking on the ridge of the roof. But it is obvious that in the end the metempsychosis is reversed, for the last quarter of what has survived of the book consists of a third-person account of Scudamour's adventures in Othertime as he later narrated it after his return. The adventures so far as they go show him in the Othertime Stinging-man's body discovering that Camilla's double in the Dark Tower does not contain the 1938 Camilla's soul, but is in love with him; passing himself off as the Othertimer whose body he is inhabiting; and giving an over-long and laboured account of Othertime scientific experiments leading up to the making of Chronoscopes of their own. But before this is fully achieved the manuscript breaks off suddenly in mid-sentence at the bottom of a page. How much more was written there is no way of knowing, for no more has survived beyond these first 32,000 words or so.

It is a tantalizing fragment, particularly as it leaves no clue to the real content of the book: there is a suggestion that the Other-timers may be infiltrating into this world, but even that is vague. Yet it is the only possible link with *Out of the Silent Planet*, and even so it reduces Ransom to a fairly minor character. MacPhee turns up again in *That Hideous Strength*, but there is not enough of what we may call '*The Dark Tower*' (Lewis gave it no name) to show whether Camilla bears any resemblance to her namesake in the same book: from the few remarks about the earthly Camilla she seems more like a forecast of Jane Studdock.

'All my seven Narnian books, and my three science fiction books, began with seeing pictures in my head,' said Lewis in 1960 (*Radio Times*, 15 July). There is no record of what pictures grew into *Out of the Silent Planet*; but it seems probable that pictures, or even actual nightmares (to which Lewis was prone throughout his life) were very much in evidence when he started to write *The Dark Tower*: the scenes witnessed in the Othertime through the Chronoscope are particularly vivid – indeed it is possible that the slowness of the connecting links and the sheer lifelessness of Scudamour's investigations in the Othertime explain why Lewis discarded the book: he was carried away by the pictures and did not know what was to happen next.

It is probable that his studies for the lectures on *Paradise Lost* between 1939 and 1941 gave Lewis the basic idea for *Perelandra*. Indeed, it is difficult to understand why Ransom's successful visit to Mars did not immediately suggest sending him to Venus, instead of endeavouring to let him conquer time as well as space. *The Dark Tower* was probably abandoned well before the end of 1939 when Lewis began work on *The Problem of Pain*, which occupied most of his available time until the following April. On 9 May 1940 he was writing to Arthur Greeves about *Out of the Silent Planet*, but making no mention of any possible sequel; and the rest of the year was taken up with various lectures and broadcast talks – both in person to Army camps, and on the wireless. On 9 November he wrote to Sister Penelope: 'I've got Ransom to Venus and through his first conversation with the "Eve" of that world; a difficult chapter. . . . I may have embarked on the impossible. This woman has got to combine characteristics which the Fall has put poles apart – she's got to be in some ways like a Pagan goddess and in other ways like the Blessed Virgin. But, if one can get even a fraction of it into words, it is worth doing' (*Letters*, p. 195). On 23 December he was writing to Arthur Greeves about the story: 'The idea is that Venus is at the Adam-and-Eve stage: i.e. the first two rational creatures have just appeared and are still innocent. My hero arrives in time to prevent their "falling" as *our* first pair did.' To another friend he wrote on 20 January 1942, 'Ransom is having a grand time on Venus at the moment'; and finally to Sister Penelope again, on 11 May, 'The Venus book is now finished except that I find the first two chapters need rewriting' (*Letters*, p. 200).

Apart from the *Paradise Lost* inspiration, the book grew out of vivid pictures of the floating islands, the golden sky, the towering rocks on the fixed land, and recollections of childhood fears and dreams of gigantic insects in endless caves. Probably the floating islands grew and developed subconsciously from a passage in Olaf Stapledon's *Last and First Men* (Chapter 13, Section I): 'In early days on Venus men had gathered foodstuff from the great floating islands of vegetable matter . . .'; and he may have got the violent rainstorms from the same source. But the world of Perelandra owes little to any previous suggestion: it is Lewis's supreme imaginative triumph in the creation of another world so vivid that any other picture of Venus becomes preposterous. The undulating islands, the golden sky, the fixed land, the curiously unearthly weather – we can see them so vividly that it is hard to believe that we have not seen them with our actual eyes.

Lewis must have seen Perelandra more clearly than any of his readers can, and probably more clearly than any of the mind-pictures out of which his stories grew: for he liked *Perelandra* best of all his works of fiction, though he considered *Till We Have Faces* his masterpiece in this kind. And Green remembers walking round 'Addison's Walk' at Magdalen in the middle of an idyllic summer night when the trees and spires stood out against a skyline lit by a low, unseen moon, and the dome of the sky was bright with stars. Brightest of all shone a superb planet: 'Perelandra!' said Lewis with such a passionate longing in his voice that he seemed for a moment to be Ransom himself looking back with infinite desire to an actual memory.[1]

Presently Green quoted some lines from 'Locksley Hall Sixty Years After' and Lewis took them up and completed the passage – surely the epitome of the whole conception of the 'Field of Arbol', of Malacandra, Thulcandra and Perelandra:

Venus near her! smiling downward at this earthlier earth of ours,
Closer to the Sun, perhaps a world of never fading flowers.
Hesper, whom the poet call'd the Bringer home of all good things.
All good things may move in Hesper, perfect peoples, perfect kings.
Hesper – Venus – were we native to that splendour or in Mars,
We should see the Globe we groan in fairest of their evening stars.
Could we dream of wars and carnage, craft and madness, lust and spite,
Roaring London, raving Paris, in that point of peaceful light?
Might we not in glancing heavenward on a star so silver-fair
Yearn, and clasp the hands and murmur, 'Would to God that we were
  there'?

This was perhaps a unique moment, for Lewis seldom revealed his deeper feelings. A more typical reaction to the heavenly bodies

---

[1] There survives an undated fragment of verse in one of Lewis's note-books which runs:

> The floating islands, the flat golden sky
> At noon, the peacock sunset: tepid waves
> With the land sliding over them like a skin:
> The alien Eve, green-bodied, stepping forth
> To meet my hero from her forest home,
> Proud, courteous, unafraid; no thought infirm
> Alters her cheek –

At first sight this might suggest that Lewis began with the idea of writing *Perelandra* as a narrative poem. But a study of the fragment makes it seem much more likely that he is writing about his own creation – perhaps on the very night described above.

came when Warren asked him one night why stars twinkled while planets did not. 'Well, obviously,' said Jack, 'because the stars are lit by gas and the planets by electricity.'

Lewis would seldom explain how he came to invent names in his stories: often, indeed, they came to him in more or less the same way as the pictures out of which the stories grew. His advice on finding new names was to spell old ones backwards and see what the result suggested: but few of his names can be traced in this way. He did admit that Thulcandra, the Silent Planet, might have been reached by a 'portmanteauword' method: 'thick', 'dull' and 'sulk' giving Thulk; on this analogy Malacandra for Mars might derive from the Latin *malo* – 'I would rather be' – 'would to God that we were there', as in Tennyson's couplet, but in this case a straightforward desire to be in an unfallen world. Perelandra has no obvious original, unless we equate it with 'Peri-landra', i.e. 'fairyland': however, it is worth noting that in the first edition of *Out of the Silent Planet* (p. 146) Venus appears as 'Parelandra', possibly from 'parallax', Lewis having 'Paradise' in mind – Tennyson's 'world of never fading flowers.' But all this is guesswork.

Perelandra repeats (p. 92) the fears which Lewis had voiced in *Out of the Silent Planet* about the way in which Weston and scientists like him would carry out a ruthless extermination of any possible inhabitants of other planets so as to preserve earth's human race at all costs. (In the *Christian Herald* for April 1958 he gave his fuller and more reasoned thoughts on inter-planetary travel, should such a thing ever come to pass, under the title 'Will We Lose God in Outer Space?', reprinted as a pamphlet by the S.P.C.K. the following year, and included in *The World's Last Night* (U.S.A., 1960) as 'Religion and Rocketry'.) In December 1943 Arthur C. Clarke (ten years later to write *Childhood's End*, which Lewis admired greatly) wrote a long letter condemning Lewis's views on science fiction and inter-planetary flight (which he was sure would come in the foreseeable future) and on the high ideals of serious scientists in the field – Clarke himself later became chairman of the British Interplanetary Society.

Lewis replied (7 Dec. 1943): 'I quite agree that most scientific-tion is on the level of cowboy boys' stories. But I think the funda-mental moral assumptions in popular fiction are a very important symptom. If you found that the most popular stories were those in which the cowboy always betrayed his pals to the crooks and deserted his girl for the vamp, I don't think it *could* be unimportant. I don't of course think that at the moment many scientists are budding Westons: but I do think (hang it all, I *live* among scientists!) that a point of view not unlike Weston's is on the way. Look at Stapledon (*Star-Maker* ends in sheer devil worship), Haldane's *Possible Worlds* and Waddington's *Science and Ethics*. I agree Technology is *per se* neutral: but a race devoted to the increase of its own power by technology with complete indifference to ethics *does* seem to me a cancer in the Universe. Certainly if he goes on his present course much further man can *not* be trusted with knowledge.' (Lewis might also have added that Stapledon's future inhabitants of Earth, when colonizing Venus in *Last and First Men*, begin by exterminating the aboriginal inhabitants of that planet.)

Lewis was taking the future of 'civilized' man very seriously at this time, as *The Abolition of Man* shows. These lectures were delivered in 1943 at the University of Durham, and both they and to some extent Durham itself supplied the background for his next story, *That Hideous Strength*, which concludes the Ransom trilogy.

Since the beginning of the Second World War in September 1939, when Charles Williams came to Oxford with the evacuated London branch of the University Press, the Thursday evening meetings of the Inklings – the informal literary gatherings of which the most regular members were Lewis and his brother, Tolkien, Coghill and Dyson – had, with the addition of Williams, entered upon their most vital period. In November 1939 Tolkien was reading early chapters of *The Lord of the Rings*, Charles Williams a nativity play, and Lewis *The Problem of Pain*. *Pere-landra* was also read chapter by chapter as written, to the accom-paniment of Williams's *All Hallows' Eve*; and by the time Ransom's last adventure was under way, Lewis was being very strongly influenced by Williams, and in particular by his prose romances or 'spiritual thrillers', as they have been most aptly called, which are set in the world of everyday and masquerade as novels, with a greater or lesser admixture of the supernatural.

That Hideous Strength has been described as a Charles Williams novel written by C. S. Lewis. This is, of course, a wild exaggeration: but it bears the seeds of critical truth. *Perelandra* obviously led up to an attack of some sort by the Bent Oyarsa through his servants, such as Devine who had not accompanied Weston to his fate on Perelandra, against what Ransom might be able to do after his return to the Silent Planet. The idea of the N.I.C.E. – the National Institute of Co-ordinated Experiments – and its ruthless appropriation and partial destruction of Edgestow (a little university town resembling Durham, though Lewis disclaimed any definite connection), was suggested by the controversy over the founding of the atomic factory of Harwell near Blewbury ('Belbury' via 'bluebell') fifteen miles from Oxford; and with this was combined what Lewis conceived to be the logical outcome of the materialist and anti-religious indoctrination creeping into education, which he had tried to expose in *The Abolition of Man*.

Any idea of a Ransom story on this earth, the planet Thulcandra in Lewis's solar system the 'Field of Arbol', must of necessity turn to the Bible for some of its inspiration. The End of the World was too vast a theme, but some such judgement of Heaven as the Confusion of Tongues in the Tower of Babel, or the destruction of the Cities of the Plain from which Lot and his family escaped (though his wife looked back), would be the obvious dénouement. Lewis combined both, admitting his debt to Gordon Bottomley's poem 'Babel' for the inspiration of the banquet at Belbury, and to a chance reading in the newspaper of a German experiment in keeping a dog's head alive by artificial means – which suggested 'The Head', through which the devils could speak to their worshippers. Doubtless, too, the late-medieval stories of Friar Bacon and Friar Bungay with their 'Brazen Head' were not forgotten.

But there was also a background 'picture', namely a dream

recorded in his diary of 12 September 1923: 'I had a most horrible dream. By a certain poetic justice it turned on the idea Jenkin and I were going to use in our shocker play: namely that of a scientist discovering how to keep consciousness and some motor nerves alive in a corpse, at the same time arresting decay, so that you really had an immortal dead man. I dreamed that the horrible thing was sent to us – in a coffin of course – to take care of . . . it was perfectly ordinary and as vivid as life. Finally the thing escaped and I fancy ran amok. It pursued me into a lift in the Tube in London . . . I am not sure that the idea of the play did not originate in another dream I had some years ago – unless the whole thing comes from Edgar Allan Poe.' (The reference to Poe is to 'The Facts in the Case of M. Valdemar', the story of the dead man kept alive by mesmerism for seven months.) In an earlier reference to the plot for the play Lewis makes it clear that the 'consciousness' was kept alive in the brain of the dead man – but the rest of the scheme bears too close a resemblance to the behaviour of Frankenstein's monster to be of much interest.

The influence of Charles Williams, altogether to the book's advantage, is shown in Lewis's decision to set the spiritual and apocalyptic adventures among ordinary people in the everyday setting of a conventional novel. Only in *The Screwtape Letters* does he show the same depth of psychological understanding and the ability to make the problems and temptations of ordinary men and women of absorbing interest. Mark's experiences with the Inner Ring at Bracton, and his attempts to get into and keep in the Inner Ring at Belbury, are an understandable extension of Lewis's disillusionment with college politics at Magdalen and perhaps exaggerated recollections of the 'Bloods' at Malvern; a theme which comes out in a number of his essays both ethical and literary – and became indeed rather a King Charles's head with him. Much more surprising is his deep and delicate understanding of Jane's pilgrimage to grace from the self-centred superficiality and synthetic agnosticism of typical modernity. The Jane of the early chapters may owe a lot to the insight gained from a study of his female pupils and some members of the Socratic Club; but there is much which seems almost uncannily accurate coming from a man with no experience of the married state. Perhaps the dedication of the book to Jane McNeill, the 'Chaney' of his early Belfast days, has some significance as far as this deeply understood character is concerned; and Mark probably owes a great deal to Lewis's own unregenerate days – 'there, but for the grace of God . . .'

The introduction of Merlin, with the tantalizing hints about the Circle of Logres, Numinor and 'the last vestiges of Atlantean magic', must strike many readers as the least successfully achieved strand in the whole web. This, apart from the inherent modern difficulty in accepting the marvellous, is partly Lewis's fault for expecting too much knowledge in his readers. They are too easily left, for example, wondering why the Companies of Good and Evil both want his help, both think that he will be of their party, not realizing the implication of Merlin's mysterious birth: he was 'the child who had no father', who was begotten by an incubus – we might almost say an eldil – who might be either good or bad, but who was described simply as a devil by writers such as Geoffrey of Monmouth. Moreover, like King Arthur himself, Merlin did not die, but was imprisoned in a tomb, in a magic sleep, by an enchantress: and from that sleep he would awake at some future date no older than when he fell into it. It is the ancient legend still believed in the case of Epimenides of Crete and the Seven Sleepers of Ephesus, used most memorably as conscious literary background in *Rip Van Winkle* and Edwin Lester Arnold's *Lepidus the Centurion*, and in the imaginative science fiction of Rider Haggard's *When the World Shook*. Indeed, Lewis may have had all these at the back of his mind – Jane's dream of the vault and the sleeper under Bragdon Wood seems too close to Louis Allenby's discovery of Lepidus to be mere coincidence.

With regard to Numinor and the True West, readers are still awaiting the publication of J. R. R. Tolkien's *The Silmarillion* for real understanding, though both have a place in the background of *The Lord of the Rings*. In the interim Professor Tolkien raises

the corner of the veil so far as to write: 'With regard to "Numinor".
In the early days of our association Jack used to come to my house
and I read aloud to him *The Silmarillion* so far as it had then gone,
including a very long poem: Beren and Luthien. Numinor was
his version of a name he had never seen written (numenor) and
no doubt was influenced by *numinous*. Other things in other works
are also derived from me: for instance Tor and Tinidril are clearly
Tor and his elf-wife Idril blended with Tinuviel (the second name
of Luthien). The Eldils also owe something to the Eldar in my
work.' Tolkien adds 'In full Q-form *Númenóre*, "West-land", the
furthest west of mortal lands' – and apparently Lewis equates it
with Atlantis.

At some time between July and October 1944 Lewis wrote to
Sister Penelope, 'I've just finished another book which concludes
the Ransom trilogy; the scene is on earth this time.' In the same
letter he told her that he had 'also had an operation for the removal
of a piece of shell I got into me in the last War, which after lying
snug and silent like an unrepented sin for twenty years or so,
began giving trouble.' A callous undergraduate when asked where
Lewis was replied, 'Oh, he's in hospital having an operation, to
see if he can solve the Problem of Pain.' And not long afterwards
another don remarked, 'Lewis and I are the most hated men in
Oxford' – both of them having achieved unacademic fame and
fortune.

That Hideous Strength was published in July 1945 and had good
sales, though Lewis himself remarked that it was hated by all the
critics, and Green was told by an ardent science-fiction enthusiast
that Lewis would almost have been lynched had he appeared at one of their meetings. This attitude was to change
completely in the next ten years, and as early as 1953 Arthur C.
Clarke was asking Lewis to give a lecture to the British Inter-
planetary Society – though he added, 'It would be only fair to
point out that your position might be somewhat analogous to
that of a Christian martyr in the arena,' although 'many of our
members admire your writings even if they may not see eye to eye
with them.' To which Lewis replied: 'I hope I should not be

deterred by the dangers! The fatal objection is that I should be covering ground that I have already covered in print and on which I have nothing to add. I know that is how many lectures are made, but I never do it. . . . But thank your Society very much for the invitation and convey my good wishes to them as regards everything but interplanetary travel . . . [P.S.] Probably the whole thing is only a plan for kidnapping me and marooning me on an asteroid! I know the sort of thing.'

(In spite of early acrimonious correspondence over space flight, Lewis was able to appreciate Clarke's most outstanding book in the genre, *Childhood's End*, of which he wrote to Joy Davidman on 22 December 1953: 'It is quite out of the range of the common space-and-time writers; away up near Lindsay's *Voyage to Arcturus* and Wells's *First Men in the Moon*. It is better than any of Stapledon's. It hasn't got Ray Bradbury's delicacy, but then it has ten times his emotional power, and far more mythopoeia . . . An ABSOLUTE CORKER!')

Meanwhile, in spite of the professional critics, those at all in tune with *That Hideous Strength* were absolutely enthralled by it. Green stayed up all night reading it – a unique occurrence – and has been more and more profoundly moved and impressed by it on each of half a dozen subsequent readings. And Dorothy Sayers wrote to Lewis on 3 December 1945: 'The book is tremendously full of good things – perhaps almost too full – the scheme at the beginning seems almost violently condensed – and I'm afraid I don't like Ransom quite so well since he took to being golden-haired and interesting on a sofa like the Heir of Redclyffe – but the arrival of the Gods is grand and (in a different manner) the atmosphere of the N.I.C.E. is superb. Wither is a masterpiece; even with some experience of official documents and political speeches, one would not have believed it possible to convey so little meaning in so many words. And the death of Filostrato is first-class – his desperate agitation at feeling that it was so unscientific, and "his last thought was that he had under estimated the terror." Mr Bultitude [the bear] of course is adorable – oh! and the marvellous confusion of tongues at the dinner. And the painful realism of that college meeting. I enjoyed it all enormously . . .'

'I think *That Hideous Strength* is about a triple conflict,' Lewis wrote to William L. Kinter of the U.S.A. on 30 July 1954: 'Grace against Nature and Nature against Anti-Nature (modern industrialism, scientism and totalitarian politics): I should be very surprised if I owe anything to Politian or Ascham. Taking the word Humanist in the old sense in which they are Humanists, I am solidly anti-Humanist: i.e. though I love the Classics I loathe Classicism.'

'What it is to have a real reader!' he wrote to Kinter; and some extracts from Lewis's letters in this correspondence will be relevant here: 'An amusing question whether my trilogy is an epic! Clearly, in virtue of its fantastic elements, it could only be an epic of the Ariosto type. But I should call it a Romance myself: it lacks sufficient roots in legend and tradition to be what I'd call an epic. Isn't it more the method of Apuleius, Lucian and Rabelais, but diverted from a comic to a serious purpose?' (14 Feb. 1951). 'No one else sees that the first book is Ransom's *enfance*: if they notice a change at all, they complain that in the later ones he "loses the warm humanity of the first," etc.' (27 Nov. 1951). ' "By the *Furioso* out of the *Commedia*" is not far wrong. My real model was David Lindsay's *Voyage to Arcturus* which first suggested to me that the form of "science fiction" should be filled by spiritual experiences. And as the *Furioso* was in some ways the science-fiction of its age, your analogy works. But mind you, there is already a science-fiction element in the *Commedia*: e.g. *Inferno* XXXIV 85–114' (28 March 1953). 'I'm afraid the name St Anne's was chosen merely as a plausible and euphonious name, and for no such deep reasons as you suggest' (30 July 1954).

With *That Hideous Strength* Lewis came virtually to the end of his science fiction. The moment it was finished he embarked on *The Great Divorce* (*Who Goes Home?* it was called at first), which began its serial publication in the *Guardian* in November 1944 before appearing in book form a year later, by which time he had written *Miracles* ("The Miracle book is finished but will not come

out until next year,' he wrote to Sister Penelope on 25 May 1945) –
though he probably rewrote a good deal of it before its publication
in 1947.

The Great Divorce, though cast in narrative form, must be
considered with *The Pilgrim's Regress* and *The Screwtape Letters*
among Lewis's theological writings, and it would be an even
greater effort to include them in science fiction than to include
Dante's *Divine Comedy*.

Lewis did in fact write three science-fiction short stories towards the end of his life, which have been collected since his
death in *Of Other Worlds* (1966). The first two, 'The Shoddy
Lands' and 'Ministering Angels', were published in the *Magazine
of Fantasy and Science Fiction* in February 1956 and January
1958, and conquer no new worlds. 'The Shoddy Lands' are those
of a rather trivial young woman's mind explored in visible form
by a dreamer for a few minutes; 'Ministering Angels', though
actually set on Mars (definitely *not* Malacandra), takes place
entirely in a scientific 'space station' set up there, and is a light-
hearted skit on the serious suggestion that if men were to spend
long periods in space or on the planets, concubines should be
supplied 'to relieve tensions and promote morale'.

The third story, 'Forms of Things Unknown', is of much
greater interest. Lewis did not publish it, perhaps meaning to
revise and simplify it after Green, to whom he read it, had pointed
out that few readers would take the point. How few has been shown
by two American scholars and students of Lewis's works, the first
of whom asked what the Gorgons were, and the second who
assumed that Medusa was the only Gorgon and that her head
could somehow be floating about on the moon – actually she, the
only mortal Gorgon, could not have lived in space any more than
an ordinary man without a space-suit, while her sisters Stheno and
Euryale, being immortal, could perfectly well have done so. But in
fact the Gorgons are not mentioned by name or as such, and the
reader is left to realize, with a cold thrill, what it is that turns all
Selenauts into stone.

The description of the landing on the moon and of the scenery and physical conditions as Jenkin, the Selenaut, explores the area where previous space voyages have disappeared so mysteriously, is brilliantly imagined and described. And this must owe a great deal to a picture, or rather an astral dream, which Lewis described in a letter to his father on 30 March 1927: 'I dreamed that I was walking among the valleys of the Moon – a world of pure white rock, all deep chasms and spidery crags, with a perfectly black sky overhead. Of course there was nothing living there, not even a bit of moss: pure mineral solitude. Then I saw, very far off, coming to meet me down a narrow ravine, a straight, tall figure, draped in black, face and all covered. One knew it would be nicer not to meet that person: but one never has any choice in a dream, and for what seemed about an hour I went on till this stranger was right beside me. Then he held out an arm as if to shake hands, and of course I had to give him my hand: when suddenly I saw that instead of a hand he had a sort of metal ring which he closed round my wrist. It was sharp on the inside and hurt abominably. Then, without a word, drawing this thing together till it cut right to the bone, he turned and began to lead me off down the same long valley he had come from. It was the sense of being on the Moon you know, the complete desolateness, which gave the extraordinary effect.'

VIII. TALK OF THE DEVIL

When the war broke out in 1939, Warren, who had remained in the Army Reserve, was called into active duty and posted to the Base Supply Depot at Havre. He was now 43, had enjoyed seven years of retirement, and the 'romance' of Army life which he had felt as a young man had palled. Even the Enemy, which had been somewhat amorphous during the First War, had become grim and dreadful in the person of Hitler – the one modern man so bad that Lewis (in 'Screwtape Proposes a Toast') put him in Hell. At the same time, Lewis had no sympathy with the modern view that killing or being killed is a great evil and he did not believe in pacifism. Expecting a Leftist and a Rightist pseudo-theology to emerge in England, he would not accept the tempting belief that his country was without fault. Thus it was that when the vicar of his parish church (Holy Trinity in Headington Quarry) prayed that God might prosper 'our righteous cause', Lewis protested against the audacity of informing God that England's cause was 'righteous'.

During the First War Lewis had not only his brother's life to worry about but his own. Now that he was left behind, in the relative security of his college, he thought primarily of Warren and whether he would come out of the war alive. His foster-sister, Maureen, later told Walter Hooper of the elaborate means he went to in order to hide his deepening sorrow from the family. Once when Mrs Moore sent her into his study to call him for tea, she found Lewis reading. This she knew to be a ruse when she noticed that the book he was holding was upside-down. Some idea of his mental anguish comes through the pages of one of his notebooks where he tried to put his prayers for his brother into a poem.

Scribbled throughout the notebook are various versions of the lines

> How can I ask thee Father to defend
> In peril of war my brother's head to-day?

Later – perhaps for the purpose of disguising his feelings from others – he emends 'brother' to 'dearest friend', and takes the poem a bit further:

> How can I ask thee, Father, to defend
> In peril of war my dearest friend to-day,
> As though I knew, better than Thou, the way,
> Or with more love than thine desired the end?
> When I, for the length of one poor prayer, suspend
> So hardly for his sake my thoughts, that stray
> And wanton, thrusting twenty times a day,
> Clean out of mind the man I call my friend;
> Who, if he had from thee, no better care
> Than mine, were every moment dead. But prayer
> Thou givest to man, not man to thee: thy laws
> Suffering our mortal wish that way to share
> The eternal will; at taste of whose large air
> Man's word becomes, by miracle, a cause.

The war advertised itself everywhere. Three schoolgirls were evacuated to the Kilns, and Mrs Moore set Lewis to hanging up blackout curtains. So great was the shortage of space near London that the Government appropriated many college buildings for the billeting of soldiers. Lewis, fearing the worst, was delighted that New Buildings, which contained his set of rooms, was not used and that there were enough undergraduates to begin Michaelmas Term.

Meanwhile, the loss of Warren was somewhat compensated for by the appearance in Oxford of another great friend. A few days before war was declared against Germany, the Oxford University Press was moved to Southfield House in Oxford, and on 4 September 1939 Charles Williams arrived and took up residence in South Parks Road – within walking distance of Magdalen College. Lewis and Williams had met occasionally on weekends in London and

Oxford, and now that Williams was living in Oxford he became a regular attender of the Inklings.

Though Williams was given something of a hero's welcome by Lewis, he was not universally admired by the Inklings: Tolkien told Walter Hooper some years later that it was characteristic of Lewis to be 'taken in' by someone – first Mrs Moore, then Williams, and later Joy Davidman. However that may be, the effect of Williams was momentous, and his attendance at the Thursday evenings in Lewis's rooms in Magdalen and on Tuesday mornings at the 'Bird and Baby' are remembered as vintage years for Lewis and his fellow Inklings.

As it has become fashionable to speak of the 'influence' of Charles Williams on Lewis and to draw parallels between the two men's books, it is not, perhaps, amiss to record a conversation Hooper once had with Lewis on the subject. After a meeting of the Inklings some years after Williams's death, Dr R. E. Havard drove Lewis and Hooper out to the Trout Inn at Godstow. Over lunch Hooper asked Lewis what he thought of the current vogue for tracing the 'influence' of Williams in his work. 'I have never', replied Lewis, 'been *consciously* influenced by Williams, never believed that I was in any way imitating him. On the other hand, there may have been a great deal of *un*conscious influence going on.' Then, bursting into laughter, he said, 'By the by, I notice that every time I have a pork pie you have one too – is that "influence"?'

It may have been partly the great *unconscious* influence of Williams that made the war years some of Lewis's most productive. Some months before the Oxford University Press moved to Oxford, Lewis received two unusual requests for a layman. One came from the Reverend T. R. Milford asking if he would preach before the University in the Church of St Mary the Virgin, and the other from Ashley Sampson requesting him to write a book on pain for his 'Christian Challenge' series.

Lewis often said that if anyone had told him in his atheist days that he would someday step into a pulpit and preach he would have considered that man raving mad. Nevertheless, he accepted the invitation, conscious while doing so of both his duty to take on whatever tasks of this kind that he was given and the curious 'about-face' actions which God sometimes requires of a once cheeky atheist. He was at this time writing his essay on 'Christianity and Culture' and the sermon is quite obviously an outgrowth of it. The vicar of St Mary's was pleased with the script Lewis sent him and he mimeographed copies to pass out after the sermon. So, on Sunday evening, 22 October 1939, Lewis climbed into the pulpit to preach to a very large congregation of dons and undergraduates, one of whom was Roger Lancelyn Green. The sermon was entitled 'None Other Gods: Culture in War Time', and Lewis chose as a text the verse 'A Syrian ready to perish was my father' from Deuteronomy 26:5. It has since appeared in his *Transposition and Other Addresses*.

Knowing that many of the undergraduates might go to war – as he had – before they completed their studies in Oxford, he set himself to answer the peculiarly relevant question, 'What is the use of beginning a task which we have so little chance of finishing?' As was typical in all Lewis's sermons, he went straight to the heart of the matter – pointing out that, since we are all going to die sometime, as we live *perpetually* on the edge of a precipice, war creates no absolutely new situation but only 'aggravates the permanent human situation so that we can no longer ignore it'. That being so, and as neither conversion nor war obliterates our intellectual and aesthetic activities, we would be foolish to allow fear to cause us to substitute a worse cultural life for a better. (It is interesting to compare Lewis's idea of culture with that which Hitler was busy inaugurating in Germany.)

Lewis went on to say that, whereas a man might have to die for his country, no man should, in any exclusive sense, *live* for his country. Religion, on the other hand, though it cannot occupy the whole of life in the sense of excluding all our natural activities, must, in another sense, occupy the whole of life – the solution to this paradox being that *whatever* we do must be done to the glory of God. 'The work of a Beethoven, and the work of a charwoman', Lewis insisted, 'become spiritual on precisely the same condition, that of being offered to God, of being done humbly "as to the Lord".'

Ashley Sampson was, during the 1930s, the owner of a small London publishing firm, the Centenary Press. Shortly before the war, another publisher, Geoffrey Bles, who had opened up a firm in 1924 and who achieved success through his publication of a translation of Vicki Baum's novel *Grand Hotel* in 1930, bought up the Centenary Press and its owner. Though he was working for Bles now, Sampson – who can truly be called the 'discoverer' of C. S. Lewis – was keenly interested in theology and, having been greatly impressed by *The Pilgrim's Regress* and its author, invited Lewis to contribute a book on pain to his 'Christian Challenge' series. This series of popular theological books, which came out during the war under the imprint of both the Centenary Press and Geoffrey Bles Ltd, contained many valuable titles: Canon Roger Lloyd's *The Mastery of Evil*, Father Gerald Vann's *The Heart of Man*, Charles Williams's *The Forgiveness of Sins*, and *The Resurrection of Christ* by Professor A. M. Ramsey (now Archbishop of Canterbury). Lewis began writing *The Problem of Pain* during the summer of 1939, and when the Inklings met on 8 November at the 'Eastgate' to dine, part of the fare consisted of a section from Tolkien's 'new Hobbit', a nativity play by Charles Williams, and a chapter from Lewis's *Problem*. It was still being written and read aloud when Lewis and Tolkien (the only two Inklings on this occasion) met in the latter's rooms in Pembroke on Thursday, 30 November. In a letter to his brother written a few days afterwards (3 December) he described his observations on the supposedly close connection between *theories* about pain and actual *pain*: 'If you are writing a book about pain and then get some actual pain, as I did in my ribs, it does *not* either, as the cynic would expect, blow the doctrine to bits, or, as a Christian would hope, turn it into practice, but remains quite unconnected and irrelevant, just as any other bit of actual life does when you are reading or writing.'

It was Lewis's interest in pain that introduced another friend into the circle of Inklings. This was Dr R. E. Havard who had been Lewis and Warren's doctor since 1934 and who shared with them an interest in literature, theology and good company. The physician referred to as 'Humphrey' in *Perelandra* was partially modelled after Dr Havard and, though the fictional doctor has little of the charm of the real one, Dr Havard, following the publication of *Perelandra*, came to be known to Lewis and his friends as 'Humphrey Havard'. He came to the first meeting of the Inklings on 1 February 1940 and, as a favour to Lewis, read a paper on his clinical experiences of the effects of pain, a portion of which Lewis afterwards used as an appendix to his book on pain.

After *The Problem of Pain* had obtained the *nihil obstat* of the Inklings – to whom it is dedicated – the manuscript went off to Ashley Sampson in the spring of 1940 and was published on 18 October of the same year. Though it has often been listed in catalogues as a medical handbook (much to Lewis's amusement), its success was immediate and continuing; it has gone through twenty hard-cover impressions and sold over 120,000 paperback copies in England alone.

The 'problem' of pain is roughly this: 'If God is *good*, why does he allow so much suffering in the world?' Lewis knew that most readers had never read a serious discussion of theology before, and, as they might never read another, he uses a technique not totally unlike that of Billy Graham in taking full advantage of his one opportunity to get everything in. He spends the first half of his book discussing the nature of God, free will, human wickedness and the Fall of man – and that with such freshness, clarity and dispelling of petty, traditional prejudices that, had only those chapters been printed, many readers might have been able to answer the 'problem' for themselves. In Chapter 6 on 'Human Pain' Lewis points out the benevolence of God in giving men the 'enormous permission to torture their fellows'. The author's purpose is not only to justify free will but to show the good and remedial effects of pain: 'God whispers to us in our pleasures, speaks in our conscience, but shouts in our pains: it is His megaphone to rouse a deaf world.' (Interestingly, the Dutch translation of the book is entitled *Gods Megafoon*.)

By the time he has got to his chapter on 'Hell', Lewis has placed God's goodness beyond attack and, then, having pictured a really bad man, asks: 'Can you really desire that such a man, *remaining what he is* (and he must be able to do that if he has free will), should be confirmed forever in his present happiness – should continue, for all eternity, to be perfectly convinced that the laugh is on his side? . . . Even mercy can hardly wish to such a man his eternal, contented continuance in such ghastly illusion.'

In his chapter on 'Animal Pain' which Lewis admits is pure speculation ('God has given us data which enable us, in some degree, to understand our own suffering: He has given us no such data about beasts'), he traces the sufferings of animals to the Fall of man and suggests that as man is to be understood only in his relation to God, the beasts are to be understood only in their relation to man and, through him, to God. 'The tame animal', he says, 'is therefore . . . the only "natural" animal – the only one we can see occupying the place it was made to occupy, and it is on the tame animal that we must base all our doctrine of beasts.'

Finally, in his last chapter on 'Heaven', Lewis brings in the darling theme of all his writings, the romantic yearning after a transcendent joy which lifts the thesis of his book once and for all to a level at which everything is seen in its full significance.

Though many find it difficult to accept Lewis's belief in a literal Satan, a literal Fall of man, and his fundamentalist doctrine of original sin (the latter seems to be coming back into fashion as, for instance, in William Golding's *Lord of the Flies*), the chapter which has attracted most attention is that on 'Animal Pain'. Lewis's gentle controversy with the late Professor C. E. M. Joad on 'The Pains of Animals' can be found in Lewis's *Undeceptions* (ed. Walter Hooper, 1971). Some of the most pointed criticism of this chapter came from Evelyn Underhill who complained in a letter to Lewis of 13 January 1941 that she found the belief that the tame animal is the only *natural* animal 'an intolerable doctrine of a frightful exaggeration of what is involved in the primacy of man'. 'Is the cow', she went on to ask, 'which we have turned into a milk machine or the hen we have turned into an egg machine really nearer the mind of God than its wild ancestors? . . . You surely *can't* mean that, or think that the robin red breast in a cage doesn't put heaven in a rage but is regarded as an excellent arrangement . . . If we ever get a sideway glimpse of the animal-in-itself, the animal existing for God's glory and pleasure and lit by His light (and what a lovely experience that is!) we don't owe it to the Pekinese, the Persian cat or the Canary, but to some wild free creature living in completeness of adjustment to nature a life that is utterly independent of man. And this, thank heaven, is the situation of all but the handful of creatures we have enslaved. Of course I agree that animals too are involved in the Fall and await redemption and transfiguration . . . And man is no doubt offered the chance of being the mediator of that redemption. But not by taming, surely? Rather by loving and reverencing the creatures enough to leave them free. When my cat goes off on her own occasions I'm sure she goes with God – but I don't feel so sure of her theological position when she is sitting on the best chair before the drawing-room fire. Perhaps what it all comes to is this, that I feel your concept of God would be improved by just a touch of wildness.'

Lewis obviously agreed with Miss Underhill about wildness for he made all the animals in his Narnian stories as natural as possible – far more like the real thing than anything in Walt Disney's films. When one of the children in *The Lion, the Witch and the Wardrobe* asks if Aslan is 'safe' she is answered, 'Safe? Who said anything about safe? 'Course he isn't safe. But he's good.' And, lest one get the impression from *The Problem of Pain* that Lewis himself treated his own pets – which did not include Pekinese, Persian, or Canaries – with exaggerated and cloying affection, Walter Hooper has given us a picture of what it was like at the Kilns during the 1960s: 'The Kilns "family" included two cats, an old ginger named Tom (a mighty hunter of mice when he was young, but then living on a pension of fish) and Snip (a Siamese which Lewis inherited from his wife and referred to as his "step-cat"). There was also a young boxer pup named Ricky who regularly left a trail of sticky saliva across Lewis's trousers.

They recognized Lewis as the undisputed head of the house, but he never made an elaborate fuss over them. He greeted Tom in the morning, stroked Snip when she jumped in his lap, and passed the time of day with Ricky. Live and let live: just what they wanted. If the door to his study was open, they knew they were welcome within: otherwise not. One summer morning when Lewis was writing at his desk by the open window, Snip took a great spring and shot through the window. She landed with a great thump on top of his desk, scattering papers in all directions, and skidded into his lap. He looked at her in amazement. She looked at him in amazement. "Perhaps", he said to me, "my step-cat, having finished her acrobatics, would enjoy a saucer of milk in the kitchen." I opened the door for poor Snip and she walked slowly out, embarrassed, but with the best grace she could manage.' ('Past Watchful Dragons: The Fairy Tales of C. S. Lewis' in *Imagination and the Spirit*, 1971.)

Years before, Lewis would have stopped to savour the success of a new book, but, once delivered of the manuscript, his attention switched to new enthusiasms and ideas. He persuaded the university to give Charles Williams an honorary M.A. and to invite him to lecture. On 29 January 1940 Williams began his term of weekly lectures on Milton in the Taylorian Building. Lewis was there of course and immensely pleased with his friend's success. He wrote to his brother on 11 February about Williams's lecture on *Comus* which, as he said, was 'nominally on *Comus* but really on Chastity . . . "The sage and serious doctrine of virginity" . . . It was a beautiful sight to see a whole roomful of modern young men and women sitting in that absolute silence which can *not* be faked, very puzzled, but spell-bound.' So unusual was it to hear virginity extolled that at the next meeting of the Inklings Hugo Dyson wryly complained that Williams was becoming a 'common *chastitute*'.

While Williams was lecturing on Milton, Warren Lewis was lying ill in a French hospital where he had been for several months. In May 1940 he was evacuated with the rest of his unit from Dunkirk and sent to Wenvoe Camp in Wales. Though it was some months before he recovered his strength, Lewis was relieved that he was at least safe and close to home. As he was only 41, Lewis was expected to join the Home Guard and in August 1940 he was issued with a rifle and uniform and began his weekly three-hour patrol on the outskirts of Oxford. Every Saturday he joined two other men at 1.30 a.m. and patrolled the area round the college sports grounds and pavilions till 4.30 a.m. – an experience he treasured as he was able to walk home in what he called the 'empty, silent, dewy, cobwebby hours' of the morning.

Meanwhile, Warren's health remained unsatisfactory and in the autumn of 1940 he was transferred to the Reserve List and sent home. Lewis and his brother had been wrenched apart so many times that, with the war growing worse every day, they hardly dared hope that this time they were permanently united. But they were – for the rest of Lewis's life.

As Lewis spent the weekends at the Kilns, it had long been his and his brother's practice to go to Holy Trinity Church in Headington Quarry on Sunday mornings. The parish priest at this time was the Reverend T. E. Bleiben who, though an able priest, was rather low-church and, thus, unrepresentative of the parish with its long tradition of Anglo-Catholicism. Because of his intense dislike of organ music Lewis usually shunned the 10.30 Sung Eucharist or Matins and went instead to the Communion service at 8.00 a.m. It was following the 8 o'clock Communion at Holy Trinity on Sunday, 15 July 1940, that he was struck by the idea for what was to become his most famous book. Writing to Warren (who was still at Wenvoe Camp) on 20 July, he said: 'After the service was over – one could wish these things came more seasonably – I was struck by an idea for a book which I think might be both useful and entertaining. It would be called "As one Devil to another" and would consist of letters from an elderly retired devil to a young devil who has just started work on his first "patient". The idea would be to give all the psychology of temptation from the *other* point of view.'

The book is of course *The Screwtape Letters*. We do not know how long he spent writing it except for what he tells us: he never wrote with more ease – and, as it turned out, with less enjoyment. If it flowed as freely as most of his books, he had probably finished it by Christmas 1940.

The plot of *Screwtape* is quite simple. It consists of a series of admonitory epistles from Screwtape, an experienced devil high in the Administration of the Infernal Civil Service, to his nephew, Wormwood, a junior colleague engaged on one of his earliest assignments on earth – which is to secure the damnation of a young man who has just become a Christian. The young man, or 'patient', lives with a very trying mother and, much to Screwtape's delight, falls under the influence of 'rich, smart, superficially intellectual and brightly sceptical people'. Later he does a number of things which, though innocent enough by normal standards, are considered suspect by the Lowerarchy of Hell: he reads a book he likes, takes an agreeable solitary walk, has tea at an old mill, and falls in love with a delightful girl in whose home he encounters 'Christian life of a quality he never before imagined'. Finally – and this is how Wormwood loses him – he is most inopportunely killed in the war while working in Civil Defence.

If this is a simple 'human' story from the novelist's usual point of view, it is anything but that to God – and, presumably, to Satan. Even those who do not hold, as Lewis did, that men are immortal and that each of us is progressing moment by moment either to Heaven or to Hell, will benefit from Lewis's angle of vision. An 'angle' he found it difficult to maintain, for in every letter he had to twist his mind into a diabolical attitude – to imagine how every temptation, pleasure, joy and sorrow looks to the devils. Lewis later said in his new preface of 1961: 'The strain produced a sort of spiritual cramp. The world into which I had to project myself while I spoke through Screwtape was all dust, grit, thirst, and itch. Every trace of beauty, freshness and geniality had to be excluded. It almost smothered me before I was done.'

What interests a great many people is, not so much that *Screwtape* is an imaginary correspondence between devils, but that Lewis believed in their existence. However, as he explained in the preface to the edition of 1961, what he does *not* believe in is the existence of a power opposite to God – that is, in Dualism. As there is no uncreated being except God, he cannot have an opposite. 'The proper question', said Lewis, 'is whether I believe in devils. I do. That is to say, I believe in angels and I believe that some of them, by the abuse of their free will, have become enemies to God and, as a corollary, to us. These we may call devils. They do not differ in nature from good angels, but their nature is depraved. *Devil* is the opposite of *angel* only as Bad Man is the opposite of Good Man. Satan, the leader or dictator of devils, is the opposite not of God but of Michael.' He goes on to say that though the belief in devils is not part of his creed, it is one of his opinions: 'It seems to me to explain a good many facts. It agrees with the plain sense of Scripture, the tradition of Christendom, and the beliefs of most men at most times. And it conflicts with nothing that any of the sciences has shown to be true.'

Though there has always been a certain amount of interest in devils, it is not perhaps unfair to say that the publication of *The Screwtape Letters* stirred up even greater curiosity. It also cleared up a mass of nonsense about their nature. In his original preface of 1942 Lewis wrote: 'There are two equal and opposite errors into which our race can fall about the devils. One is to disbelieve in their existence. The other is to believe, and to feel an excessive and unhealthy interest in them.' When Wormwood asks Screwtape whether the 'patient' ought to know of his existence or not, he is told, 'I do not think you will have much difficulty in keeping the patient in the dark. The fact that "devils" are predominantly *comic* figures in the modern imagination will help you. If any faint suspicion of your existence begins to arrive in his mind, suggest to him a picture of something in red tights, and persuade him that since he cannot believe in *that* . . . he therefore cannot believe in you.'

At the same time that he was writing *Screwtape*, Lewis was busy with two other books in which he wanted to demonstrate why Christians are committed to believing that 'the Devil is an ass'. In the first book, his *Preface to 'Paradise Lost'* (1942), in his chapter on 'Satan', he suggests that those who consider him the 'hero' of Milton's poem have confused a 'magnificent poetical treatment' with what a real being like Satan would be like if we actually met him. Of the progressive degradation of Satan who 'thought himself impaired' by being inferior to his Creator, Lewis says: 'In the midst of a world of light and love, of song and feast and dance, he could find nothing to think of more interesting than his own prestige. And his own prestige, it must be noted, had and could have no other grounds than those which he refused to admit for the superior prestige of Messiah . . . It is like the scent of a flower trying to destroy the flower.'

At the end of Milton's 'temptation scene', which lasts only 200 lines, Eve falls. Lewis in *Perelandra* takes up the same biblical story from Genesis 3, albeit on a different planet with a different Eve, and devotes a hundred pages to it. His Eve is far more intelligent than Milton's; but then so is his Satan. Though Lewis's hero, Ransom, feels defenceless in the face of Satan's dizzying barrage of logic, illogic and half-truths, he eventually sees that the fallen archangel, by choosing to make Evil his 'Good', has come to regard intelligence 'simply and solely as a weapon, which it had no more wish to employ in its off-duty hours than a soldier has to do bayonet practice when he is on leave. Thought was for it a device necessary to certain ends, but thought in itself did not interest it' (p. 146).

Lewis complained that *Screwtape* gave a lop-sided view of life because, ideally, Screwtape's advice to Wormwood ought to have been balanced by archangelical advice to the 'patient' from his guardian angel. This cannot, however, be seen as a serious defect in the book because Screwtape himself, despite his malign ingenuity, throws out numerous back-handed compliments about the 'Enemy' (i.e. God): 'Whenever there is prayer, there is danger of His own immediate action. He is cynically indifferent to the dignity of His position . . . and . . . pours out self-knowledge in a quite shameless fashion' (Letter 4). 'He really *does* want to fill the universe with a lot of loathsome little replicas of Himself – creatures whose life, on its miniature scale, will be qualitatively like His own, not because He has absorbed them but because their wills freely conform to His. . . . We are empty and would be filled; He is full and flows over. Our war aim is a world in which Our Father Below has drawn all other beings into himself: the Enemy wants a world full of beings united to Him but still distinct' (Letter 8). 'I know we have won many a soul through pleasure. All the same it is His invention, not ours. He made the pleasures: all our research so far has not enabled us to produce one' (Letter 9). 'When the creation of man was first mooted and when, even at that stage, the Enemy freely confessed that he foresaw a certain episode about a cross, Our Father very naturally sought an interview and asked for an explanation. The Enemy gave no reply except to produce the cock-and-bull story about disinterested love which He has been circulating ever since. This Our Father naturally could not accept. He implored the Enemy to lay His cards on the table, and gave Him every opportunity. He admitted that he felt a real anxiety to know the secret; the Enemy replied "I wish with all my heart that you did". It was, I imagine, at this stage in the interview that Our Father's disgust at such an unprovoked lack of confidence caused him to remove himself an infinite distance from the Presence with a suddenness which has given rise to the ridiculous enemy story that he was forcibly thrown out of Heaven. . . . If we could only find out what He is really up to!' (Letter 19).

Not a few critics have complained that, considering the world's woes – wars, famines and the like – Lewis has Screwtape aim at very small targets in his attempt to secure the 'patient's' damnation. But Lewis has supplied us with the answer to this charge. In Letter 12 Screwtape pulls Wormwood up rather sharply: '. . . like all young tempters, you are anxious to be able to report spectacular wickedness. But do remember, the only thing that matters is the extent to which you separate the man from the Enemy. It does not matter how small the sins are provided that their cumulative effect is to edge the man away from the Light and out into the Nothing. Murder is no better than cards if cards can do the trick. Indeed the safest road to Hell is the gradual one – the gentle slope, soft underfoot, without sudden turnings, without mile-stones, without signposts.'

Once when Walter Hooper asked if there were any book which had given him the idea for *The Screwtape Letters*, Lewis took off his bookshelves Stephen McKenna's *Confessions of a Well-Meaning Woman* (1922) and gave it to him to read. McKenna's once-popular book had been, he said, his only 'model' and had suggested how he might go about writing an 'infernal correspondence'. It consists of twelve letters from Lady Ann Spenworth to an un-named 'friend of proved discretion'. Lady Ann is the daughter of an earl and her husband the younger of two sons of another peer – the rub being that their son Will is unable to inherit either family title unless various uncles and cousins come to grief in some way or another. Though Lady Ann does not confess to having anything so crude as this in mind, her letters betray her as being an un-scrupulous and catty hypocrite, bent (though she says just the opposite) on destroying their lives. *Her* grief, other than the fact that her relatives remain in blooming health, comes in the form of a poor, but pretty, Yorkshire girl whom her son marries – the daughter, wails Lady Ann, of 'one of these rugged, north-of-England clergymen who always have the air of intimidating you into a state of grace' (p. 158). 'The connection may not be obvious', Lewis wrote in the 1961 preface to *Screwtape*, 'but you will find there the same moral inversion – the blacks all white and the whites all black – and the humour which comes of speaking through a totally humourless *persona*.'

The fact remains that, bad as Lady Ann Spenworth is, she does not understand evil as well as Lewis who, pressed for information about how he knew so much about temptation, replied in his 1961 preface: 'Some have paid me an undeserved compliment by supposing that my *Letters* were the ripe fruit of many years' study in moral and ascetic theology. They forgot that there is an equally reliable, though less creditable, way of learning how temptation works. "My heart" – I need no other's – "sheweth me the wicked-ness of the ungodly." '

No one will ever know just how much personal experience went into *Screwtape*, but members of an Oxford Senior Common Room do not usually find their so-called 'ivory tower' existence, however plush the surroundings, free of thorns. Lewis did nothing to hide the fact that he found his colleagues at Magdalen, though no worse, certainly no better than men of other professions. Then there was Mrs Moore whose faults, if they were never spoken of by Lewis, did not escape the notice of his friends. Though her brother, W. J. Askins, was the dean of Kilmore Cathedral in Ireland, Mrs Moore was an atheist in later life (blaming it on Paddy's death) and chided Lewis and Warren for participating in 'blood feasts' at the local parish church. Lewis doubtless encountered many mothers who resented their children becoming Christians, but if Mrs Moore was as bitter about his conversion and subsequent fame as a Christian apologist as she is said to have been, it is hard to reject the idea that Lewis consciously or unconsciously had her in mind when, in Letter 3, Screwtape asks how the patient's mother accepted his conversion: 'Is she at all jealous of the new factor in her son's life? – at all piqued that he should have learned from others, and so late, what she considers she gave him such good opportunity of learning in childhood? Does she feel he is making a great deal of "fuss" about it – or that he's getting in on very easy terms? Remember the elder brother in the Enemy's story.'

Lewis's ability to ferret out those sins which lie hidden, like tiny cancers, so close to a man's heart probably owes a great deal to a decision made near the time he thought of writing *The Screwtape Letters*. Though Lewis's theology was 'high' from the standpoint of being completely and utterly orthodox, he had not been brought up to make auricular confessions to a priest – except, that is, for the 'general confessions' contained in the services of Matins, Evensong and Holy Communion. The difficulty he found with these Prayer Book confessions is that one could be as specific or (as is usually the case) as 'general' as one likes. It was shortly after Lewis conceived the idea of his *Letters* that he was attracted by the Exhortation in the service of Holy Communion which states that if any man 'cannot quiet his own conscience' he may go to a priest and 'open his grief' in order that he 'may receive the benefit of absolution together with ghostly counsel and advice'.

He decided to do just this and on 24 October 1940 he wrote to his friend Sister Penelope of the Community of St Mary the Virgin in Wantage saying, 'I am going to make my first confession next week . . . The *decision* to do so was one of the hardest I have ever made . . . I begin to be afraid that I am merely indulging in an orgy of egoism.' Some years later he told Walter Hooper that a moment after he had dropped the letter into the pillar-box he got cold feet and tried to fish it out. As this turned out to be impossible he felt he had no course but to go through with the confession and, so, hied himself down to the Anglican priests of the Society of St John the Evangelist in Cowley – popularly known as the 'Cowley Dads' – where he was given a *directeur* whom he made his regular confessor till the priest's death many years later. Shortly after his first confession, he reported back to Sister Penelope (4 Nov. 1940): 'Well – we have come through the wall of fire and find ourselves (somewhat to our surprise) still alive and even well. The suggestion about an orgy of egoism turns out, like all the enemy propaganda, to have just a grain of truth in it, but I have no doubt that the proper method of dealing with that is to continue the practice, as I intend to do. For after all, everything – even virtue, even prayer – has its dangers and if one heeds the grain of truth in the enemy propaganda one can never do anything at all.'

Lewis had long given up what he considered a pernicious and time-wasting habit – that of following the 'news'. The one paper, or weekly news-magazine, he did read, however, was the *Guardian*. It had been founded in 1846 to uphold Tractarian principles and 'to show their relevance to the best secular thought of the day' and ceased publication in 1951 when it was taken over by the *Church Quarterly*. Following his conversion, Lewis decided that any monies made from specifically religious writings should go to charities, for, as he told Walter Hooper, 'I felt that God had been so gracious in having me that the least I could do was give back all the money made in His service.' So, even before he was paid for his first contribution to the *Guardian*, an essay entitled 'Dangers of National Repentance' (March 1940), he arranged with the editor to have all monies owing to him to be sent to any charity he might name.

The 31 *Screwtape Letters* were sent as a single manuscript to the editor of the *Guardian* who published them in weekly instalments from 2 May 1941 through to 28 November. Lewis was paid £2 per letter, all of which £62 went direct from the editor into a fund for 'Clergy Widows'.

Lewis's friend and 'discoverer', Ashley Sampson, read the *Letters* as they came out and, with his usual acumen for 'spotting a winner', had no trouble in persuading Geoffrey Bles to snap them up before Lewis had any other offers. Lewis sent Bles a 'fair copy' of the manuscript in his own hand (he could not afford a typist) and, as there was yet no complete printed copy of all the *Letters*, he sent the original manuscript to Sister Penelope with the request (9 Oct. 1941) that, 'If it is not a trouble I should like you to keep it safe until the book is printed (in case the one the publisher has got blitzed) – after that it can be made into spills or used to stuff dolls or anything.'

Lewis was showered with praise even before all the *Letters* had appeared in the columns of the *Guardian*. One subscriber, delighted with Lewis's ironic mockery of the Lowerarchy, wrote to the editor (*Guardian*, 3 Oct. 1941) suggesting that, as Screwtape had no degree higher than a B.S., some 'grateful university now welcome him *in gradum Doctoris in Satanitate dishonoris causa*'. There were, however, dissenting voices as well; one, that of a country clergyman who, Lewis learned with glee, wrote to the editor cancelling his subscription on the ground that 'much of the advice given in these letters seemed to him not only erroneous but positively diabolical'. Lewis was beginning to feel that he had hit his target.

He had indeed. The first 2,000 copies of *Screwtape* were published by Bles in February 1942 and disappeared almost at once. The book was reprinted twice in March and, then, so great was the clamour for copies, was reprinted six more times before the year was out. Lewis's New York publishers, Macmillan & Co., brought out an American edition in 1943 which immediately became a 'bestseller'. *The Screwtape Letters* has been translated into fifteen languages, and the paperback sales in England and America have now passed the million mark.

Not a few of the hundreds who have reviewed *Screwtape* have adopted in their reviews Lewis's idea of an 'infernal correspondence'. One of the cleverest is that of Charles Williams who, in *Time and Tide* (21 March 1942), has one devil, 'Snigsozzle', write a letter to another, 'Scorpuscle', in which the former suggests that the best counter-irritant to the publication of Screwtape's 'cursedly clever' letters is 'to make the infernal text a primer in our own Training College'. As a postscript he adds, 'You will send someone to see after Lewis? – some very clever fiend?'

Almost overnight it seemed, Lewis was internationally famous. Money began to roll in and he, not understanding the difference between gross and net profit, celebrated his good fortune by a lavish scattering of cheques to societies and individual lame dogs. Before the situation got completely out of hand, Owen Barfield, who ran his own legal firm in London, intervened and helped him set up a Charitable Trust – generally referred to as the 'Agape Fund' – into which he was thereafter to pay two-thirds of his royalties for the purpose of helping the poor.

IX. 'MERE CHRISTIANITY'

It is commonly supposed that Lewis came to prominence as a speaker on Christianity because of his immense popularity as the author of *The Screwtape Letters*. The truth is that the most important of his speaking engagements began a little further back. *The Problem of Pain* had been finding some grateful and influential admirers, one of whom was the Director of Religious Broadcasting for the B.B.C., Dr James W. Welch, who wrote to Lewis on 7 February 1941:

Dear Mr Lewis,

I address you by name because, although we have never met, you cannot be a stranger after allowing me – and many others – to know some of your thoughts and convictions which have been expressed in your book *The Problem of Pain*. I should like to take this opportunity of saying how grateful I am to you personally for the help this book has given me.

I write to ask whether you would be willing to help us in our work of religious broadcasting. The microphone is a limiting, and often irritating, instrument, but the quality of thinking and depth of conviction which I find in your book ought surely to be shared with a great many other people; and for any talk we can be sure of a fairly intelligent audience of more than a million. Two ideas strike me:

(1) You might be willing to speak about the Christian, or lack of Christian, assumptions underlying modern literature . . .

(2) A series of talks on something like 'The Christian Faith As I See It – by A Layman': I am sure there is need of a positive restatement of Christian doctrines in lay language . . .

Lewis had no interest whatsoever in the radio as such, a harsh contraption the sound of which he cringed at every time he heard it bellowing from his gardener's bungalow. He cared even less for travelling up to London for, sharing his father's provincialism to some extent, he regarded a trip to London in very much the same way that another man might look upon a voyage to the moon.

Nevertheless, the invitation interested him, for he had long regarded England as part of that vast 'post-Christian' world in need of a special missionary technique – one which must take into account the fact that many people were under the impression that they had rejected Christianity when, in truth, they had never had it. Once when asked to describe the difficulties of presenting the Faith to modern unbelievers, Lewis wrote: 'The ancient man approached God (or even the gods) as the accused person approaches his judge. For the modern man the roles are reversed. He is the judge: God is in the dock' (*Undeceptions*, p. 200). Could someone, he wondered, trouble the conscience of those who feel no guilt and then 'translate' the gospel into language that they can understand? On 10 February 1941 Lewis accepted the invitation:

Dear Mr Welch,
    Thanks for your kind remarks about my book. I would like to give a series of talks as you suggest, but it would have to be in the vacation. Modern literature would not suit me. I think what I mainly want to talk about is the Law of Nature, or objective right and wrong. It seems to me that the New Testament, by preaching repentance and forgiveness, always *assumes* an audience who already believe in the Law of Nature and know they have disobeyed it. In modern England we cannot at present assume this, and therefore most apologetic begins a stage too far on. The first step is to create, or recover, the sense of guilt. Hence if I give a series of talks I should mention Christianity only at the end, and would prefer not to unmask my battery till then. Some title like 'The Art of being Shocked' or 'These Humans' would suit me. Let me know what you think of this and also how many talks and at what dates (roughly) you would like.

Within the next few days it was agreed that Lewis would give four fifteen-minute talks. Knowing exactly what he wanted to say, Lewis had no trouble in writing his radio scripts. The only hitch he encountered was gauging his material so that every talk was neither more nor less than fifteen minutes. The series was announced in the *Radio Times* as *Right and Wrong: A Clue to the Meaning of the Universe?* and during the month of August 1941 Lewis journeyed up to London every Wednesday evening and spoke over the air from 7.45 to 8.00 p.m.

He was overwhelmed by letters even before finishing his four talks and sought the advice of the B.B.C. Dr Welch had not imagined that his Oxford don would be so sensational and, in an attempt to lighten his burden, gave him an additional fifteen minutes over the microphone on 6 September for a 'Talk in Answer to Listeners' Questions'. This had the 'reverse' effect of stimulating more interest and inquiries. Writing about it to Arthur Greeves on 23 December, Lewis said: 'As the aftermath of those Broadcast Talks I gave early last summer I had an enormous pile of letters from strangers to answer. One gets funny letters after broadcasting – some from lunatics who sign themselves "Jehovah" or begin "Dear Mr Lewis, I was married at the age of 20 to a man I didn't love" – but many from serious inquirers whom it was a duty to answer fully.'

Lewis had by this time been going to confession for over a year and believed very firmly that people must be convinced of the unwelcome diagnosis of sin before they can welcome the news of the Remedy. One would, however, get a distorted picture of his apologetics if one imagined that a sense of sin was the main concern of his religion. On Sunday, 8 June 1941, Lewis preached his best-known sermon, 'The Weight of Glory' – perhaps the most sublime piece of prose to come from his pen.

Paxford was asked to drive his beloved 'Mr Jack' to the Church of St Mary the Virgin where he was to preach. It was the first time that Paxford had seen his master in the pulpit and, recounting the experience to Walter Hooper, he recalls the University Church being so packed that some students could only find room by perching in the windows. 'But what was the sermon like?' inquired Hooper. 'Gor blimey!' he answered, 'Mr Jack really give it to 'em!'

'If we consider', Lewis began, 'the unblushing promises of reward and the staggering nature of the rewards promised in the Gospels, it would seem that Our Lord finds our desires, not too strong, but too weak. We are half-hearted creatures, fooling about with drink and sex and ambition when infinite joy is offered us, like an ignorant child who wants to go on making mud pies in a slum because he cannot imagine what is meant by the offer of a holiday at the sea. We are far too easily pleased.'

Lewis considered the mere hankering for immortality a despicable reason for turning to Christ. He believed that, until a certain spiritual level had been reached, the promise of immortality operates as a bribe which inflames the very self-regard which it is the business of Christianity to cut down and uproot. On the other hand, for those who *begin* with a vision of God and who try to obey him, Heaven turns out to be the consummation of their earthly discipleship. Having thrown out hint after hint about the joys of the redeemed soul's union with God, he concluded his sermon with a perspective of mankind so comprehensive in its sweep that it illuminates everything he was to write thereafter:

It is a serious thing to live in a society of possible gods and goddesses, to remember that the dullest and most uninteresting person you talk to may one day be a creature which, if you saw it now, you would be strongly tempted to worship, or else a horror and a corruption such as you now meet, if at all, only in a nightmare. All day long we are, in some degree, helping each other to one or other of these destinations. It is in the light of these overwhelming possibilities, it is with the awe and the circumspection proper to them, that we should conduct all our dealings with one another, all friendships, all loves, all play, all politics. There are no *ordinary* people. You have never talked to a mere mortal. Nations, cultures, arts, civilizations – these are mortal, and their life is to ours, as the life of a gnat. But it is immortals whom we joke with, work with, marry, snub, and exploit – immortal horrors or everlasting splendours . . . Next to the Blessed Sacrament itself, your neighbour is the holiest object presented to your senses. If he is your Christian neighbour he is holy in almost the same way, for in him also Christ *vere latitat* – the glorifier and the glorified, Glory Himself, is truly hidden.

Immediately following the broadcasts on *Right and Wrong*, the Dean of St Paul's wrote to the Reverend Maurice Edwards, then Chaplain-in-Chief of the Royal Air Force, announcing that he had a lectureship in his patronage which, in the unusual circumstances of war, he could make a sort of travelling lectureship. The Dean went on to suggest that, as C. S. Lewis was at a loose end at Magdalen, perhaps the Chaplain-in-Chief could make use of him.

Early in the winter of 1941 the Chaplain-in-Chief wrote asking

Lewis if he would accept invitations to speak to the members of the R.A.F., and shortly afterwards the Chaplain-in-Chief and his assistant, Charles Gilmore, went to Oxford to call on him. When Walter Hooper inquired for details of this meeting, he was supplied with the following reminiscences by Charles Gilmore (letter of 4 November 1972): 'I well remember going up to Oxford one winter's day with Maurice Edwards and spending an evening in C. S. Lewis's rooms to discuss details. Lewis was diffident of himself but keen to try. I remember that he mentioned that the whole project might well be aborted because the call-up age would reach him the following year. We fixed up details of expenses to be paid by the public purse, and the lectureship could provide his fees.'

Besides the fact that Lewis was still carrying in his body some shrapnel from the First War, the Government decided that he was far too valuable as a teacher to go back into service. The Chaplain-in-Chief may have known this and, shortly after the meeting in Oxford, he informed the chaplains of the Royal Air Force that Lewis would be available at the weekends to speak on the Christian faith.

Invitations poured in and, though there is no complete record of all the Air Force bases Lewis visited, we learn from a letter to Sister Penelope of 15 May 1941 that he gave his first talks the month before to the R.A.F. at Abingdon. 'As far as I can judge', he wrote, 'they were a complete failure. I await instructions from the Chaplain-in-Chief about the Vacation . . . jobs one dare neither refuse nor perform. One must take comfort in remembering that God used an *ass* to convert the prophet . . .'

Surely one of the most unusual jobs Lewis dared perform at this time was to visit the nuns of the Community of St Mary the Virgin at Wantage. At Sister Penelope's prompting, the Mother Superior invited him to come over and speak to the junior Sisters. Having been assured that there would be no oubliettes and chained skeletons in the Gate House where he was to stay for two nights – the first layman in the history of the convent – Lewis travelled over on Monday, 20 April, and spoke to the Sisters on 'The Gospel in our Generation'. Unfortunately, no notes of these lectures survive, but one nun remembers him saying that 'whereas Zacchaeus "could not see Jesus for the press", we today often cannot see Him for the Press with a capital P!'

Lewis remembered with far less pleasure an occasion on which he spoke to the Women's Auxiliary Air Force and was piqued to observe a burly female sergeant who sat and knitted throughout his lecture.

Lewis had hitherto counted on at least a fortnight's holiday in the summer when he could get over to Ireland for a rest. The summer of 1941 was so heavily booked with appointments with the R.A.F. that there was not time even for a weekend jaunt with his brother. Besides this, his broadcasts in August had proved such a success that the B.B.C. pressed him to give another series after Christmas and Lewis, who believed that delays made for more work, acted like a shot and had them written by the time term began in October.

Though weary to the bone and much in need of a holiday, Lewis saw more of Britain during the summer than he had at any other time. 'All through the Vacation', he wrote to Arthur Greeves on 23 December, 'I was going round lecturing to the R.A.F. – away for 2 or 3 days at a time and then home for 2 or 3 days. I had never realized how tiring perpetual travelling is (specially in crowded trains). One felt all the time as if one had just played a game of football – aching all over. None the less I had some interesting times and saw some beautiful country. Perthshire, and all the country between Aberystwyth and Shrewsbury, and Cumberland, are what chiefly stuck in my mind. It also gave me the chance in many places to see and smell the sea and hear the sound of gulls again, which otherwise I would have been pining for.'

When the United States came into the war, a good many American chaplains were posted with their men to various R.A.F. bases throughout Britain. Lewis's *Screwtape* was a bestseller in both Britain and the States but he had met few Americans before. As, however, both countries were united in a common cause, he was as pleased to accept their invitations as he was those of his own people and soon came to know a good many as friends. What he was not prepared for was the unashamed lionization which some Americans feel for famous men. One American chaplain was anxious to provide his men with a distinguished speaker and went to Oxford and called on Lewis at Magdalen. He was giving a tutorial at the time but broke off to come to the door. Would he, the priest asked, come and speak to his men? Yes, of course, said Lewis, and made a note of the appointment in his diary. Unaware that Lewis was so modest, the chaplain went on to say, 'With a name like yours – well, we are bound to draw a crowd!' Lewis winced, struck through the appointment and closed the door without uttering a word.

The best over-all summary of Lewis's impact as a lecturer with the R.A.F. comes from Charles Gilmore, the Commandant of the Chaplains' School, who saw him often during the war. In his letter of 4 November 1972 Gilmore wrote: 'Lewis was a distinct success in the Royal Air Force but, as I should judge, within a limited sphere. The larger stations contained a sufficient number of men (and women) both interested in what he had to say and capable of appreciating it. Thus Halton, Cranwell, Hereford, Locking provided him with audiences not so different in intellectual capacity from those which filled the Examination Schools in the High, but at the average station he would speak to an audience of a dozen or so – perhaps none the worse for that . . . Lewis came to lecture at the Royal Air Force Chaplains' School in its early days at Magdalene Cambridge (1944). This is the College where ten years later he was to hold a professorial Fellowship. I well remember his first lecture to the chaplains on a refresher course. Some had returned from the field, some were nightly seeing off crews who did not return; many were shaken in the concept of their calling, others were finding it for the first time. Action at levels heroic and very raw seemed all-important; theology had been evacuated to safe reception areas, and Nicaea was the mythological capital of cloud-cuckoo land. "To be young was very heaven." To such a crowd came Clive Staples Lewis, choosing to speak on "Linguistic

Analysis of Pauline Soteriology!" He began diffidently and seemed even to be searching for words. A few people shifted uneasily, a future bishop surreptitiously filled in a clue in "The Times" crossword. Then, quietly, Lewis struck fire with some intolerable phrase about redemption and everyone came alive. The rest of the morning was not really long enough to cover the subject in discussion. I recollected then that Lewis too had been a soldier and knew his audience.'

Gilmore enjoyed as well the playful side of this giant intellectual and recalls one occasion on which Lewis stayed overnight at Magdalene. The next morning, said Gilmore, 'We were both to catch a train to Town and, having an hour to spare, we strolled to the Fellows' Garden on a beautiful summer morning. For some reason I had my brief case with me, and after ten minutes placed it carefully on a garden seat where it would be in sight wherever we walked. I remarked that I was putting it down tenderly because it contained a full bottle of whisky, a rare treasure in those days. He regarded me gravely: "I don't think that to be a very safe remark," he said. "We are alone in this garden, I am bigger than you, and the inference is appalling!" . . . I often saw him after that. We used to walk to the railway station from the College when we had to return to Oxford. He would bid me study again Chesterton's *Everlasting Man*; would anxiously ask if the chaplains had really got it into their heads that the ancients had got every whit as good brains as we had . . . He certainly made his mark on the Chaplains save on those who themselves made no mark on anyone.'

What Lewis was attempting in his next broadcasts on *What Christians Believe* was a small-scale elucidation of Christian theology: to explain as clearly and concisely as he could what Christianity is about. To avoid saying anything that was peculiar to himself or unacceptable to the main body of Christendom, he sent the script of his talks to four clergymen of the Anglican, Methodist, Presbyterian and Roman churches asking for their criticism. The only two who took exception were Dom Bede Griffiths, the Roman Catholic, and the Reverend Joseph Dowell, a

Methodist padre in the R.A.F. Dom Bede complained that Lewis had gone too far about the comparative unimportance of theories of the Atonement, and Dowell thought he had not said enough about faith.

By Christmas 1941 the broadcasts had been vetted and were read over the air on five Sunday evenings early in the new year: 11 and 18 January and 1, 8, 15 February 1942 from 4.45 to 5.00 p.m. Like a million others, Joseph Dowell heard Lewis speak over the microphone and, writing to Hooper on 2 December 1968, he recalls the impression the talks made on him: 'They were magnificent, unforgettable. Nobody, before or since, has made such "impact" in straight talks of this kind. His own words to me – "I had to go like a bull at a gate" – were apt enough in that he felt he had to crash the barriers in order to get into a common field of thought and communication.'

The clarity of Lewis's thought, his ability to incapsulate a great many facts into a few words, is perhaps nowhere better illustrated than in these broadcasts. His second talk ends with this synopsis of the Faith: 'Enemy-occupied territory – that is what this world is. Christianity is the story of how the rightful king has landed, you might say landed in disguise, and is calling us all to take part in a great campaign of sabotage.'

One of the most famous examples of Lewis's inexorable logic, a passage often quoted from the pulpit, at retreats, and in Confirmation instructions, concerns St Augustine's argument that Christ was 'either God or a bad man':

I am trying here to prevent anyone saying the really foolish thing that people often say about Him: 'I'm ready to accept Jesus as a great moral teacher, but I don't accept His claim to be God.' This is the one thing we must not say. A man who was merely a man and said the sort of things Jesus said would not be a great moral teacher. He would either be a lunatic – on a level with the man who says he is a poached egg – or else he would be the Devil of Hell. You must make your choice. Either this man was, and is, the Son of God: or else a madman or something worse. You can shut Him up for a fool, you can spit at Him and kill Him as a demon; or you can fall at His feet and call Him Lord and God. But let us not come with any patronising nonsense about His being a great human teacher. He has not left that open to us. He did not intend to.

C. S. Lewis was now before the notice of 'everyman'. By the end of the summer of 1942 *The Problem of Pain* was in its eighth impression and *The Screwtape Letters* in its sixth. Two other books appeared during July, *A Preface to 'Paradise Lost'* and *Broadcast Talks* (combining *Right and Wrong* and *What Christians Believe*). His popularity with the R.A.F. continued to grow and the B.B.C. had already contracted him to write a third series of broadcasts for the autumn. Much as he wanted to get over to Ireland for a holiday, his sympathy for those fighting overseas made him all the more anxious to pull his own weight at home. Not only in college, but at the Kilns where he was needed more than ever: the year before, his foster-sister Maureen had married Leonard Blake, the music-master at Malvern College, and Mrs Moore who was in poor health was finding a great deal to grumble about. The strain of overwork is evident in a letter Lewis wrote to Arthur Greeves during the summer: 'Writing, writing, writing – letters, notes, exam papers, books, lectures. I've enough rheumatism in my right hand now to prevent me from sleeping on that side.'

His third series of broadcasts, *Christian Behaviour*, was completed during the summer of 1942 and delivered on the B.B.C. on eight consecutive Sunday afternoons from 20 September to 8 November at 2.50–3.05 p.m. Lewis was now, along with Mgr Ronald Knox and Dorothy L. Sayers, whose play-cycle *The Man Born to be King* was being broadcast at this time, a radio star – and such 'hot' literary property that Bles had an enlarged edition of *Christian Behaviour* in the shops by 19 April 1943. Most of the reviews of the book were extremely laudatory and evidence that Lewis had again hit his target. Robert Speaight, writing in the *Tablet* (26 June 1943), said: 'Mr Lewis is that rare being – a born broadcaster; born to the manner as well as to the matter. He neither buttonholes you nor bombards you; there is no false intimacy and no false eloquence. He approaches you directly, as a rational person only to be persuaded by reason. He is confident and yet humble in his possession and propagation of truth. He is helped by a speaking voice of great charm and style of manifest sincerity.'

Lewis consented to write one last set of talks for the B.B.C. entitled *Beyond Personality: The Christian View of God*. His other broadcasts had been delivered 'live' over the microphone, but the seven fifteen-minute talks which make up *Beyond Personality* were pre-recorded on disks and played over the air on consecutive Tuesday evenings at 10.15–10.30 p.m. from 22 February to 4 April 1944. They were published by Bles on 9 October of the same year.

Because of the loud and insistent clamour for more broadcasts, not only in England but in America and various countries of the Commonwealth, the B.B.C. urged Lewis to return to the air. He refused, making it clear that for the moment he had said all he had to say and was, therefore, unavailable for any more broadcasts during the 'foreseeable future'. He chose instead to allow all three volumes of radio talks to be published together in a single volume, *Mere Christianity* (1952) – the word 'mere' denoting 'essential' (not used as a term of derision) – to which he appended several new chapters.

It is not perhaps too outlandish to claim that what Karl Barth, Paul Tillich and Karl Rahner did for specialists in their works of 'systematic theology', Lewis did for laymen – whatever their creed – in *Mere Christianity*. In it he provides as clear a statement of catholic Christianity, the beliefs 'common to nearly all Christians at all times', as has yet been written. If you could take only one of Lewis's books to a desert island, this is probably the one to choose. *Mere Christianity* is one of the works which has caused Lewis to be celebrated as one of the most 'original' exponents of the Christian faith in this century. The interesting thing, the thing which cannot be too heavily emphasized in any study of the man or his works, is that though the settings of some of his books are strange and wonderful, his greatest claim to 'originality' rests in his total espousal of what Screwtape wryly denounced as the 'Same Old Thing' and Richard Baxter (from whom Lewis borrowed the term) called 'mere Christianity'. Believing, as Lewis did, that 'all that is not eternal is eternally out of date', he never hedged, re-interpreted or in any way diluted the 'faith once given to the saints'. However modern or unusual the dress of his apologetics, Lewis was a thoroughgoing supernaturalist who appealed to the reason as well as the imagination in explaining the Incarnation, Christ's effectual sacrifice, the Resurrection, the Trinity, Heaven and Hell and the eternal seriousness of Christian decision.

Lewis believed that science progresses when scientists do not hush up or turn their backs on troublesome phenomena, and that there will be progress in Christian knowledge only as long as we accept the challenge of the difficult or repellent doctrines. Two of the 'repellent' or, at least, unpopular doctrines he writes about in *Mere Christianity* are chastity and Christian marriage. 'There is no getting away from it,' he says in his chapter on 'Sexual Morality', 'the Christian rule is, "Either marriage, with complete faithfulness to your partner, or else total abstinence." ' Our standards of decency have sunk so low in the last decade that many people, radical clergymen included, regard this – despite its basis in Scripture – as excessively prudish and 'puritanical'. Still, there are numerous others who have held out against indifference to truth and moral action because Lewis was not afraid to take up an unpopular stance. But he by no means considered chastity the centre of morality. Of the 'Animal' self and the 'Diabolical' self, he believed the Diabolical self to be the worse of the two. 'That is why', he says with his inimitable gumption, 'a cold, self-righteous prig who goes regularly to church may be far nearer to hell than a prostitute. But, of course, it is better to be neither.'

Lewis believed that marriage between Christians is for life; but, recognizing as he did that the majority of people are not Christians, he thought there ought to be two distinct kinds of marriage: one governed by the State with rules enforced on all citizens, the other governed by the Church with rules enforced by her on her own members. On the relationship between husbands and wives, Lewis accepted St Paul's injunction: 'Wives, submit yourselves unto your own husbands, as unto the Lord. For the husband is the head of the wife, even as Christ is the head of the church' (Ephesians 5:23). This view was almost as unpopular in the Forties as it is today, and Lewis asked his readers to remember that if two people simply cannot agree, *one* must have a 'casting vote' if they are to remain united. The headship of women Lewis considered unnatural and no more likely to appeal to women in general than it is to men in general: 'Even a woman who wants to be the head of her own house does not usually admire the same state of things when she finds it going on next door.'

It was Lewis's belief in the hierarchical superiority of men which led many to think of him as a misogynist. One of those who came to share this view was E. R. Eddison to whom Lewis wrote a fan letter in mock-heroic English on 16 November 1942 praising Eddison's *Worm Ouroboros* as 'the most noble and joyous book I have read these ten years'. Eddison was delighted to find such a distinguished admirer and sent him a copy of his second romance, *Mistress of Mistresses*. Lewis, however, could not stomach Eddison's glorification of his female characters in this novel and when he wrote to Eddison on 19 December to thank him for the book he could not forbear complaining of the author's 'hyperuranian whores and transcendental trulls'. Eddison suggested that Lewis must be a misogynist to which Lewis retorted (29 Dec.) that 'it is a thing openlie manifeste to all but disards [idiots] and verie goosecaps that feminitee is to itself an imperfection, being placed by the Pythagoreans in the sinister column with matter and mortalitie. Of which we see dailie ensample in that men do gladlie withdraw into their own societie and when they would be either merrie or grave stint not to shutte the dore upon Love herself, whereas we see no woman . . . but will not of good will escape from her sisters and seeke to the conversation of men, as liking by instincte of Nature so to receyve the perfection she lacketh.' The friendship between the two men ripened as a result of this good-natured fencing and Eddison was deeply honoured when Lewis gave him a dinner-party in Magdalen on 17 February 1943 on which occasion he was introduced to Tolkien, Charles Williams and Warren Lewis. Though Lewis's attitude was to alter considerably after his marriage, it is probably true, as Owen Barfield said in a meeting of the New York C. S. Lewis Society in 1972, that Lewis could properly be called a misogynist on at least the 'theoretical level', though decidedly not so in his personal relations with individual women.

Students in Oxford did not need to turn on the radio or buy copies of his books to know how Lewis felt about Christianity. Towards the end of Michaelmas Term 1941, a young lady from Somerville College complained that no one in Oxford seemed ready to discuss the questions agnostics raised about God. Luckily, she complained to the right person – the indefatigable Miss Stella Aldwinckle who immediately had a notice put up exhorting 'all atheists, agnostics, and those who are disillusioned about religion or think they are' to meet her in the Somerville J.C.R. After a few meetings she came to the conclusion that 'an open forum for the discussion of the intellectual difficulties connected with religion in general and with Christianity in particular was the obvious solution, and Mr C. S. Lewis the obvious President'. Interest spread quickly to other colleges, and so it was that the Oxford University Socratic Club was formed. Lewis readily accepted the position of president (a position he retained till he went to Cambridge in 1954) and Stella Aldwinckle has been its chairman from the founding of the club till it ended in 1972.

In his preface to the first *Socratic Digest* (1942–43), Lewis wrote: 'By stages which must have been very swift (for I cannot remember them), we found that a new society had been formed, that it was attempting the difficult programme of meeting once a week, that it was actually carrying this programme out, that its numbers were increasing, and that neither foul weather nor crowded rooms (they were lucky who found seats even on the floor) would reduce the size of the meetings. This was the Socratic Club . . . Those who founded it do not for one moment pretend to be neutral. It was the Christians who constructed the arena and issued the challenge. It will therefore always be possible for the lower (the less Athenian) type of unbeliever to regard the whole thing as a cunningly – or not even so very cunningly – disguised form of propaganda. The Athenian type, if he had this objection to make, would put it in a paper and read that paper to the Socratic itself. He would be welcome to do so – though I doubt whether he would have the stomach if he knew with what pains and toil the committee has scoured *Who's Who* to find intelligent atheists who had leisure or zeal to come and propagate their creed.'

The first official meeting of the Socratic Club was held in Somerville College on 26 January 1942 when Dr 'Humphrey' Havard read a paper answering the question 'Won't mankind outgrow Christianity in the face of the advance of Science and Modern Ideologies?' After that the meetings were held in one or other of the Oxford colleges, and the usual procedure was to have two speakers at each meeting. Should the first be a Christian, he would be answered by an atheist, or vice versa. Meetings began at 8.15 p.m. and, after both speakers had had their say, they ended with a general discussion which usually went on to 10.30 p.m., when Miss Aldwinckle had to bring them to a halt lest they run on into the small hours of the morning. As Lewis said, it was difficult to dig up enough atheists who would come and propagate their creed, and when none could be found the debate would be between Christians who held widely differing views. Anyone who was a student in Oxford between 1942 and 1954 would have seen the club's bright green posters in the Lodge of his or her college announcing the topics and speakers for that term – and, proudly displayed at the top of each poster, the words: 'President: C. S. LEWIS, M.A.'.

Such a masthead was enough to ensure a large turn-out and though Lewis was undoubtedly the wittiest and most exciting speaker in the Socratic Club he by no means tried to hog all the attention. During his 22 years as president, he was the first speaker on only eleven occasions when he spoke on the following subjects:

1 'Christianity and Aesthetics' (16 Nov. 1942)
2. 'If We Have Christ's Ethics Does the Rest of the Christian Faith Matter?' (8 Feb. 1943)
3. 'Science and Miracles' (15 Nov. 1943)
4. ' "Bulverism": or The Foundation of Twentieth-Century Thought' (7 Feb. 1944)
5. 'Is Institutional Christianity Necessary?' (5 June 1944)
6. 'Is Theology Poetry?' (6 Nov. 1944)
7. 'Resurrection' (14 May 1945)

8. 'Nature and Reason' (15 Oct. 1945)
9. 'Religion without Dogma?' (20 May 1946)
10. 'A First Glance at Sartre' (3 Nov. 1947)
11. 'On Obstinacy in Belief' (30 April 1953)

As president, however, it usually fell to Lewis to make the first reply in discussion. And, though it was a matter of courtesy to invite an eminent atheist visitor to speak first, everyone knew that it was more exciting for the eminent atheist to sound the battle-cry before Lewis stepped in like a new Goliath and defeated the opposition with the brilliant cut-and-thrust of his unanswerable logic. The Reverend Dr Austin Farrer (who was Chaplain of Trinity College at this time) was a frequent speaker at the Socratic and in *Light on C. S. Lewis* said: 'The great value of Lewis as apologist was his many-sidedness. So far as the argumentative business went, he was a bonny fighter. His writing gave the same impression as his appearances in public debate. I was occasionally called upon to stop a gap in the earlier programmes of Lewis's Socratic Club. Lewis was president, but he was not bound to show up. I went in fear and trembling, certain to be caught out in debate and to let down the side. But there Lewis would be, snuffing the imminent battle and saying "Aha!" at the sound of the trumpet. My anxieties rolled away. Whatever ineptitudes I might commit, he would maintain the cause; and nobody could put Lewis down.'

Though no minutes of the Socratic meetings were kept till Valerie Pitt became secretary in 1945, there are a good many Socratic evenings which have passed into legend and demonstrate what a fiercely energetic society the Socratic Club was. Many people still remember the evening of 24 January 1944 when one of the largest crowds ever to attend – 250 people – gathered in Lady Margaret Hall to hear Lewis answer that great erstwhile atheist C. E. M. Joad who read a paper 'On Being Reviewed by Christians'. It was in the heart of winter but the discussion between the two men became so hot that they were both soon dripping with perspiration. Joad eventually begged leave to remove his coat, but when Stella Aldwinckle suggested Lewis do the same he whispered to her that he had a large hole in his shirt, and so had to carry on in his heavy tweed jacket.

Lewis enjoyed few things more than the rough and tumble of 'rational opposition'. Despite the seriousness of the issues at stake, blows were given and received with good humour on both sides, and many Socratic members will recall the evening on which the first speaker was a Relativist who is said to have ended his talk with the assertion: 'The world does not exist, England does not exist, Oxford does not exist, and I am confident that *I* do not exist!' When Lewis was asked to reply, he stood up and said, 'How am I to talk to a man who's *not there*?'

On 15 November 1948 the Socratic Club had as their guest speaker the celebrated biologist Professor J. B. S. Haldane, whose views Lewis had frequently attacked in print. An enormous audience had gathered in the Taylorian Institute that night to hear Professor Haldane's paper on 'Atheism' – but principally to watch Lewis make mincemeat of this most famous of his enemies. Professor Haldane may have feared a public defeat by Lewis. Whatever his reasons, no one ever found out what would have happened for, as the secretary recorded in the Socratic Minute Book: 'The speaker unfortunately had to leave early and ended with an impressive running panegyric of atheism of which the last word was perfectly timed to coincide with his exit.'

The Socratic was the most flourishing and influential society in Oxford during Lewis's years as president. Amongst its many good effects, it succeeded in making Christianity both vital and interesting to scores upon scores of undergraduates and dons who might otherwise never have heard either the Faith or atheism discussed rationally. If a history of the Socratic Club ever comes to be written, it must include not only the names of Lewis and Stella Aldwinckle, but those of many others who played a part in making it one of the toughest arenas in the academic world for a discussion of religion and philosophy. A partial list of those who were active in the Socratic (many of whom were or became Lewis's life-long friends) includes: G. E. M. Anscombe, I. M. Crombie, Martin D'Arcy, V. A. Demant, Austin and Katherine

Farrer, Michael Foster, Colin Hardie, Elizabeth Jennings, E. L. Mascall, Gervase Mathew, Basil Mitchell (who succeeded Lewis as president), T. M. Parker, Valerie Pitt, H. H. Price, Dorothy L. Sayers, Gerald Vann, Charles Williams, and J. Z. Young.

Shortly after his first broadcasts on *Right and Wrong* in which Lewis defended the existence of an objective Moral or Natural Law, a number of papers were read to the Socratic Club which caused him to realize how seriously its objectivity was being questioned. Consequently, when the University of Durham invited him to give the annual Riddell Memorial Lectures for 1943, he chose to vindicate morality from the charges brought against it.

Besides an immense amount of reading in philosophers and educationalists from Plato to the present, Lewis spent many hours in the Bodleian poring over the mammoth *Encyclopaedia of Religion and Ethics*. On 8 February 1943 he read a paper to the Socratic which anticipated the lectures he was to give at Durham. It is entitled 'If We Have Christ's Ethics Does the Rest of the Christian Faith Matter?' and, according to the secretary's minutes reproduced in the *Socratic Digest* (1942–43), Lewis maintained that 'Christian moral principles' are not different from 'moral principles', and that the real problem is how to *obey* them: 'To ask whether the rest of the Christian Faith matters when we have Christ's ethics presupposes a world of unfallen men with no need for redemption. "The rest of the Christian Faith" is the means of carrying out, instead of merely being able to discourse on, the ethics we already know.'

Lewis and his brother journeyed up to Durham together on 23 February. Having imagined Durham to be an ugly colliery-cum-manufacturing town, Warren recorded in his diary that 'its exquisite beauty came upon us with an impact I shall long remember.' Lewis's three Riddell Memorial Lectures were given on 24 February and published in January of the following year as *The Abolition of Man: Reflections on Education with Special Reference to the Teaching of English in the Upper Forms of Schools*. It was not his purpose in these lectures to show the relation between Christianity and morality as he had in the Socratic paper, but to demonstrate that there is such a thing as the *Tao* (or Way or Morality or Natural Law) which most men in all ages have discovered and passed down like the independent testimony of a single civilization.

In the opening lecture Lewis uses as a springboard from which he launches his attack on those who explain away morality two elementary text-books intended for pupils in the upper forms of schools. Both books had only recently been published and, as Lewis had no wish to pillory the authors, he concealed their titles under obviously fictitious names. Thirty years having passed, it is not perhaps unfair to reveal that the book Lewis refers to as by one 'Orbilius' is E. G. Biaggini's *The Reading and Writing of English* (1936); the so-called *Green Book* by 'Gaius' and 'Titius' is *The Control of Language* (1940) by Alec King and Martin Ketley. The last two authors, in particular, appear to take it for granted that all values are subjective and trivial, and that all sentences containing a predicate of value (such as 'This waterfall is sublime') are merely statements about the emotional state of the speaker. By so doing, says Lewis, they destroy man's chest – the seat of emotions organized by trained habit into stable sentiments, and the indispensable 'liaison officer' between man's head (the seat of reason) and his belly (the seat of instincts). 'In a sort of ghastly simplicity', says Lewis, 'we remove the organ and demand the function. We make men without chests and expect of them virtue and enterprise. We laugh at honour and are shocked to find traitors in our midst. We castrate and bid the geldings be fruitful.'

From there he goes on to argue that the principles of the *Tao* are unprovable because they are as basic and obvious as axioms are to the world of theory. 'From propositions about fact alone', he says, 'no practical conclusion can ever be drawn. *This will preserve society* cannot lead to *do this* except by the mediation of *society ought to be preserved*.' With the word 'ought' the *Tao* reappears through the side door and we are back where we started.

In answer to those innovators who suggest that instinct should be the basis of morality, Lewis asks – *which* instinct? 'Telling us to obey instinct is like telling us to obey "people". People say different things: so do instincts . . . Each instinct, if you listen to it, will claim to be gratified at the expense of all the rest.' The dreadful consequence of allowing any instinct *carte blanche* is that, in the end, our conquest of Nature turns out to be Nature's conquest over man. 'We have been trying, like Lear, to have it both ways: to lay down our human prerogative and yet at the same time to retain it. It is impossible. Either we are rational spirit obliged for ever to obey the absolute values of the *Tao*, or else we are mere nature to be kneaded and cut into new shapes for the pleasures of masters who must, by hypothesis, have no motive but their own "natural" impulses.'

Lewis's most reliable critic, Owen Barfield, had nothing but praise for *The Abolition of Man* and on 22 January 1944 wrote to his friend saying, 'It is a real triumph. There may be a piece of contemporary writing in which precision of thought, liveliness of expression and depth of meaning unite with the same felicity, but I have not come across it.' The book was not such an instant success as *Screwtape*. Now, however, when even liberal clergymen are hurrying to join the innovators who would 'free' man from morality, orthodox Christians of every denomination are turning to it as perhaps the best defence of Natural Law ever to be written. As we have seen, Lewis went on to 'spell' the whole thing out in his novel *That Hideous Strength*.

Not long after his lectures at Durham, Lewis was working on, not only *That Hideous Strength*, but another book – *The Great Divorce* – the germ of which had been maturing in his mind for some years. On 17 April 1932 Warren had recorded in his diary: 'Jack has an idea for a religious work based on the opinion of some of the Fathers that while punishment for the damned is eternal it is intermittent; he proposes to do a sort of infernal day excursion to Paradise.' Lewis first came upon the idea of a 'Refrigerium', a respite granted to the souls of the damned, in one of the sermons of the seventeenth-century Anglican divine, Jeremy Taylor, whose *Works* Arthur Greeves had given him in August 1931. As he was reading the books during September '31, it was probably then that he came upon the passage in Taylor's sermon on 'Christ's Advent to Judgement' which he says furnished him with the idea for *The Great Divorce*. 'The church of Rome amongst other strange opinions', said Taylor, 'hath inserted this one into her public offices; that the perishing souls in hell may have sometimes remission and refreshment, like the fits of an intermitting fever: for so it is in the Roman missal printed at Paris, 1626, in the mass for the dead; "*Ut quia de ejus vitae qualitate diffidimus, etsi plenam veniam anima ipsius obtinere non potest, saltem vel inter pisa tormenta quae forsam pantitur, refrigerium de abundantia miserationum tuarum sentiat*" ' (*Whole Works*, ed. R. Heber (London, 1822), Vol. V, p. 45).

Another source for Lewis's 'Refrigerium' story, and which Taylor very conveniently mentions in the same sermon, is the fourth-century Latin poet and hymn-writer Prudentius Aurelius Clemens. In his beautiful 'Hymn for the Lighting of the Lamp' found in his *Liber Cathemerinon*, Prudentius says: 'Often below the Styx holidays from their punishments are kept, even by the guilty spirits . . . Hell grows feeble with mitigated torments and the shadowy nation, free from fires, exults in the leisure of its prison; the rivers cease to burn with their usual sulphur.'

It may be asked why Lewis was so long in getting round to writing *The Great Divorce*. The truest answer may be that, though he had found a vehicle for his story and had worked out its theological implications, he had not, until now, been able to 'picture' it in his mind – which was the way inspiration worked in him. Even then, he doubtless felt some resistance to writing about something so terrible as some men's final rejection of God. Sister Penelope may have inadvertently triggered Lewis into getting his story on to paper for, in replying to a letter of hers, he said on 24 October 1940: 'About Hell; how do we get over Matthew 7:13, 14? ["Enter ye in at the strait gate: for wide is the gate, and broad is the way, that leadeth to destruction, and many there be which go in thereat: Because strait is the gate, and narrow is the way, which leadeth unto life, and few there be that find it."] But I agree we *must* get over that one somehow or go mad. And leaving that one out, perhaps we can accept your argument that tho' Hell exists, we are not absolutely forced to hold that anyone will reach it. But wouldn't the same, in logic, on the same grounds, hold of Heaven?'

By the end of the summer of 1944 Lewis had finished the fourteen chapters which make up *Who Goes Home? or The Grand Divorce* – as the story was then called – and they appeared in weekly instalments in the *Guardian* from 10 November 1944 to 14 April 1945. 'Who goes home?' is a cry shouted by the policeman on duty through the lobbies and corridors of the House of Commons when it has concluded its sitting and is about to close its doors. When Lewis discovered that several authors had already used it as a title, he altered it to *The Great Divorce: A Dream* and it was published in November 1945.

Though it cannot, of course, compare in scope and plenitude with Dante's great poem, the book can certainly be said to be Lewis's *Divine Comedy* and the parallels between the two books are numerous. As the subtitle suggests, the book is told in the form of a dream and opens with the narrator (Lewis) walking through the dismal, wet streets of Hell – the description of which suggests that he had read Thisted's *Letters from Hell* (translated by Julie Sutter with a preface by MacDonald, 1885) which stood on his bookshelves. From Hell, Lewis and a number of quarrelsome people are conveyed by a celestial omnibus to the outskirts of Heaven where each is invited to remain permanently.

Against the diamond-hard reality of Heaven, the damned appear as 'man-shaped stains on the brightness of that air'. Each ghost is met by a 'bright spirit' who is there to conduct him to the Celestial City. Lewis himself is met by George MacDonald who, Virgil-like, acts as his guide. With one exception, all the ghosts prefer to return to Hell – thus actualizing the terrible truth MacDonald points out which is that 'There are only two kinds of people in the end: those who say to God, "Thy will be done", and those to whom God says "*Thy* will be done." Without that self-choice there could be no Hell. No soul that seriously and constantly desires joy will ever miss it.'

Dante had several heretical Popes in Hell, and Lewis has an apostate Anglican bishop. The episcopal ghost, though once a

Christian, has become so wedded to the passing whims of liberal theology that he prefers to return to Hell and continue writing books about the 'spirit of sweetness and light and tolerance' rather than see God face to face.

Though *The Great Divorce* is undoubtedly a maturer and more serious work than *Screwtape*, most people prefer the charm and wit of the latter. Anticipating that he would be accused of a lack of compassion, Lewis asks his guide if the loss of one soul does not give the lie to all the joy of those who are saved. To this Mac-Donald replies: 'Son, son, it must be one way or the other. Either the day must come when joy prevails and all the makers of misery are no longer able to infect it: or else for ever and ever the makers of misery can destroy in others the happiness they reject for themselves. I know it has a grand sound to say ye'll accept no salvation which leaves even one creature in the dark outside. But watch that sophistry or ye'll make a Dog in the Manger the tyrant of the universe.'

Between the time when *The Great Divorce* was serialized in the *Guardian* and that when it made its appearance in book form, Lewis met an enemy and lost a friend. Charles Williams had long been amused by Lewis's dislike of T. S. Eliot and the raking over the coals Lewis had given Eliot in his *Preface to 'Paradise Lost'*. Eager to see what would happen if he got his two friends together, Williams arranged for them to meet over tea at the Mitre Hotel. Fr Gervase Mathew was among those who were invited to witness this historic occasion. Though Lewis can hardly be said to have been a vain man regarding his physical appearance, and once told Walter Hooper how much easier he would find life when his hair fell out, he was anything but amused by Eliot's opening remark: 'Mr Lewis, you are a much *older* man than you appear in photographs.' Whatever possessed Eliot to say such a thing no one knows. Lewis stood facing him with the poker-face he sometimes assumed. Having botched it the first time, Eliot tried again: 'I must tell you, Mr Lewis, that I consider your *Preface to "Paradise Lost"* your best book.' This being the very book in which he had attacked him, Lewis could not believe Eliot meant him any good will. After that the conversation dwindled to small-talk and, according to Fr Mathew, a very bad time was had by all except Charles Williams who is said to have enjoyed himself hugely.

There is a small reminder of this disastrous tea-party in one of Lewis's notebooks. 'Mr Eliot', he scribbled, 'has asked me not to write about his literary criticism. Very well. I obey.' Beyond that, he seems to have put Eliot out of his mind till they met years later under more congenial circumstances.

However unpleasant that meeting might have been, few events were to be so unpleasant for Lewis as that which followed on its heels. The war ended on 9 May 1945 and the next day Charles Williams was seized with pain. He was rushed to the Radcliffe Infirmary and on 14 May he was operated on. The next day, Tuesday, meant a meeting of the Inklings at the 'Bird and Baby'. It turned out to be one of the saddest they were ever to remember. None of them had any idea that Williams's trouble was serious and, as the Infirmary is only a few minutes' walk from the 'Bird and Baby', Lewis went up to see him before the others arrived. On reaching the Infirmary he discovered that Williams had just died.

After the funeral Charles Williams's body was buried in St Cross churchyard where it lies beneath a white stone bearing an epitaph he had written for himself – 'Under the Mercy'. Writing to Sister Penelope shortly afterwards (28 May), Lewis said: 'You will have heard of the death of my dearest friend, Charles Williams, and, no doubt, prayed for him. For me too, it has been, and is, a great loss. But not at all a dejecting one. It has greatly increased my faith. Death has done nothing to my idea of him, but he has done – oh, I can't say what – to my idea of death. It has made the next world much more real and palpable.'

Among the numerous salutes to Williams's memory was a course of lectures on Williams's Arthurian poems which Lewis gave to the University during Michaelmas Term 1945, and which were later published as *Arthurian Torso* (1948). Long before this Lewis, Warren, Barfield, Tolkien, Gervase Mathew and Dorothy L. Sayers had been writing a collection of essays which they planned to offer Williams on his return to London after the war. As Lewis said in the preface to these *Essays Presented to Charles Williams* (1947): 'Death forestalled us; we now offer as a memorial what had been devised as a greeting.'

Lewis often worked on several books at the same time, and it ought now to be clear that publication dates do not serve as an infallible guide as to when his books were written. The same month that Charles Williams died, he completed his most important work of straight theology – *Miracles: A Preliminary Study* – which he began writing during the summer of 1943. The manuscript of *Miracles* was sent to Bles in the spring of 1945 but was not published till May 1947.

During this interval Lewis was awarded an honorary degree of Doctor of Divinity by the University of St Andrews – a very rare and unusual compliment to be paid a layman. Lewis was pleased at being offered the degree but dreaded the fuss and bother of having to go up and get it. As, however, St Andrews is situated on the eastern coast of Scotland, Lewis and his brother used the occasion as an excuse for a little jaunt. When they arrived at St Andrews on Thursday, 27 June 1946, they went immediately to explore the coastline. 'All along the high watermark of the beach', Warren recorded in his diary, 'ran a line of rather blackguardly-looking crows whom Jack supposed to have been ordered sea air by their doctors.' At the graduation ceremony the next day, there was a bishop who invited Lewis home afterwards for refreshments. Lewis told Hooper some years later that as they were about to go in the bishop turned and said: 'Well, Lewis, what about a mouthful – ' (as he paused Lewis imagined a large glass of whisky) ' – of *prayer*?' The mouthful of prayer was, however, followed by several of whisky and Lewis felt a bit more easy in his stiff shirt and graduation robes.

Looking back, it seems inevitable that Lewis should have written a book on miracles. They proved one of the chief reasons why he found Christianity unacceptable when he was an atheist, and part of the groundwork of his faith after he was converted. A belief in the miraculous is, of course, assumed in all his theological books up till now, but it may have been Dorothy L. Sayers who prodded him into writing a full-length book on the subject. In a letter of 13 May 1943 she complained to Lewis that 'there aren't any up-to-date books about Miracles. People have stopped arguing about them. Why? Has Physics sold the pass? or is it merely that everybody is thinking in terms of Sociology and international Ethics?' She thought Lewis was the person to remedy the situation, and he may have thought so too as he began his book a few weeks after he received her letter.

One can get a good idea of what Lewis's book on miracles is *not* about from his letter to Sister Penelope of 28 May 1945. 'The truth is we shall never get on', he complained, 'till we have stamped out "religion". "Religion" as it is called – the vague slush of humanitarian idealism, Emersonian Pantheism, democratic politics and material progressiveness, with a few Christian names and formulae added to taste like pepper and salt – is almost the great enemy. If one can't talk to a Christian then give me a real believing member of some other religion or an honest clear-headed sceptic like J. S. Mill. One can at least get some *sense* out of them.'

Lewis's first blow at this 'vague slush' comes in the second and third chapters of the book where he defines *miracle* as 'an interference with Nature by supernatural powers', and those who believe that Something Other than Nature exists as supernaturalists. He goes on to use the *reductio ad absurdum* argument as a means of attacking the naturalists. Believing, as they claim to do, that Nature means absolutely 'everything that happens', all of which came about by the blind working of chance, it must therefore follow that even their *thoughts* must also be the working of chance and the accidental by-products of atoms moving in their brains. That being so, why, Lewis asks, should the naturalist believe that one thought is more 'valid' than another, or that it should give a correct account of all the others?

Having established the validity of thought, Lewis proceeds to get rid of several Red Herrings, one of which is the notion that St Joseph was such an ignoramus as not to know where babies come from. 'No doubt the modern gynaecologist knows several things about birth and begetting which St Joseph did not know. But those things do not concern the main point – that a virgin birth is contrary to the course of nature. And St Joseph obviously knew *that*. . . . If there ever were men who did not know the laws of nature *at all*, they would have no idea of a miracle and feel no particular interest in one if it were performed before them. Nothing can seem extraordinary until you have discovered what is ordinary' (Ch. 7). Miracles, he goes on to show, do not break the laws of Nature but are instances of something being 'fed into' Nature by the very One who created her. Not only that, miracles help us know what the story of the world is *about*. The Incarnation, for instance, 'far from denying what we already know of reality, writes the comment which makes that crabbed text plain: or rather, proves itself to be the text on which Nature was only the commentary. In science we have been reading only the notes to a poem; in Christianity we find the poem itself' (Ch. 14).

Miracles, though it has the common touch, is a much tougher book than *Mere Christianity* and was written for a more educated audience. As expected, it was joyfully received by all those of the orthodox persuasion. At the same time, it afforded reviewers a delightful field-day: for the publication of Lewis's philosophic defence of miracles coincided almost exactly with the late Bishop of Birmingham's *Rise of Christianity* in which he tried to explain away the miraculous. It is impossible to be certain, but it is quite likely that the free-thinking Bishop (E. W. Barnes) was the model for the episcopal ghost in *The Great Divorce*.

While Lewis's praises were being sung by most readers of *Miracles*, Miss G. E. M. Anscombe, the Roman Catholic philosopher, was sharpening her pen for an attack. It came on 2 February 1948 at a meeting of the Socratic Club when Miss Anscombe read her 'Reply to Mr C. S. Lewis's Argument that "Naturalism" is Self-refuting' – a criticism of Chapter 3 of *Miracles*. It was afterwards published along with Lewis's answer in the *Socratic Digest* (No. 4, 1948). The meeting is said to have been the most exciting and dramatic the Socratic has ever seen. According to Derek

Brewer, who dined with him two days later, Lewis was 'deeply disturbed' and described the meeting 'with real horror. His imagery was all of the fog of war, the retreat of infantry thrown back under heavy attack.' Some who were at the meeting contend that Lewis lost to Miss Anscombe, others say that the lady came out second best. Even the contestants said different things: Lewis told Walter Hooper he was not defeated, and Miss Anscombe told Hooper that he was. One certain result of the disagreement was that Lewis revised Chapter 3 of *Miracles* before it was published as a Fontana paperback in 1960.

For a long time now what Lewis called in one of his poems 'The plann'd and unplann'd miseries' of life had begun to deepen. By 1947 Mrs Moore had nearly lost the use of her legs and supervised the running of the Kilns from her upstairs bedroom. 'He is as good as an extra maid in the house,' she said of Lewis – and indeed he must have been, for he was called upon to settle endless disputes between the two resident maids, one of whom was having psychiatric treatment. This meant a great curtailment of his freedom to move about, and especially outside Oxford. One of the few exceptions he made was when the Marquess of Salisbury invited him on 8 March 1947 to join a group, which included the two Archbishops, who were meeting in London to discuss the future of the Church of England. In replying to the Marquess on 9 March, Lewis said: 'My mother is old and infirm, we have little and uncertain help, and I never know when I can, even for a day, get away from my duties as a nurse and a domestic servant (there are psychological as well as material difficulties in my house). But I will come if I possibly can.' Lewis did go to the meeting which was held in Lambeth Palace on 26 March 1947.

Lewis was by now the most popular spokesman for Christianity in the English-speaking world and, though it was difficult for him to stray outside Oxford, this did not prevent his numerous fans from coming to see him. In the summer of 1948 Professor Chad Walsh – a long-time friend of Lewis's future wife – came over from America to gather materials for a book he was writing. The result of his numerous meetings with Lewis was Chad Walsh's delightful and aptly titled *C. S. Lewis: Apostle to the Skeptics* (1949). It is clear from Walsh's book that Lewis had achieved the feat which, before his time, might have been considered impossible: by confining himself to the essentials of the Christian faith and defending supernaturalism in its fullest rigour he had won the respect of fundamentalists, Anglo- and Roman Catholics, and all other thoroughgoing believers. He appealed, furthermore, to sophisticated sceptics who would have been scandalized at having any other religious books on their coffee tables than those of the witty and urbane Lewis. To them he was, as Charles Moorman says in his *Arthurian Triptych* (1960), 'a cocktail-party *advocatus Christi*'.

Except for a few Romans who had reservations about certain finer points of his otherwise impeccable orthodoxy, Lewis won the respect of that communion. His acceptance by the most extreme fundamentalists happened without his knowing it. Shortly after the war the hottest of all hot-gospellers from the 'Bible Belt' of South Carolina, Dr Bob Jones Jr, visited Lewis in Oxford. By a remarkable coincidence Walter Hooper was introduced to Dr Jones in 1953. Hooper popped a peppermint into his mouth to hide any smell of tobacco and asked the ultra-conservative what he thought of C. S. Lewis. 'That man', said Dr Jones fiercely, 'smokes a pipe, and that man drinks liquor – but I *do* believe he is a Christian!'

Shortly after the publication of *Miracles* Lewis began writing his chronicles of Narnia which form the subject of the next chapter. Other than a volume of sermons entitled *Transposition and Other Addresses* (1949), he did not attempt a full-length work of theology till the autumn of 1952. It was to have been a book on prayer, but after writing a dozen or so pages he abandoned it. A few years later Geoffrey Bles's new partner, Jocelyn Gibb, made him dig it out of storage and begin again.

In the summer of 1948 Mrs Moore had to retire permanently into a nursing home. 'She is in no pain', Lewis wrote to Sister Penelope on 31 August 1948, 'but her mind has almost completely gone . . . There is no denying – and I don't know why I should deny to you – that our domestic life is both more physically comfortable and more psychologically harmonious.' Lewis visited Mrs Moore every day till she died – aged 79 – on 12 January 1951. Her body was buried in the churchyard of Lewis's parish church in Headington Quarry.

As much as Lewis revelled in 'rational opposition' he several times during the war years said 'no doctrine of the Faith seems so spectral and unreal to me as that which I have just successfully defended'. It is not perhaps surprising that his next book, *Reflections on the Psalms*, should be so much quieter in tone than its predecessors. It was written during the autumn of 1957 and, such was the magic of his name by now, had sold 11,000 copies before its publication in September 1958.

Lewis was no Hebraist and so worked from the Coverdale translation of the Psalms as found in the Book of Common Prayer (Lewis's own copy of the Prayer Book was the one his grandfather, Thomas Hamilton, had taken with him to India in 1852) as well as the translation by James Moffatt (1924). Though Lewis enjoyed the co-operation of his friend Austin Farrer in writing the book, he made it clear in his introductory chapter that he was writing 'as one amateur to another, talking about difficulties I have met, or lights I have gained, when reading the psalms'. 'This is not', he went on to say, 'what is called an "apologetic" work . . . A man can't always be defending the truth; there must be a time to feed on it.' One of the most flattering results of his *Reflections* is that he was shortly afterwards made a member of the committee appointed by the Convocations of Canterbury and York to revise the psalms for *The Revised Psalter* which appeared in 1963.

Once a book was through the press Lewis usually forgot about it; of the many he had written by this time, he owned only a few. There was hardly time for him to forget *Reflections on the Psalms* before the Episcopal Radio-TV Foundation of Atlanta, Georgia, asked him in 1957 to make some tape-recordings to be played over the American air. The request came from the Bishop of South Florida (H. I. Louttit) and was backed up by Chad Walsh and the foundation's executive director, Mrs Caroline Rakestraw. In his reply to the Bishop, Lewis said: 'The subject I want to say something about in the near future, in some form or the other, is the four Loves – Storge, Philia, Eros, and Agape. This seems to bring in nearly the whole of Christian ethics.'

By the summer of 1958 Lewis had completed the script of his ten talks on the four Loves (Affection, Friendship, Eros, and Charity) and Mrs Rakestraw met Lewis in London where the recording took place on 19–20 August. Lewis afterwards used the radio script as a basis for a book entitled *The Four Loves*. The latter was completed in June 1959 and published in March 1960.

After the tapes were taken to Georgia the Episcopal Radio-TV Foundation launched a huge publicity campaign which, however unintentionally, led many people to suppose that C. S. Lewis was planning to visit the United States for the purpose of talking over the radio. Regardless of how they interpreted the publicity, it was enough for his fans that they would soon hear his voice over the air. Then the blow fell. Though the facts are hard to get at, Lewis was given to understand that various bishops in the Episcopal Church discovered – on reading transcripts of the tapes – that what Lewis had to say about Eros was 'too frank for the American people'. The talks were not cancelled but they were not perhaps broadcast as widely as they might have been.

There are two people whose names Lewis could not pronounce correctly – or did not wish to because of the fun it gave him to mispronounce them. One is Mrs Clare Boothe Luce whom he referred to as 'Clara Bootlace'; the other, Mrs Rakestraw, whom he called 'the very nice Mrs Cartwheel'. It fell to Mrs Rakestraw to explain to Lewis why some of her backers found his talks on Eros objectionable. Though it is entirely possible that Lewis misunderstood the issue, he told Walter Hooper that Mrs Rakestraw said to him, 'Professor Lewis, I'm afraid you brought sex into your talks on Eros', to which he replied, 'My dear Mrs Cartwheel, how can you talk about Eros and *leave it out?*' However imperfect his grasp of the situation might have been, he told Hooper that it struck him as unthinkable that a country which peddled so much pornography could not bear to hear a Christian discussion of sex. Lewis thought one of the 'offensive' passages might have been that in which he said: 'Now the act of love – Venus, as our ancestors called it – has even on those terms its own inherent kind of gravity. But it is also possible to take it too seriously or with the wrong kind of seriousness, and especially today. A preposterous and ludicrous solemnization of sex has been going on almost since my life began. Nothing is more needed on this subject at the moment than a good outbreak of belly laughter . . . The technicians, so to call them, have so bedeviled us with the immense psychological importance of getting this act right, and the all but impossibility of doing so, that one imagines some young couples now go to it with the complete works of Freud, Krafft-Ebing, Dr Stopes, Havelock Ellis, laid out on bedtables all around them.'

The happy outcome of what, at first, seemed an unpromising episode is that Caroline Rakestraw persisted with her work and in 1970 the Episcopal Radio-TV Foundation issued for sale an album containing cassettes of Lewis's *Four Talks on Love*.

Lewis was lucky in his publishers but none of them, perhaps, knew how to shepherd Lewis's energies so well as did Jocelyn (Jock) Gibb who took over the management of Geoffrey Bles Ltd after Bles retired in 1954. Without his gentle and kindly perseverance Lewis might never have written his last book. What began in 1952 as a slightly dull and rather academic work on prayer suddenly caught the author's imagination and almost, as it were, wrote itself. *Letters to Malcolm: Chiefly on Prayer* was completed in May 1963 and a typescript sent to Gibb a few weeks later. 'Respect and admire you as I do', Gibb wrote on 13 June, 'this "Letters to Malcolm" . . . has knocked me flat. Not quite; I can just sit up and shout hurrah, and again, hurrah. It's the best you've done since *The Problem of Pain*. By Jove, this is something of a present to a publisher!'

When Walter Hooper met the Archbishop of Canterbury in 1964 the Archbishop's first words were, 'Who is Malcolm?' Those who have asked the same question will now know they are in wise and good company. In few of his books was Lewis so successful in the art of illusion as in these 22 letters. Even the actual recipient of his *Letters to an American Lady* (1967) is less believable than the imaginary Malcolm with whom his creator argues and shares reminiscences, and whom he sometimes needs to comfort. Malcolm might have been supposed to be Owen Barfield – till he is discovered to be their mutual friend.

When Jock Gibb asked for suggestions in writing a blurb for the book-jacket, Lewis said (28 June): 'I'd like you to make the point that the reader is merely being allowed to listen to two very ordinary laymen discussing the practical and speculative problems of prayer as these appear to them: i.e. the author does *not* claim to be teaching . . . Some passages are controversial but this is almost an accident. The wayfaring Christian cannot quite ignore recent Anglican theology when it has been built as a barricade across the high road.'

Two of the modernists whom Lewis believed to be active in building the barricade were the 'de-mythologizers', Rudolf Bultmann and the former Bishop of Woolwich (or 'Woolworth', as Lewis preferred to call J. A. T. Robinson). 'Never . . . let us think', Lewis says to Malcolm in Letter 4, 'that while anthropomorphic images are a concession to our weakness, the abstractions are the literal truth. Both are equally concessions; each singly misleading, and the two together mutually corrective. Unless you sit to it very lightly, continually murmuring "Not thus, not thus, neither is this Thou", the abstraction is fatal. It will make the life of lives inanimate and the love of loves impersonal. The naïf image is mischievous chiefly in so far as it holds unbelievers back from conversion. It does believers, even at its crudest, no harm. What soul ever perished for believing that God the Father really has a beard?'

It was very difficult to draw Lewis out on the subject of liturgy, but he makes it clear in his first letter that he has little sympathy for those priests who have the 'Liturgical Fidget' and attempt to lure people to church by 'incessant brightenings, lightenings, lengthenings, abridgements, simplifications and complications of the service'. 'My whole liturgiological position', he says, 'really

boils down to an entreaty for permanence and uniformity.'
Fortunately for Lewis, his own vicar, Fr R. E. Head, was as
opposed to the 'fidget' as he was and it was from him that Lewis
learned a great deal about what the revisers of the Prayer Book
were up to.

After his explicit references to Purgatory in *The Great Divorce*
a TV interviewer asked Lewis if he planned to join the Roman
communion. 'After all', he said, 'you do believe in Purgatory.'
'But not', answered Lewis, 'the *Romish* doctrine!' (He was referring
to Article XXII in the Prayer Book.) Rather than go on denying
the rumours that he was leaving the Anglican for the Roman
Church, Lewis decided to explain his views on Purgatory to
Malcolm: 'Our souls *demand* Purgatory, don't they? Would it not
break the heart if God said to us, "It is true, my son, that your
breath smells and your rags drip with mud and slime, but we are
charitable here and no one will upbraid you with these things, nor
draw away from you. Enter into the joy"? Should we not reply,
"With submission, sir, and if there is no objection, I'd *rather* be
cleaned first." "It may hurt, you know" – "Even so, sir." . . . My
favourite image on this matter comes from the dentist's chair. I
hope that when the tooth of life is drawn and I am "coming
round", a voice will say, "Rinse your mouth out with this." *This*
will be Purgatory' (Letter 20).

In the last chapter of the last book he wrote – his final letter to
Malcolm – Lewis speculates on what is implied in the doctrine
of the resurrection of the body. He was very ill at the time and
rewrote the chapter a number of times. What, he asked, did St
Paul mean by, 'It is sown in corruption; it is raised in incorrup-
tion'? He could not believe that men reassumed the bodies they
had worn on earth, nor could he believe that the richness of a lifetime would be dissolved into something so 'spiritual' that it
resembled a gas. Finally it came to him. 'What the soul cries out
for', he says to Malcolm, 'is the resurrection of the senses. Even in
this life matter would be nothing to us if it were not a source of
sensations. . . . At present we tend to think of the soul as somehow
"inside" the body. But the glorified body of the resurrection as I

conceive it – the sensuous life raised from its death – will be inside the soul. As God is not in space but space is in God. . . . Guesses, of course, only guesses. If they are not true, something better will be' (Letter 22).

Lewis gave the manuscript of *Malcolm* to Walter Hooper and watched him closely as he read it. 'If anyone thinks I have in any way lost my faith in Christ's promises', he said, 'will you point them to what I've said in *The Last Battle*?'

And that takes us to the next chapter.

X. THROUGH THE WARDROBE

'I am almost inclined to set it up as a canon that a children's story which is enjoyed only by children is a bad children's story. The good ones last,' said C. S. Lewis in his lecture 'On Three Ways of Writing for Children' at the Bournemouth Conference of the Library Association in 1952. And he pointed out at the same time that 'where the children's story is simply the right form for what the author has to say, then of course readers who want to hear that, will read the story, or re-read it, at any age. I never met *The Wind in the Willows* or the Bastable books till I was in my late twenties, and I do not think that I have enjoyed them any the less on that account.'

In fact, as we have seen, Lewis seems to have read relatively few children's books as a child: after the usual nursery rhymes and fairy tales, and the earlier Beatrix Potter (the first, *Peter Rabbit*, appeared when he was four; the thirteenth, *Samuel Whiskers*, when he was ten), he seems to have moved on to adventure stories. The one notable exception was E. Nesbit, whose Psammead series and two Arden serials he read in the *Strand Magazine* where they appeared between 1902 and 1909, together with several of her short tales of magic. The absence of the Bastable books suggests that he did not purchase her works in volume form and knew only those in the *Strand*, except when he chanced on an odd short story in any other publication.

Lewis's love of E. Nesbit's stories was life-long. In his diary for 29 January 1923 he noted: 'I dreamed that in a station waiting room I found a children's story which I had never seen before, by E. Nesbit; and became so interested that I missed my train.' (Lewis never missed a train by his own fault: in later years it became a joke among his Oxford friends that he liked to be on the platform half an hour before the train went – and they tried again and again to make him miss his train to Cambridge. They never succeeded. He, on the other hand, entered fully into the spirit of the game, and tried to make those who were seeing him off fail to leave the train before it started: he succeeded once, and his friend had to walk back to Oxford from Wolvercote.)

Perhaps Mark's experience in *That Hideous Strength* (pp. 446–7) when he finds the run of the *Strand Magazine* in the hotel sitting-room echoes an earlier experience of Lewis's: 'In one of these he found a children's serial story which he had begun to read as a child, but abandoned because his tenth birthday came when he was half-way through it and he was ashamed to read it after that. Now, he chased it from volume to volume till he finished it. It was good. The grown-up stories to which, after his tenth birthday, he had turned instead of it, now seemed to him, except for *Sherlock Holmes*, to be rubbish.' For Lewis admitted in his lecture that, 'When I was ten, I read fairy tales in secret and would have been ashamed if I had been found doing so. Now that I am fifty I read them openly.' And in the histories of Boxen which he and his brother created as boys, though the characters were 'dressed animals' they were treated as grown-up human beings and their interests, pursuits and dialogues were intended to be as 'adult' as possible, however dull and unromantic adult preoccupations appeared to be.

Lewis himself was not able to recollect exactly why he began to write fantasy stories for young readers. 'I am not quite sure', he said in the lecture quoted above, 'what made me, in a particular year of my life, feel that not only a fairy tale, but a fairy tale addressed to children, was exactly what I must write – or burst.' Nor was the urge very strong at first, for he seems to have begun his first children's story early in the war, and then to have left it for nearly ten years.

As with the Ransom stories, the Narnian tales 'began with seeing pictures in my head. At first they were not a story, just pictures. The *Lion* all began with a picture of a Faun carrying an umbrella and parcels in a snowy wood. The picture had been in my mind since I was about sixteen. Then one day when I was about forty, I said to myself: "Let's try to make a story about it." At first I had very little idea how the story would go. . . .'

Unfortunately Lewis kept no early drafts of stories, once the final form was achieved, nor even the manuscripts of the finished books themselves, and we have only a few early Narnian fragments preserved by chance, mostly in notebooks kept since they also contained references for his more academic works.

What we now know as *The Lion, the Witch and the Wardrobe* seems to have been begun at the end of 1939. On 2 September Lewis wrote to his brother, who had been recalled to the Army on the outbreak of war, about the children evacuated to the Kilns. 'Our schoolgirls (i.e. evacuees) have arrived and all seem to me to be very nice, unaffected creatures and all most flatteringly delighted with their surroundings. They are fond of animals, which is a good thing'; and on 18 September he amplified. 'I have said that the children are "nice", and so they are. But modern children are poor creatures. They keep coming to Maureen and asking, "What shall we do now?" . . . Shades of our childhood!'

The evacuees gave Lewis a setting for the story, and he began on an odd sheet which has survived in the manuscript of *The Dark Tower*, and which has notes for *Broadcast Talks* on the other end of it:

'This book is about four children whose names were Ann, Martin, Rose and Peter. But it is most about Peter who was the youngest. They all had to go away from London suddenly because of Air Raids, and because Father, who was in the Army, had gone off to the War and Mother was doing some kind of war work. They were sent to stay with a kind of relation of Mother's who was a very old Professor who lived all by himself in the country.'

It is uncertain whether Lewis wrote much – or indeed any – more of the story at this time. The next reference to it was a casual remark to Chad Walsh in the summer of 1948. 'He talks vaguely of completing a children's book he has begun "in the tradition of E. Nesbit",' when he had finished *Surprised by Joy. (C. S. Lewis: Apostle to the Skeptics* (1949), p. 10.)

By this time Lewis had probably taken up the book again, having seen more mental pictures: 'a queen on a sledge', perhaps even 'a magnificent lion'. He had also been stimulated, perhaps subconsciously, by reading the manuscript of a friend's book of a similar kind, to continue with his own tale – and in doing so, seems to have drawn some ideas from what he had read.

On 6 September 1945 Lewis attended the wedding of the eldest daughter of David Nichol Smith, at that time Merton Professor of English Literature. After the ceremony, at the reception in the Senior Common Room at Merton, Roger Lancelyn Green found him rather out of his element and only too delighted to withdraw into a window-alcove and talk about fiction and fairy tales. (Green had recently submitted a thesis on 'Andrew Lang and the Fairy Tale' for the degree of Bachelor of Letters – and Lewis was reported to have remarked at the English Faculty Meeting at which it was discussed, 'Much better let him write a fairy tale about B. Litts!')

During the conversation Green told Lewis about a fantasy he had just written called *The Wood that Time Forgot*; Lewis showed great interest in this, and asked to read it. Green lent him the typescript and Lewis wrote him two packed pages of criticism a couple of weeks later, and invited him to dinner later that term to discuss the book in particular and 'imaginative fiction' in general. Lewis kept the typescript until Green lunched with him again on 17 September the following year, when he returned it with much good advice and the assurance that it ought to be published. Green tried in vain to turn the story into 'a fairy tale for grown ups', and finally revised the book, scrapped the last two chapters and wrote four new ones to give it a completely different ending – of which Lewis approved very highly. But the book remains unpublished to this day – and would pass no publisher's reader, as it would appear to owe too much to *The Lion, the Witch and the Wardrobe*.

It is, in fact, the earlier part of the book which set Lewis to work again on his 'children's book in the tradition of E. Nesbit'. The story tells of three children and an undergraduate friend who find their way out of an ordinary Oxfordshire wood, along a stream which comes through a tunnel under an embankment, into a wood cut off by Time from the surrounding world. In it they find Elena, the girl who has become partly a succuba and whose age is also suspended by Time, who is pursued by Agares, a kind of fallen angel or minor devil (out of Reginald Scot's *Discoverie of Witchcraft*) following her perpetually until she and Randal, the undergraduate, with the aid of the children, meet and finally by saving each other save themselves. ('The later chapters are splendidly conceived,' wrote Lewis after reading the revised book. 'The idea – almost the epigram – that Elena can reach Heaven only by recovering earth, comes from a depth that does not make itself felt in anything else of yours that I have seen.') But the important part in the story, there from the beginning, is the visit paid by the children to Agares in his house, where he seems to be just a kindly old man, and the sweet raspberry-cordial-like drink which tempts one of the children to side with the enemy. That, and the whole atmosphere of the wood, seem to have given Lewis at least the seeds of the Pevensie children's incursion into the Narnian forest, the character of the White Witch, and her temptation of Edmund by means of the magic Turkish Delight.

And somewhere, after he had suddenly begun writing again and was deep into Narnia, 'suddenly Aslan came bounding into it. I think', Lewis records, 'I had been having a good many dreams of lions about that time. Apart from that, I don't know where the Lion came from or why He came. But once He was there He pulled the whole story together, and soon He pulled the other six Narnian stories in after Him.' The Lion and the Lamb had come very close together at the end of Chapter 9 of *The Problem of Pain*: perhaps Aslan (the Turkish for 'lion') was already stirring in the author's subconscious.

On 10 March 1949 Green dined with Lewis in Magdalen and thereafter followed a 'wonderful talk until midnight: he read me two chapters of a story for children he is writing – very good indeed, though a trifle self-conscious'. Nonetheless it was a memorable occasion which the listener remembers vividly, and remembers too his awed conviction that he was listening to a book that could rank with the great ones of its kind.

Lewis stopped reading with the remark that he had read the story to Tolkien, who had disliked it intensely: was it any good? Green assured him that it was more than good, and Lewis had the complete story ready to lend him (in the original manuscript) by the end of the month. (Tolkien met Green shortly after and remarked: 'I hear you've been reading Jack's children's story. It really won't do, you know! I mean to say: "*Nymphs and their Ways, The Love-Life of a Faun*". Doesn't he know what he's talking about?')

But Lewis was finding his way into a completely new world, and one that only he could have created – and insisted on creating. There have been many stories from *Alice* onwards in which the nursery-rhyme or fairy-tale characters play a part; from *Only Toys!* and *Winnie-the-Pooh* in which the child's most beloved secret companions come to life: but only Lewis could take all myth and ransack it for his *dramatis personae*, taking what he needed wherever he found it throughout literature, but making it so much his own that whatever 'original' researchers may find, there is no thought of anything like plagiarism.

And he was convinced from the start about what he was doing, though not at first quite able to convince all his readers. Green remembers reacting against the appearance of Father Christmas in *The Lion, the Witch and the Wardrobe* and urging Lewis to omit him somehow as breaking the magic for a moment: he still does not seem to fit quite comfortably into his place, but the rightness of introducing him seems more certain on each re-reading.

The 'self-consciousness' which Green noted was most apparent in the first two stories, and took the form of an occasional forced jocularity, and a more frequent attempt at children's colloquialisms – which too often sounded like recollections of E. Nesbit – though were as likely to be from Lewis's own childhood. His knowledge of actual children was slight, and his own two stepsons did not arrive on the scene until after the Narnian stories were completed. Doubtless Maureen, Mrs Moore's daughter, whom he could have observed from childhood onwards, gave him some insight into the mind of a girl: and most of his girls seem more deeply studied than his boys. He had also a number of godchildren whom he met from time to time, and with whom he was sometimes able to get on very friendly terms; but children played a very small part in his life, and he saw them to a great extent 'through the spectacles of books'.

Being rather more in touch with contemporary children, Green was able to suggest a number of small alterations and improvements, ranging from the deletion of 'Crikey!' as a common exclamation among the young ('the word "Crikey!" fell from more than one pair of lips', as Oswald Bastable says in *The Treasure Seekers*) to the omission of bird's-nesting from among the Pevensie children's occupations – Lewis being unaware of the revolution against 'egg-collectors' achieved by Arthur Ransome.

In spite of Aslan's pull, Lewis found it very hard to write a second Narnian story. He began by trying to discover what had gone before the meeting of the Pevensies with the White Witch, and how the lamp-post came to be standing on the edge of Narnia. From the literary point of view it stood 'hard by the Sea of Dreams' in Kipling's poem in *The Brushwood Boy*:

> Over the edge of the purple down
> Where the single lamplight gleams;

but the creator was interested only in discovering how it found its way into Narnia.

So he began a story of the boy Digory who could understand what the trees and animals said, until he cut off a branch from the oak tree to help Polly, the girl next door, in the building of a raft; and of the visit of his godmother Mrs Lefay who is obviously endowed with magic arts and has a rabbit in her bag called Coiny . . . But there the story stuck, and Lewis was not sure what came next, and was dissatisfied with the turn it was taking. In June 1949 he read it to Green, who liked the beginning, but felt that Mrs Lefay was getting perilously near the kind of burlesque fairy-tale character in the kind of stories such as *The Rose and the Ring* and some of E. Nesbit's short 'Unlikely Tales' which Lewis liked least. Lewis agreed, and the story was set aside (by an irony of fate it is the only MS fragment of a Narnian story to survive) – the more readily because he had thought of a splendid beginning for an adventure that was to be a sequel to *The Lion, the Witch and the Wardrobe*. There were many stories, both traditional and invented, Lewis pointed out, in which people are summoned by magic across time or space – but they are always told from the side of the magician, or the possessor of the charm which does the summoning: what would it be like to be on the other end – to be pulled suddenly by magic into another land or another age – or both? And so the story of Prince Caspian was begun: *Drawn into Narnia* was its original title, which was changed on the advice of the publisher who thought it would be difficult to say, but relinquished with regret, the second choice (also vetoed by the publisher) being *A Horn in Narnia* (since it was Queen Susan's magic Horn which drew the children back to the rescue of Prince Caspian).

The manuscript of the new story was finished by December 1949, and Green had read it and suggested corrections and returned it with his report by 31 December when Lewis had a lunch party in 'The Wilde Room' at Magdalen to meet Pauline Baynes who was to illustrate the first story: the choice was due to the excellent illustrations which she had just produced for Tolkien's *Farmer Giles of Ham*.

Before the end of February 1950 *A Horn in Narnia* was in typescript and the manuscript of *The Voyage of the 'Dawn Treader'* ready for Green to read. The former was taken to be read to Professor Lawson's children, with enthusiastic results; the latter needed hardly any revision and was written obviously in the white heat of inspiration with hardly a correction in the clear, neat hand which Green was learning to know so well, and which still brings a thrill of memory and regret whenever he sees it.

At the end of March illustrations for *The Lion, the Witch and the Wardrobe* were coming in and being discussed, and Lewis asked Green to write a blurb for the jacket. This he did 'with much difficulty' on 2 April, and Lewis wrote a couple of days later: 'Thanks very much for the blurb: I shall send it to Bles to-day – It seems excellent to me, but like you I don't really understand Blurbology.' And it was not, finally, used.

Proofs of *The Lion* were being handed round at the 'Bird and Baby' on 22 June, and on 26 July Green 'spent most of the day reading Lewis's new story *Narnia and the North* [*The Horse and his Boy*], which is very enthralling – almost the best of the four'. And next day he 'dined in Magdalen S.C.R. with Lewis, and then a wonderful evening talking until after 1 a.m. Began by discussing *To Narnia and the North*, made several suggestions etc. Some talk of *The Golden Cat* [Green's latest children's story], which Lewis liked; much literary talk, also of life after death, war, killing, the ethics of such things: we got on to life after death by way of Kipling's "On the Gate" and a Wells story of a similar kind.'

The almost weekly meetings with Lewis in 1950 ceased when Green left Oxford at the end of August to live in Cheshire. But he went with a standing invitation to stay with Lewis each term, and was paying his first visit to the Guest Room at Magdalen on 13 November when he 'started reading Lewis's newest story in MS'. He read more of the story the next day, and after dinner in Hall, 'back to his rooms where we sat talking until about 12.30: usual sort of subjects – children's books, romances of other worlds; I discoursed upon Edgar Rice Burroughs; we planned a story of a trip to Mercury – but couldn't get very far with it.'

He was staying again at the beginning of March 1951 when he 'finished reading the new Narnian story, which is every bit as good as the rest', and left notes for possible alterations. About one of these Lewis wrote to him on 6 March: 'You are quite right about a wood fire. Wood keeps on glowing red again in the places you have already extinguished – phoenix-like. Even the large webbed feet of a Marsh-wiggle couldn't do it. Yet it must be a flat hearth, I think. *Does* peat go out easily by treading? As an Irishman I ought to know, but don't. I think it will have to be a coal fire in a flat hearth. After all, Underland might well use coal, whereas wood or charcoal would have to be imported.'

It was impossible to change it completely, but Lewis cut out the original description of a great log fire and simply let Puddleglum stamp 'on the fire, grinding a large part of it into ashes on the flat hearth' (*The Silver Chair*, p. 163).

Besides such alterations and corrections there was much discussion about the titles of the stories. (Green christened the whole series *The Chronicles of Narnia*, on the analogy of Andrew Lang's *Chronicles of Pantouflia*, and the name stuck.) Thus *Night under Narnia* (Green's title) when Lewis decided to publish it as the fourth book (though written fifth) provoked several suggestions. 'Bles, like you, thinks *The Wild Waste Lands* bad', Lewis wrote to Green on 26 September 1952, 'but he says *Night under Narnia* is "gloomy". George Sayer and my brother say *Gnomes under Narnia* would be equally gloomy, but *News Under Narnia* would do. On the other hand my brother and the American writer Joy Davidman (who has been staying with us and is a great reader of fantasy and children's books) both say that *The Wild Waste Lands* is a splendid title. What's a chap to do?' The final decision was, of course, *The Silver Chair*.

When Geoffrey Bles, the publisher, received the story originally called *Narnia and the North*, he again disliked that title, and Lewis wrote to him on 13 April 1953: 'What are your reactions to any of the following? *The Horse and the Boy* (which might allure the "pony-book" public) – *The Desert Road to Narnia* – *Cor of Archenland* – *The Horse Stole the Boy* – *Over the Border* – *The Horse Bree*. Suggestions will be welcome.' To which Bles replied, 'I like best *The Horse and the Boy*, but what about *The Horse and his Boy*, which is a little startling and conveys the idea of your other title *The Horse Stole the Boy*?' – and his suggestion was followed.

Another question raised by Bles was that of the gender of some of the creatures in Narnia, which seemed to be getting muddled, and Lewis wrote on 20 March 1953: 'My idea about *He* and *It* was that the semi-humanity would be kept before the imagination by an unobtrusive mixture of the two. Your reaction, however, shows that such a mixture could not be unobtrusive or else that I, at any rate, could not make it so. Of course I cherish a secret hope that you are merely playing the "normalizing scribe", well known to textual critics . . .'

There were also criticisms of illustrations: those for *The Silver Chair* Lewis considered 'the best set Miss Baynes has done for us yet. There is, as always, exquisite delicacy: and I think the faces (human faces) are greatly improved.' He found it hard to discard the few by which Bles wanted to cut the size of the book, but suggested one which was 'ruined by the utterly un-numinous, foreshortened Aslan in the background', another in which 'the travellers ought to be carrying packs, not parcels in their hands like trippers', and a Gnome who was 'too like a brat out of Dickens's London', and asked for one alteration: 'could the shield be painted out in Chinese white and thus obliterated? Knights didn't wear shields on the *right* arm.'

'It is delightful to find (and not only for selfish reasons) that you do each book a little better than the last,' wrote Lewis to Pauline Baynes on 21 January 1954 after seeing the illustrations for *The Horse and his Boy*. 'Both the drawings of Lasaraleen in her litter were a rich feast of line and of fantastic – satiric imagination: my only regret was that we couldn't have both. Shasta among the tombs (in the new technique which is lovely) was just what I wanted. The pictures of Rabadash hanging on the hook and just turning into an ass were the best comedy you've done yet. The Tisroc was superb: far beyond anything you were doing five years ago. I thought that your human faces – the boys, King Lune, etc. – were, this time, really good.' Lewis had been very disappointed with the children in the illustrations to the earlier books, whom he considered ugly and unintelligent: 'I know you made the children rather plain – *in the interests of realism* – but do you think you could possibly pretty them up now?' he had written when the illustrations for *Prince Caspian* were commissioned. And he detested the modern trend in children's book illustration for making the characters as vulgar and moronic as possible, whatever their cultural or hierarchic background: typically, he described the jacket picture to Green's *The Luck of Troy*, supposedly depicting young

Nicostratus, the son of Menelaus and Helen, as 'a beatnik in running shorts'.

Meanwhile Lewis was turning back to the story he had always intended to write, about the beginnings of Narnia: why the lamp-post stood in 'Lantern Waste', and how the White Witch came to be such an evil power in the land. The 'Lefay Fragment' gave him little more than his two characters, who at first supplied the name for the book, *Polly and Digory*; and the idea that Digory should be the Professor Kirke of *The Lion, the Witch and the Wardrobe*, as a boy, set the story back to the period of Lewis's own childhood: the period of E. Nesbit and Conan Doyle.

A little under half of the book was written by the end of May 1951 when Green was staying again at Magdalen. Lewis read the first chapter aloud, pausing at 'In those days Mr Sherlock Holmes was still living in Baker Street and the Bastables were looking for treasure in the Lewisham Road,' with a diffident: 'Is it all right to say that in a story?' and then handed over the manuscript, which Green read eagerly into the small hours, after the usual evening of enthralling talk.

He was in Magdalen again at the end of October, and about three-quarters of the book was written. But on this occasion he took it upon himself to criticize not merely lines and incidents, but a whole section of the story. In the version which Green read on 31 October, and spent the evening of 2 November 1951 in discussing with Lewis, Digory paid several visits to the dying world of Charn during which he stayed in a farm cottage with an old countryman called Piers and his wife, who spoke with a rather laboured 'Loamshire' accent, were a little too simple and honest and far too long-winded; but, most of all, seemed to him quite out of harmony with the rest of the book. And when the end of Charn came, Piers and his wife became the Adam and Eve of the newly created Narnia, becoming king and queen of the Talking Animals, to be the parents of the future race of Narnians.

Lewis was not at first convinced, and set the book aside to consider. In fact he had finished *The Last Battle* before lending the revised typescript to Green in February 1954. Green noted at the time: 'It seems the best of the lot (but each does on reading) – and is certainly vastly improved by the omission of the long section about Piers the Plowman – which I take some credit for persuading Jack to cut out. It's a single unity now, and irresistibly gripping and compelling . . .' And Lewis wrote to him on 22 February: 'I was relieved that *Polly and Digory* got your *nihil obstat*. I was afraid you might object to Uncle Andrew as a character more amusing to adults than to children. You can always feel a paternal interest in this tale, for it owes more than half its merit to your shrewdness in discerning and honesty in pointing out, the fatal "sag" in the original draft.'

The Magician's Nephew, as the book was finally called, owes a great deal of its excellence to the completely natural conversation and behaviour of the children: here at least any feeling that Lewis is remembering his own childhood (or being reminded by his recollections of E. Nesbit's characters) makes not for less but for more verisimilitude: for Polly and Digory are his contemporaries, and there is no danger of their talk being out of date. As Lewis said later in 1954 in his Inaugural Lecture at Cambridge, 'I may yet be useful as a specimen . . . Use your specimens while you can. There are not going to be many more dinosaurs.'

In spite of the excellence of *The Magician's Nephew*, the critics were probably right in waiting to award *The Last Battle* the honour of the Carnegie Medal for the best children's book of 1956. This, *The Last Chronicle of Narnia* as it was first called, did not follow the rest for more than a year after the first version of *The Magician's Nephew* was finished and set aside for further consideration. Green was reading the first 40 pages of it (more than half the book, in Lewis's neat handwriting on very large folio sheets) early in February 1953, and on 11 March Lewis wrote to Geoffrey Bles, 'You will hear with mixed feelings that I have just finished the seventh and really the last of the Narnian stories.' It was revised and ready to be typed by the end of May.

It has often been asked whether Lewis had planned the whole Narnian series from the beginning, or even wrote each book with the next in mind; and whether he set out from the start to 'put across' certain lessons in simple Christianity and then looked about for the most suitable form in which to clothe them. Lewis himself answered the last question in his article 'Sometimes Fairy Stories May Say Best What's To Be Said' in the *New York Times Book Review* on 18 November 1956 (collected in *Of Other Worlds* (1966), pp. 35–8): 'At first there wasn't even anything Christian [about the pictures which grew together to form *The Lion, the Witch and the Wardrobe*], that element pushed itself in of its own accord.' And again of the first story, 'suddenly Aslan came bounding in . . .'

With regard to *The Chronicles of Narnia* as a whole, there was certainly no idea of more than one book to begin with – though naturally the possibility of a sequel was present in his mind when *The Lion, the Witch and the Wardrobe* was drawing to a close. But it was only a hazy idea – and Green inadvertently held it up for a little while by asking how the lamp-post came to be in Narnia, which led Lewis off on the first abortive attempt which survives as the 'Lefay Fragment'. *Prince Caspian* led on to *The Voyage of the 'Dawn Treader'*, and there the series stopped for the moment – though not the inspiration, for Lewis then paused to tell the purely Narnian tale of *The Horse and his Boy*, before returning to Eustace, who at the end of the *Voyage* had been promised a return to Narnia, which became *The Silver Chair*.

Already Lewis was departing slightly from statements made in the first chronicle: the Pevensies were the only 'Sons of Adam and Daughters of Eve' who had come into Narnia, but in *Prince Caspian* the Telmarines are descended from a boat-load of pirates from earth who got in by way of a magic cave in the South Seas. This incursion was, of course, centuries later than the Pevensies' first visit, and so does not contradict completely; but the introduction of Frank the Cabby and his wife Helen from London, in place of Piers the Plowman and his wife from Charn, in *The Magician's Nephew*, does go contrary to the original statement. Presumably the rather clumsy contrivance of Digory's apprenticeship to the farmer and his wife in a world other than earth shows Lewis's original attempt to conform to his first ideas of Narnia –

and it obviously seemed worth assuming that readers would have forgotten a relatively unimportant point in the *Lion* in order to achieve so much better a plot in *The Magician's Nephew*.

It is unfortunate that Lewis recorded so few of the 'pictures' out of which the Narnian stories grew: 'a faun carrying an umbrella, a queen on a sledge, a magnificent lion', almost make up the sum total. The door which Aslan made in the air in *Prince Caspian*, and with it the Stable Door in *The Last Battle*, may owe something to a dream recorded in his diary on 27 April 1923. 'I dreamed first that I was sitting in the dusk on Magdalen Bridge. Then I went up a hill with a party of people. On top of the hill stood a window – no house, a window standing alone . . .' The names Caspian and Jadis were remembered from the version of the Cupid and Psyche story which Lewis was writing in verse in 1923: only here their sexes were reversed:

> Now I say there was a prince
> Twin brother to this Psyche, fair as she,
> And prettier than a boy would choose to be,
> His name was Jardis. Older far than these
> Was Caspian who had rocked them on her knees,
> The child of the first marriage of the king.

The literary inspirations are even more tenuous. Again and again one can find echoes from legend and literature, ancient and modern – and those of us who have 'read the right books' will find more than those who have not. But such echoes are of little importance, save to suggest what books Lewis had read or to make us marvel at his wide reading and retentive memory. But however much his reading may have suggested to him, Lewis can never be accused of copying another author, save in trifling instances, which were usually subconscious anyway.

Thus Lewis probably came across E. Nesbit's short story 'The Aunt and Amabel' when it appeared in *Blackie's Christmas Annual* for 1909 (published for Christmas 1908, when he was ten) in which Amabel finds her way into her magic world by the same door as the Pevensies – 'the station was *Bigwardrobeinspareroom*', which is close to Mr Tummus's 'far land of Spare Oom . . . bright

city of War Drobe'. But Lewis had forgotten the Nesbit story
entirely until reminded of it. Occasionally echoes come through
from slighter recollections: Queen Jadis's account of her destruction of Charn and its people has a tantalizing ring of Oro's similar
description in *When the World Shook*, and the passage under the
eaves by which Polly and Digory get into Uncle Andrew's study
is surely a continuation of that used by Stalky & Co., in 'An
Unsavoury Interlude' – though for once the illustration contradicts
the text, and Lewis failed to spot it until too late.

But it is unsafe to follow such echoes far: how far was the
Underland in *The Silver Chair* suggested by Haggard's under-
ground cities of Mur and Nyo – or by Joseph O'Neill's *Land
Under England*? But Lewis might equally well have been thinking
of Athanasius Kircher's *Mundus Subterraneus* (1665) or Ludwig
Holberg's *Nicolai Klimii Iter Subterraneum* (1741) – or even Jules
Verne's *Voyage au Centre de la Terre* (1864) and Bulwer Lytton's
The Coming Race (1871)! Rider Haggard's remark about Andrew
Lang can suitably be applied to Lewis in this context – up to a
certain point: 'Whenever he sets to work to create, his wide
knowledge and his marvellous memory – and little worth studying
in ancient or modern literature has escaped him – prove positive
stumbling blocks in his path.' Lewis was at least as widely read
and had a similar memory ('the best-read man any of us is ever
likely to meet,' said Austin Farrer at his memorial service in
Magdalen) – but he was a creator, while Lang was seldom more
than an inventor: it could almost be said that Lang used what he
had read, but what he had read used Lewis – hence, like Ransom,
we feel in Narnia 'a sensation not of following an adventure but of
enacting a myth.'

'Were all the things which appeared as mythology on Earth
scattered through other worlds as realities?' Ransom asks himself
in *Perelandra*, and *The Chronicles of Narnia* seem to be the
affirmative answer to this question. For Lewis is making a new
mythology that grew out of and embraced the old and gave it a
new life in another world: he could no more be accused of plagiarism for introducing fauns and centaurs, dryads and hamadryads,

Bacchus and Silenus and satyrs, than Homer could. Homer had the myths and legends, the lays and folk tales of the old Mycenaean world to use in the *Odyssey*: he probably got the Sirens from some lost lay of the Argonauts, the Cyclops from a current folk tale, and so on. But Lewis, besides the literary and legendary legacy of the ancient world, had also all that lies between it and us: he had the plenteous riches of the Arthurian Cycle – it gave him the mystic table on which lay the Stone Knife, with which Aslan was slain by the White Witch, in Ramandu's kingdom, from the Grail Castle of the Fisher King, in the same way as the classical tales gave him the faun and the centaur. There are Talking Animals as in Aesop or Beatrix Potter or Kenneth Grahame; Queen Jadis visits late-Victorian London for one crowded hour rather as the Queen of Babylon does in Nesbit's *The Amulet*; Eustace turns into a dragon rather as Maurice had into a cat or Kenneth into a carp in other Nesbit stories – but all these incidents in *The Chronicles of Narnia* render Lewis's new world no less original than the introduction of playing-cards, chess-pieces, nursery rhyme and proverbial characters does in *Wonderland* and *Through the Looking-Glass*. Indeed the technique is similar, though Lewis Carroll was inventing lands of brilliant and convincing nonsense, and C. S. Lewis lands where fantasy and adventure merge inevitably into the numinous, where vice can be disguised as Turkish Delight and Aslan can be the Narnian Christ with perfect propriety.

For the Bible is, of course, the basic source-book, though most readers, even of mature age, recognize little of it except in Aslan's death and resurrection – and Lewis intended it to be recognized only subconsciously: 'supposing that by casting all these things into an imaginary world, stripping them of their stained-glass and Sunday School associations, one could make them for the first time appear in their real potency? Could one not thus steal past those watchful dragons? I thought one could.'

But *The Chronicles of Narnia* should not be treated as an allegory: they bear no literary relation either to *The Pilgrim's Progress* or to *The Pilgrim's Regress*, and it would spoil their effect to attempt to interpret them allegorically or symbolically –

certainly for children. They are and must be read simply as stories.

However, as adults will be analysing, a simple example of how this can be done was given by Walter Hooper in answer to such an attempt (in the *Oxford Times*, 2 Feb. 1968): '*The Last Battle* is modelled pretty closely on Our Lord's apocalyptic prophecy in St Matthew xxiv, but it is the end of Narnia, not of this world, that Lewis is writing about. Aslan (who is Christ) is holding his Last Judgement for that world – the entire Narnian creation. The only people from this world who are present are those who were killed in the railway accident: Digory, Polly, Peter, Edmund, Lucy, Mr and Mrs Pevensie, Eustace and Jill. The last two take an active part in the last battle; the others are reborn in the new Narnia on the other side of the Stable door. Susan was not killed in the railway crash, but even if she were, it is doubtful if she would have been with the others. Her interests are narrowly confined to the Shadowlands (this world) and she is, of her own free will, "no longer a friend of Narnia." Lewis is taking into consideration the fact that many people drift into apostasy. The new Narnia, of which the old was only a "shadow or a copy" is Heaven. Jutting out from the mountains of Aslan are all the *real* countries, one of which is that inner England which, Lewis believed, will never be destroyed. A better understanding of this can be had by reading the chapter on the resurrection in Lewis's *Letters to Malcolm* . . .' – or in Plato's *Phaedo*.

And so the stories can be read and enjoyed on at least two levels: by the child who perhaps knows nothing of the Bible, of classical or Arthurian myth and legend, of any of the authors whose works Lewis knew; and by the reader who knows many at least of these and senses many more. The first has a series of enthralling adventure stories, full of magic and fantasy, and complete in themselves. The second – usually the older reader – finds an added dimension and an additional enjoyment. 'What you see and hear depends a good deal on where you are standing: it also depends on what sort of person you are.'

'People won't write the books I want, so I have to do it for myself: no rot about "self-expression",' wrote Lewis to Chad Walsh in 1948 – unconsciously echoing Arthur Ransome's words written ten years earlier: 'You write not *for* children but for yourself, and if, by good fortune children enjoy what you enjoy, why then you are a writer of children's books.' The fact that both writers wrote primarily to please themselves, and that neither had children of their own or even a child audience, produces one similarity between their books – however different they are in other respects: there are no private jokes or allusions as, for example, in *Alice* or *Pooh*. There are virtually no personal 'originals' either: Lewis told Walter Hooper that the character of Puddleglum the Marsh-wiggle 'is modelled after his gardener, Paxford – an inwardly optimistic, outwardly pessimistic, dear, frustrating, shrewd countryman of immense integrity. But unlike Paxford, Puddleglum is so much *more* the type of man of which Paxford is typical.' In fact Puddleglum is based on Paxford but no nearer to being a real portrait than MacPhee is to William Kirkpatrick: and these seem to be the only originals to whom Lewis admitted.

Nor apparently do the Narnian stories contain any private references, other than those with a literary flavour, such as an occasional submerged quotation or an invention like the pavender, that Narnian fish which is based on a perhaps inaccurate recollection of Warham St Leger's humorous poem 'A False Gallop of Analogies'. Very occasionally a personal prejudice appears a little too strongly, as in the excessive unpleasantness of the school whence Eustace and Jill escape into Narnia in *The Silver Chair*, or the attack on 'civilization' in *The Last Battle* which upset at least one critic when the book was published. (But Lewis added a special footnote to Green's 'Bodley Head Monograph' (1963) which quoted this criticism: 'The critic means by *civilization* things like big cities and offices. I mean things like justice, mercy, free speech, honour and courtesy. It is unfortunate that English uses the word in both senses.')

The critical reception of the seven books was varied and usually guarded. But the readers' reception both in Great Britain and the

United States, if slow at first, was enthusiastic and with a mounting and widening enthusiasm that makes them still, nearly 25 years after their publication, among the most popular children's books of the day – and Lewis still the bestseller in the Puffin paperback series, where his nearest rivals include E. Nesbit, Hugh Lofting, Arthur Ransome, Alan Garner and a very few others.

The adverse adult criticism is usually caused by other than purely literary reasons; such critics may be divided roughly into the sceptics and the sentimentalists. The first attack the stories for their Christianity, the second for their presentation of some of the children as unpleasant characters – Edmund for his early treachery, Eustace before his experience as a dragon, and so on. Both are also inclined to object to Lewis's 'cruelty': Aslan's sacrifice, Eustace's sufferings when the dragon's hide is torn from him, Peter's killing of the wolf, and so on. And those who dislike, for either reason, do so very thoroughly and can see few virtues in the series – even condemning them as dull and badly written, condescending, cliché-ridden, devoid of any characterization.

But vast numbers of children read the stories with delight and live imaginatively in Narnia, even turning into play and acting the events. And very few find anything wrong unless it is pointed out to them by 'watchful dragons' among their elders. Most of the criticisms were answered by Lewis more or less before they were made in his Library Association lecture 'On Three Ways of Writing for Children', which was written at least by March 1952 when he read it to Green. ('I think the Bournemouth Lecture was a success,' he wrote to him on 1 May. 'One librarian said I had *almost* converted him to fairy tales, he having hitherto taken the "real life" stunt for granted. . . .') As for the 'cliché' and the 'condescension' – it would be surprising if it were not possible to find any such faults in a collection of seven books by a writer, however skilled, who was venturing into an untried field and then using it to produce work which was, as a whole, new and unique in that kind. Lewis took a little time to escape from the influence of E. Nesbit (a slipshod writer as far as style was concerned, and one who delighted in clichés) and put in certain things which he considered to be part of the literary form with which he was experimenting. Green was able to suggest the quiet excision of most of these – and some of the blame must attach to him for the few which remain – though Lewis would occasionally argue cogently for their retention, and keep them.

The immense popularity of the books is also shown by the change they brought about in what were conceived to be the reading habits, likes and dislikes of children. In the years before *The Lion, the Witch and the Wardrobe*, publishers returned the manuscripts of such books with the almost stereotyped form: 'the modern child is not interested in magic and fantasy.' From 1950 onwards came the swing of the pendulum back to fantasy and fairy tale, the myth and the mythopoeic which has not yet spent itself. There had been no swing so pronounced since the publication of Andrew Lang's first two fairy books in 1889 and 1890 ushered in the re-conquest of Fairyland and the golden age of Nesbit.

In spite of anything that can be said against them, and considering *The Chronicles of Narnia* as dispassionately as possible, it seems safe to say that C. S. Lewis has earned by them a place among the greatest writers of children's books and – surprising as it would have seemed to him – he will probably be remembered as a literary creator for them even more than for *The Screwtape Letters* and *Perelandra*.

XI. SURPRISED BY JOY

Lewis was already writing his autobiography *Surprised by Joy: The shape of my early life* in March 1948, and presumably had the title and the theme of 'Joy' almost from the first, although the final typescript was not ready for the publisher until March 1955. This being so, it is a curious coincidence that in 1956 he should have married a woman whose name was Joy. It was a coincidence not overlooked in Oxford at the time of his marriage where the smart thing to say was 'Do you know what's happened to C. S. Lewis? He's been surprised by Joy!'

Although she had written to him a number of 'fan' letters, Lewis did not meet Joy Davidman until September 1952 – and whatever dreams she may have entertained, marriage was far indeed from his thoughts at the time.

After some months in hospital Mrs Moore having finally died on 17 January 1951 at the age of 79, Lewis was freer than he had ever been since his undergraduate days. 'I specially need your prayers,' he wrote to Sister Penelope on 5 June, 'because I am (like the pilgrim in Bunyan) travelling across "a plain called Ease". Everything without, and many things within, are marvellously well at present.' He was in the full flush of his creative powers; Narnia was nearing completion, the 'O.H.E.L.' volume was off his hands in June 1952; he was enjoying summer holidays in Ireland with his brother, and his other friends saw more of him than at any other period.

In November 1951, for example, he paid his first visit to Roger Lancelyn Green in Cheshire on his way back to Oxford from a trip to Ireland, and together they planned a longer excursion the following year to visit some of the ruined castles of North Wales. The plan was for them to meet at Woodside (Birkenhead) and go by boat to Beaumaris in Anglesey for the night – and at the end of March 1952 Lewis was writing to Green in playful vein: 'Hearken, Little Brother, to the wisdom of Baloo. Neither you nor I will write to the Bulkeley Arms for rooms for us both, for the modern hotel keeper would then be very likely to put us both in one room without warning or remedy. But you will write for your room and I will write (today) for mine. And then, by the permission of Allah, he will think he had to do with a Mr Green of Bebington and a Mr Lewis of Oxford who have no connection.'

When they met on 9 September the weather was too bad for the sea trip, but they went by train to Bangor and on by bus to Beaumaris. Lewis insisted on keeping up the pretence that neither knew the other was to be there, and they arrived separately at the hotel, met by chance in the bar, and greeted each other with well-simulated surprise and delight.

A long time was spent in exploring the castle, which impressed Lewis greatly; and then they sat on the top of Rusticoker Tower and hatched the plot of a story in which they were the only survivors of a world-cataclysm but later found a party of children and with them founded a new civilization. The main incentive was to work out how much they could remember in the way of religion, literature, history and general knowledge to pass down to the new civilization of which the children would be the founders when they grew up and began to re-people the earth. Of course the book was never written: but they both got great enjoyment out of devising it (and continued planning it in Conway Castle the next day on their way back to Bebington).

That evening Lewis was opening a pile of letters which had accumulated while he was in Ireland and been sent in a parcel to await his arrival at Beaumaris. Among them was a curious large envelope with writing all over the back of it in red ink. Lewis held it up and said: 'I'd better tell you about this so that you'll be able to contradict any false rumours. This is from a mad woman who constantly writes, and tells people that we are engaged to be married. I now don't even open the letters.' (The following year the woman put an announcement of her wedding to Lewis in the papers and turned up at the Kilns. Lewis was not even there, and she was taken away and the persecution ceased.)

By a curious chance the woman who did eventually marry Lewis turned up at the Kilns – as an invited guest – the week after the Beaumaris visit.

Helen Joy Davidman was 37 at this time, and was already known as a poet of considerable merit; she and her husband William Gresham were recent converts to Christianity, their conversion having been in part due to Lewis's books. The Greshams had two sons, aged eight and seven at that time, but their marriage was not turning out well, and Joy had come to England to get away from the trouble and see whether some months of separation would help to heal it.

'The adult convert to Christianity is of course a characteristic figure of our age,' wrote Lewis in the foreword to her book on the Ten Commandments, *Smoke on the Mountain* (1955). 'Joy Davidman is one who comes to us from the second generation of unbelief; her parents, Jewish in blood, "rationalists" by conviction. This makes her approach extremely interesting to the reclaimed apostates of my own generation; the daring paradoxes of our youth were the stale platitudes of hers. "Life is only an electro-chemical reaction. Love, art, and altruism are only sex. The universe is only matter. Matter is only energy. I forget what I said energy is only"; thus she describes the philosophy with which she started life. How, from the very first, it failed to accommodate her actual experience, how, as a result of this discrepancy, she was for some years almost "two people", how Communism, too, broke up under the impact of realities more formidable even than itself, must be read in her own words . . . The essay describes exactly how "the universe" – indeed, something much more important than it – broke in. For of course every story of conversion is a story of a blessed defeat.'

Undoubtedly Lewis found Joy a splendid companion from the first. The vivacity and depth of her mind, the quick and logical response to argument, and the considerable breadth of literary knowledge embracing many fields in which he was deeply interested made this inevitable. They struck fire from one another and their intellectual enjoyment of each other's company was never in doubt.

Mrs Phoebe Hesketh remembered her first meeting with Lewis in June 1953 'when I and my husband took him and Joy, along with our son and Herbert Palmer, to dinner at the Eastgate. He was in a state of exhilaration, with his brain ticking over at top speed so that he turned out the wittiest of Alexandrines – to the amazement of Herbert Palmer who was incredulous of such verse off the cuff. Anyway he had us in fits of laughter, and lifted up our spirits so that we were transported beyond ourselves.'

But presently it appeared that Joy had other ideas than those of simple intellectual friendship, and Lewis took fright. Joy was no longer invited to stay at the Kilns: Lewis was even known to have hidden upstairs and pretended to be out when he saw her coming up the drive.

Obviously her marriage with William Gresham was deteriorating faster in absence than it had ever done when they were together. And after she had been away for about a year, Joy heard from him that he too had been seeking consolation elsewhere. She returned at once to America, allowed Gresham to divorce her for desertion, so that he could re-marry as he was eager to do, and she returned to England in the summer of 1954 with her two sons of whom she had complete custody. She settled in Belsize Park, London, and sent her sons David and Douglas to Dane Court, the well-known preparatory school at Pyrford in Surrey.

In 1955 Joy moved to Oxford, living in Old High Street, Headington, a mile or so from the Kilns, and was a frequent visitor once more. Chad Walsh and his wife visited Oxford that summer and ' "smelt marriage in the air", though neither of them talked of it'. But he was probably wrong – at least as far as Lewis was consciously concerned – though his autobiography was submitted to the publisher in April and published in September of that year, with the title *Surprised by Joy*: presumably the possibility of the double meaning had not yet occurred to him.

But Joy was having a profound influence on his work, notably

on a new work of fiction which was being written during 1955 and
ready in typescript for the publisher by the beginning of February
1956, with the title *Bareface*, followed a few weeks later by a
descriptive note, later revised somewhat in the volume as published: 'In one sense the author has worked on this book most of
his life, for this re-interpretation of an old story (readers need not
know which when they begin) had lived with him and pestered
him to make it ever since he was an undergraduate. Suddenly,
last Spring, the form presented itself. All came into focus: and
had drawn into it many sympathies that had found no vehicle in
earlier books – for the ugly woman, the barbarous idolater, the
humane sceptic, and (above all) the friends and lovers of those
who have a vocation or even a faith.'

The publisher objected to the title and warned Lewis, half
jokingly, that it might be mistaken for a Western. 'I don't see why
people (I mean, people who are interested in what I do next)
would be deterred from buying it if they *did* think it a Western,'
replied Lewis on 16 February. 'Actually, I think the title cryptic
enough to be intriguing. (The point, of course, is that Orual after
going literally bareface in her youth, is made really and spiritually
bareface, to herself and to all the dead, at the end.)'

But on 29 February he wrote, 'One other possible title has
occurred to me: *Till We Have Faces*. (My heroine says in one
passage "How can the gods meet us face to face till we have
faces?") I must, however, warn you that no one on whom I've
tried it thinks it an improvement on *Bareface*.' The second title
was finally used, with Lewis's full approval, though he insisted
that '*Bareface* was better *per se*'.

As Lewis said, the idea of re-telling the story of Cupid and
Psyche from Apulcius with a new twist had been an early one
which he had never managed to achieve. In his diary for 9 September 1923 he wrote: 'My head was very full of my old idea of a
poem on my own version of the Cupid and Psyche story in which
Psyche's sister would not be jealous, but unable to see anything
but moors when Psyche showed her the Palace. I have tried it
twice before, once in couplet and once in ballad form.' The first

of these may have been the idea of 'a masque or play of Psyche and Caspian', which he was trying to work out during a walk by Shotover on 23 November 1922; of the second about 70 lines survive, which show that Caspian was Psyche's sister, 'the child of the first marriage of the King', who had brought up Psyche (and her brother Jardis – Lewis's addition to the legend) since they were babies.

The fragment, so far as it goes, parallels the earlier part of the legend as adapted in *Till We Have Faces*: it is not just the anger of Venus because Psyche is being worshipped as a goddess instead of her, that causes the people to sacrifice her,

> . . . but summer rains
> Withheld and harvest withering on the plains.
> The streams were low, and in the starving tribe
> Ran murmurs that of old a dearer bribe
> Had charmed the rain. Forgotten customs then
> Stirred in their sleep below the hearts of men
> Thrusting up evil heads.

And when Psyche has been left in chains on the hillside,

> When fear had done his worst in the girl's heart
> That some strange helper came and took her part . . .

From the fragment it is also possible that Jardis was to have some vision of the truth which he concealed under the usual story of the jealous sisters, which story, says Lewis, is

> . . . like the work of some poetic youth,
> Angry, and far too certain of the truth,
> Mad from the gleams of vision that claim to find
> Bye ways to something missed by all mankind.
> He thinks that only envy or dull eyes
> Keep all men from believing in the prize
> He holds in secret. In revenge he drew
> – For portrait of us all – the sisters two,
> Misunderstanding them . . .

But the fragment breaks off after the proemion and half a dozen lines (in two versions) of the beginning of the actual narrative, and it is almost certain that no more was written.

When the form came to him at length and he began writing *Till We Have Faces*, Lewis combined Caspian and Jardis into one person, Psyche's elder sister Orual (the sisters have no names in Apuleius – the only classical authority for the story) who is in a sense both man and woman: almost the personification of Filia and Eros – friendship and sexual love – about which Lewis was already beginning to think deeply as they grew in his understanding towards their place in *The Four Loves*.

There is a great deal of Joy Davidman in the character of Orual – though how consciously Lewis used her is uncertain; and, of course, he only *used* her, as a creative writer does: he did not draw a portrait of her. Orual's spiritual journey from Ungit-worship through apostasy and by way of the Platonism taught by the Fox, to her final surrender to God (almost a fore-shadowing of Christ, one of the 'good dreams' which Lewis felt had been permitted from time to time in the pagan world) parallels Joy's pilgrimage from her Jewish background by way of atheism and Communism, until her conversion to Christianity. There is also in a sense the physical Joy, the middle-aged and not particularly good-looking woman whom Lewis was able to treat for a long time almost as one of his men friends: just as Bardia treats Orual; but although Orual accepts and reciprocates this kind of love – Filia – another kind – Eros – is present on her side though not on his.

The theme of friendship with the unattractive woman was explored in *Till We Have Faces*, but not exhausted. It merged into the theme of the beautiful woman married for love in the ordinary sense, and then the sudden question: if we jump forward ten years or so – the opposite problem to that of *Mary Rose* – and find her suddenly middle-aged, no longer physically attractive, does love survive? And then, is the love of friendship and affection stronger, better even, than physical love?

Lewis was asking this question before *Till We Have Faces* was even published. On 28 May 1956 Green travelled with him from Oxford to Cambridge on the slow through-train – the 'Cantab Crawler' as they nicknamed it – and noted that during the three-hour journey they had a 'delightful talk, mainly on Classical

Myths, re a story he has written, and one he plans to write about Helen after Troy, and about my *Helen of Sparta* which he suggests re-naming *Mystery at Mycenae*'. The story of Helen became the fragment published in *Of Other Worlds* as 'After Ten Years' (Lewis gave it no name). This he began shortly afterwards, but abandoned until 1960 directly after his visit to Greece. On 3 May of that year Green, again at Cambridge, spent 'all evening until midnight with Jack – mainly talking about the story he's writing of which he read me all that he had done – about Helen and Menelaus, beginning with Menelaus in the Horse (he'd written the first few pages some time ago and read it to me)'. The story got hardly any further, mainly because Joy's death the following month seemed to cut off his creative ability; but also because he was becoming less and less sure of the story's course. One of the odd little group of Greek books which Orual was able to secure in Glome was 'a poem in honour of Helen by Hesias Stesichorus' and, although neither his *Helen* nor his *Palinode* have survived, the theme is well known: that Helen remained in Egypt while her double or *eidolon* or *ka* went to Troy with Paris and caused the disastrous war – and that Menelaus found the real Helen in Egypt on his way home, still innocent and beautiful (as in Euripides' play *Helen*) – the legend which Rider Haggard and Andrew Lang had already adapted in *The World's Desire* which had been an early favourite of Lewis's.

When Lewis began *After Ten Years* the idea seems to have been that, after Menelaus had found Helen at the fall of Troy – Helen grown old and commonplace and an utter disappointment after his dreams of ten years – he was to find her young and beautiful as before the war, when he reached Egypt on the way home; and there make his choice between the two, the elderly, tired Helen being the real woman. By the end of August 1960 Lewis had written one more chapter, a trial section from the Egyptian portion of the book: but he was not decided what the *eidolon* was to be:

'Daughter of Leda, come forth,' said the old man.
And at once it came. Out of the darkness of the doorway

There the fragment breaks off in mid-sentence – and there Lewis's invention or inspiration failed him – or Joy's death had shown him that he was working in the wrong direction, but did not reveal what the solution should be.

But this was far in the future when, in the full flush of inspiration, he wrote *Till We Have Faces*, and dedicated it to Joy Davidman in 1956: it was certainly his most unexpected book, and his greatest *tour de force*; to many readers, and probably to himself, his best work of fiction (even if *Perelandra* remained his favourite) – and his nearest approach to failure with his reading public since *Dymer*. 'The great disappointment of his career has been the reception in England of *Till We Have Faces* – in America it's been received rather better,' wrote Jane Gaskell of an interview with Lewis published in *Books and Bookmen* in November 1958.

One reason for its cool reception, even among those who bought Lewis's other books by the hundred thousand, is probably that (except perhaps in the visions of the last few chapters) *Till We Have Faces* is utterly unlike anything Lewis ever wrote. One looks again and again for his style, his mode of argument, his outlook; but broadly speaking one looks in vain. For he has succeeded to an amazing degree in becoming someone else, Orual, while he wrote – and at the first reading this is curiously off-putting. But it is a book that grows on the reader at each reading, and at each reading the mythic quality has a deeper and deeper effect.

It is natural that such a book should have proved peculiarly tempting to those who would analyse and allegorize and interpret; and indeed researchers of this kind were busy on it immediately, particularly in America.

One of the first of these was Professor Clyde S. Kilby. Lewis replied to his interpretation in a letter dated 10 February 1957, five months after the book's publication, and though it is included in the published *Letters* (pp. 273–4), it is of so much importance that it must be reprinted here:

An author doesn't necessarily understand the meaning of his own story better than anyone else, so I give my account of *Till We Have Faces* simply for what it is worth. The 'levels' I am conscious of are these.

(1) A work of (supposed) historical imagination. A guess at what it might have been like in a little barbarous state on the borders of the Hellenistic world of Greek culture, just beginning to affect it. Hence the change from the old priest (of a very normal fertility mother-goddess) to Arnom; Stoic allegorizations of the myths standing to the original cult rather as Modernism to Christianity (but this is a parallel, not an allegory). Much that you take as allegory was intended solely as realistic detail. The wagon men are nomads from the steppes. The children made mud pies not for symbolic purposes but because children do. The Pillar Room is simply a room. The Fox is such an educated Greek slave as you might find at a barbarous court – and so on.

(2) Psyche is an instance of the *anima naturaliter Christiana* making the best of the Pagan religion she is brought up in and thus being guided (but always 'under the cloud', always in terms of her own imagination or that of her people) towards the true God. She is in some ways like Christ because every good man or woman is like Christ. What else could they be like? But of course my interest is primarily in Orual.

(3) Orual is (not a symbol) but an instance, a 'case' of human affection in its natural condition, true, tender, suffering, but in the long run tyrannically possessive and ready to turn to hatred when the beloved ceases to be its possession. What such love particularly cannot stand is to see the beloved passing into a sphere where it cannot follow. All this I hoped would stand as a mere story in its own right. But –

(4) Of course I had always in mind its close parallel to what is probably happening at this moment in at least five families in your home town. Someone becomes a Christian, or in a family nominally Christian already, does something like becoming a missionary or entering a religious order. The others suffer a sense of outrage. What they love is being taken from them. The boy must be mad. And the conceit of him! Or: is there something in it after all? Let's hope it is only a phase! If only he had listened to his natural advisers. Oh come back, come back, be sensible, be the dear son we used to know! Now I, as a Christian, have a good deal of sympathy with those jealous, suffering, puzzled people (for they do suffer, and out of their suffering much of the bitterness against religion arises). I believe the thing is common. There is very nearly a touch of it in Luke II. 38, 'son, *why hast thou* so dealt with us?' And is the reply easy for a loving heart to bear?

Luke
2:38

This letter shows how far Lewis was on his way to the achievement of his book on *The Four Loves* of which the first version (originally given as recorded lectures broadcast in America) was written in 1958. All four, Affection, Friendship, Eros, and at least the foreshadowing of Charity, are explored in Orual: level 4 in the letter is closely paralleled on pages 59–60 of *The Four Loves*, and many passages in the novel foreshadow the more analytical treatment of the study. And finally, the choice offered on page 80 of *The Four Loves* is that which Menelaus was to face in *After Ten Years*.

Lewis in fact learnt of love as he learnt to love. He knew all too much of Affection run riot from his years with Mrs Moore. He knew and valued Friendship as it is valued and known by all too few in the present age. Eros in its wilder, saltier forms he had known in youth, he had fought against with quiet acceptance since his conversion – even to the point of abstaining from certain foods because of their aphrodisiac qualities; Eros in a deeper, gentler form was already beginning imperceptibly to draw him towards Joy. Charity he had sought – and found it more nearly perhaps than the majority of us.

Before *The Four Loves* grew into being he was finishing his *Reflections on the Psalms* (1958) which he had already been considering ten years earlier. And in this too Joy Davidman, with her Jewish background, was proving a help and an inspiration.

The progress of the relationship between Lewis and Joy was and remains, as it should be, their own secret. To begin with he had accepted her as a friend. 'In a profession (like my own) where men and women work side by side, or in the mission field, or among authors and artists, such Friendship is common,' he wrote in *The Four Loves*. 'To be sure, what is offered as Friendship on one side may be mistaken for Eros on the other, with painful and embarrassing results. Or what begins as Friendship in both may become also Eros.' Somehow the state of 'while the one eludes must the other pursue' came to an end: Joy ceased to pursue and Lewis to elude. Joy also was ill, and becoming more seriously so; at first it was thought to be acute rheumatism, but early in 1957 it was diagnosed as cancer of the bone.

Meanwhile, early in 1956 the Home Office refused to renew Joy's permit to remain in Great Britain, no reason being given. She was in desperate straits, with two boys at school, and only one means to avoid extradition for herself and her sons. Lewis took the only course possible to secure her right to remain, by marrying her at the Oxford registry office on 23 April 1956 and thus giving her, and with her his two step-sons, British nationality.

This, as two days later he told Green (whom he was now treating as his future biographer), was a pure matter of friendship and expediency. A registry office wedding was simply a legal form and had nothing to do with marriage. And he caused his solicitor friend Owen Barfield to draw out a document stating the reasons for which he was entering into the civil contract.

Joy became rapidly worse, and on 5 February 1957 he was writing to Green 'my wife lies ill – indeed almost certainly dying. Pray for us.' On 21 March 1957 a bedside marriage to a dying woman was celebrated in the Churchill Hospital at Oxford by the Reverend Peter Bide. Again this ceremony was performed partly because Joy did not want to die in hospital, and Lewis could not bring her to the Kilns unless he was married to her in the sight of God as well as in the sight of man.

In May he wrote, 'Joy is home, only because hospital can do no more for her – completely bedridden. But thank God, no pain, sleeping well, and often in good spirits.' There was still no question but that she was dying without any hope of recovery.

And then began what Lewis described as the nearest thing to a miracle he had ever experienced. When Green met Joy for the first time, on 21 June 1957, she was in bed in the sitting-room, with a day and night nurse in attendance. On 24 September he and his wife, taking their elder son to Dane Court for his first term, called at the Kilns to pick up Douglas Gresham, and found Joy up, but in an invalid chair. On 10 December Lewis wrote, 'Joy is now walking: with a stick and a limp, but we never dreamed of getting so far.' By 27 March 1958 when Green dined at the Kilns he found Joy 'up and about, miraculous as it seems'. And on 26 July, 'Jack and Joy turned up to see Douglas' at the end of term display and prize-giving at Dane Court.

'My case is definitely arrested for the time being – I may be alright for three or four years,' Joy had written to Chad Walsh on 6 June 1957. 'There's a faint hope [the bone] may knit enough to let me hobble around a little in a caliper. . . . Jack and I are managing to be surprisingly happy considering the circumstances; you'd think we were a honeymoon couple in our early twenties, rather than our middle-aged selves. . . . I never before had the experience of keeping a fairly large household staff happy – I feel quite the lady of the manor! For ten weeks we had, in addition to the gardener, housekeeper, and daily woman, two nurses. . . .'

As soon as Joy was on her feet, with no immediate fear of a relapse, she set about putting the Kilns to rights and bringing comfort into what had become a rather uncomfortable abode. 'When Mrs Lewis arrived, it hadn't been decorated for thirty years,' Jane Gaskell learnt. 'We were afraid to move the bookcases in case the walls fell down. Jack's friends called it "The Midden" . . .' ' "The Kilns" is now a real home,' Joy wrote to Green in May 1958, 'with paint on the walls, ceilings properly repaired, clean sheets on the beds – we can receive and put up several guests. . . . I've got a fence round the woods and all the trespassers chased away; I shoot a starting pistol at them and they run like anything! We'd love a visit.'

In August of the same year Lewis wrote to another friend, Mrs Watt: 'We had a holiday – you might call it a belated honeymoon – in Ireland and were lucky enough to get that perfect fortnight in July. We visited Louth, Down, and Donegal, and returned drunk with blue mountains, yellow beaches, dark fuchsia, breaking waves, braying donkeys, peat-smell, and the heather just beginning to bloom. We flew to Ireland, for though both of us would prefer ship to plane, her bones and even mine could not risk a sudden lurch. It was the first flight either of us had ever experienced, and we found it – after our initial moment of terror – enchanting. The cloud-scape seen from above is a new world of beauty – and then the rifts in the clouds through which one sees "a glimpse of that dark world where I was born" . . .'

This brief halcyon period was perhaps the happiest time of Lewis's life. The male friendships in which he had always delighted remained unimpaired; he had received from Cambridge the Chair which his own university had failed to award to him, and was happier in Magdalene than he had been of late at Magdalen, finding the smaller Cambridge college much closer to the Oxford of his youth; in term-time he had both the Combination Room and the frequent visits of older friends who travelled to his new university with him on a Monday afternoon following the gathering at the 'Bird and Baby' to spend the evening with him; and he had his own home at the Kilns for most weekends in term-time and throughout the vacations, with a wife who as friend was able and eager to meet him and any friend of his on equal terms as if she too were an Inkling, but was also fast becoming the lover whom he had failed to find.

'I never expected to have, in my sixties, the happiness that passed me by in my twenties,' he said to Nevill Coghill, looking at Joy across the grassy quadrangle when he had brought her to lunch with him in Merton in the summer of 1958.

It was a delight to visit the Kilns in 1958 and 1959 and see the sheer happiness and contentment that Lewis was finding in his brief St Martin's summer: the solicitude for his wife, the simple delight in her company, the argument, badinage and rollicking fun that betokened the perfect relationship. Lewis the Family Man was a role he accepted with kindly amusement – 'see how I have dwindled into a husband!' he quoted with delight; and there was a merry twinkle in his eye when he and Joy turned up to the plays and prize-givings at Dane Court, or discussed the achievements and short-comings of the young with other parents.

It could not last. Both knew that it was not likely to last. 'The blow has fallen,' he wrote to Chad Walsh on 21 October 1959. 'Joy's last X-ray check revealed that cancer has returned in several parts of the skeleton.' And to Green a month later: 'This last check is the only one we approached without dread – her health seemed so complete. It is like being recaptured by the Giant when you have passed every gate and are almost out of sight of his castle. Whether a second miracle will be vouchsafed us, or, if not, when the sentence will be inflicted, remains uncertain. It is quite possible she may be able to do the Greek trip next spring. Pray for us.'

To visit Greece was Joy's great ambition. Lewis professed to take no interest in foreign travel, had never been outside the British Isles, except to France as a boy and during the First World War, and declared that to see the site of a great story or historical event would detract rather than add to his pleasure in it. But he was eager to take Joy if it were possible, and when Green, who had been there on a 'Wings' tour in April 1959, offered to make all arrangements for a similar tour in April 1960, he jumped at the chance.

With the return of Joy's cancer the trip became more and more risky and problematical. But, although experiencing a slowly increasing amount of pain, she professed herself willing and eager to go, if he would take the risk. And when the time came Lewis took it gladly for her sake, both of them hiding from the Greens how desperate her condition was, though of course they realized that Joy was suffering considerably, and that a cure was no longer probable.

And now Roger Lancelyn Green retells the story of that trip to Greece, from his diary kept at the time, and from his recollections of one of the most memorable experiences of his life.

'*Sunday 3 April 1960.* June and I to London Air Port with "Wings" Party (about 30 altogether) where we found Jack and Joy Lewis waiting for us, with Douglas to see us off, having driven there directly from Oxford. A very rough flight; our little Viking (Hunter Clan) had to make an extra landing at Naples, between those at Lyon and Brindisi. The four of us made merry on Chianti in large quantities while the 'plane was refuelling. We arrived very late at Athens, after midnight and unfortunately with a long walk from the 'plane to the Airport buildings, which was rather painful for Joy. We immediately learnt the Greek for a Wheel-chair – which we shall demand in future. We drove straight to the Hotel Cosmopolis, near Omonia Square.

'*Monday 4 April.* A cloudy morning. Jack and Joy did not accompany the party to Marathon. But they joined us for lunch at the "Hellenikon", and on the afternoon tour of Athens. Joy was able to get right up to the Acropolis, where she and Jack found a seat on the steps of the Propylaea and sat drinking in the beauty of the Parthenon and Erechtheum – columns of honey gold and old ivory against the perfect blue sky, with an occasional white cloud. We met again for dinner at the "Hellenikon", Joy having gone back to the hotel to rest, while June and I explored the Agora and Plaka on foot.

'*Tuesday 5 April.* All of us made an early start by coach. We went via Eleusis and Megara without stopping, to the Corinth Canal where we paused for twenty minutes for drinks. Then on into Argolis: poor weather and some rain. But when we got to Mycenae we had ideal weather: a great lowering dark cloud over the citadel, but blue sky beyond. Jack was immensely impressed by the entrance between the towering walls of Cyclopean masonry and through the Lion Gate: I shall never forget the way he paused suddenly and exclaimed: "My God! The Curse is still here," in a voice hushed between awe and amazement.

'Jack and Joy did not get further than the Grave Circle. But they came to the Treasury of Atreus, the most impressive of all Mycenaean buildings, and we had a merry lunch at "La Belle Helene", the old guest house which was still more or less as when Schliemann had stayed there, and were introduced to the genuine Wine of Nemea known as "Lion's Blood". The drive back to Athens took us by way of Old Corinth.

'*Wednesday 6 April.* This was the most memorable day on the whole tour, and one which Jack said afterwards was among the supreme days of his life – the last of the great days of perfect happiness. The four of us set out on a private excursion in a car with a driver who had just a few words of English. We went via Daphni, where we paused to see the little Byzantine church and the ruins of the temple of Apollo. Then on the Thebes road as far as the pass over Mount Cithairon where we stopped at a taverna for ouzo. After June and I had climbed up to see the Classical ruins of Eleutherai Castle, we drove down to the head of the Gulf of Corinth, a superbly lovely drive down and down through vine-yards, and richly scented pine woods with many of the trees tapped for resin, and through olive groves shining silver in the sunlight to the tiny village of Aegosthena, with the ruins of another Classical castle. After exploring the ruins we settled down at the one tiny taverna right on the shore, with Cithairon towering up on one side and the mountains behind Megara on the other, for a marvellous meal. To accompany our pre-luncheon ouzo we had pickled octopus, and the meal itself began with fried red mullets which our host brought to us still wet from the sea before cooking; and after these fried squid, the tenderest I have ever found in Greece, followed by ewe's milk cheese and fresh oranges. And with this came measure after measure of retsina freshly drawn from the great cask in the half-cellar at the back of the taverna.

'We sat there for several hours, the usual vivid conversation lapsing into contented silence broken only by the gentle lapping of the waves, the pervading hum of bees and the call of cicadas: the misty blue of the Gulf and the miraculously clear light of Greece working a charm of absolute contentment. It was with an effort that we tore ourselves away from Aegosthena and went back towards Athens and then up into the valleys and foothills of the Parnon range trying to reach the castle of Phyle. When the road gave out, June and I scrambled uphill and finally saw the castle far away on its hilltop. Then we rejoined the Lewises and drove back to Athens in the soft evening light just in time for dinner – "after a supreme day".

'*Thursday 7 April.* Some of us went to the National Museum in the morning, and then after lunch we flew to the Island of Rhodes and settled in at the comfortable Hotel Thermai, where June and I enjoyed the "usual hilarious dinner with Jack and Joy, sampling several new Cretan wines."

'*Friday 8 April.* In the morning we went on an excursion round the Old City, while the Lewises did a little exploring on their own. In the afternoon we all went to Kamiros, an attractive site on a hillside looking towards Turkey, which combined Mycenaean, Classical, Hellenistic and Roman ruins.

'*Saturday 9 April.* All day excursion to Lindos. Jack and Joy did not climb up to the Citadel, but had a pleasant time wandering round the little Greek village still mostly unspoilt by tourism.

A very pleasant evening, the four of us drinking ouzo and having several stimulating arguments. Splendid verbal sparring between Jack and Joy, each enjoying it to the full: we could barely keep up with them.

'*Sunday 10 April*. A quiet morning wandering by the harbour, and attending part of an Easter service in the Orthodox Cathedral. After lunch the whole party flew to Herakleon (late Candia) in Crete. A comfortable hotel, but no food supplied. We set out for dinner at the scheduled restaurant, only to find that it was being re-built and we had a mile walk to a terrible tourist resort called "The Glass House" on the edge of the harbour. We were kept waiting hours for a very indifferent meal, and the band blared away deafeningly. Joy finally began flicking bread-pellets at the nearest musician, and the four of us whiled away the time by writing alternate lines of the following doggerel:

[Jack]	A pub-crawl through the glittering isles of Greece,
[Joy]	I wish it left my ears a moment's peace!
[June]	If once the crashing Cretans ceased to bore,
[Roger]	The drums of England would resist no more.
[Jack]	No more they *can* resist. For mine are broken!
[Roger]	To this Curates' shields were but a token,
[June]	*Our* cries in silence still above the noise –
[Joy]	He has been hit by a good shot of Joy's!
[Jack]	What aim! What strength! What purpose and what poise!

'*Monday 11 April*. An excursion to Knossos all morning. Jack and Joy got only to the entrance to the Palace of Minos whence a good view of the whole could be obtained. In the afternoon they hired a car for the excursion to Mallia, as the step of the coach was so high that Joy had hurt herself getting up and down in the morning. Mallia being all on the level they were both able to enjoy it fully. In the evening we refused to go to "The Glass House" and went off, the four of us, to the nearby "Irakleon Club" – the only decent eating place – where we had dolmades, squid, globe artichokes and plenty of Minos wine: we had a very happy time.

'*Tuesday 12 April*. All day excursion across the island to

Gortyna, Phaistos and Agia Triada. The Lewises went by car with a French couple from the hotel who wanted to share one. At lunch on a balcony overlooking the Phaistos ruins we all sat at a big table: Minos wine "off the wood" flowed in abundance, and Jack was the life and soul of the party, keeping "the table in a roar". We stopped again at Gortyna on the way back, and I had the drinks waiting for Jack and Joy by the time the party had thought of ordering theirs. We'd realized for some time that Joy was often in pain, and alcohol was the best alleviation: so I had become adept at diving into the nearest taverna, ordering "tessera ouzo", and having them ready at a convenient table by the time June had helped Jack and Joy out of coach or car and brought them in.

'The orange harvest was in progress, and whenever the coach or car got held up the Cretans would come to welcome us and give us beautiful fresh oranges.

'*Wednesday 13 April.* We had a splendidly smooth flight to Pisa, with views of Melos and much of the Peloponnese as we flew over it fairly low. Touched down at Brindisi, where the Chianti was far from good. In Pisa, June and I left the party and went off to stay with relations at Cesanello.

'*Thursday 14 April.* We rejoined the Lewises for lunch at "Hotel Nettuno", and flew back to London in the afternoon. They had a car waiting for them, and my last sight of Joy was of Jack wheeling her briskly in an invalid chair towards the waiting car.'

There was no doubt of the success of the trip. 'Greece was wonderful,' wrote Lewis to Jocelyn Gibb on 9 May 1960. 'We badly need a word meaning "the-exact-opposite-of-a-disappointment". *Appointment* won't do!'

And on 23 May he wrote to Chad Walsh: 'It looked very doubtful if Joy and I would be able to do our trip to Greece, but we did. From one point of view it was madness, but neither of us regrets it. She performed prodigies of strength, limping to the top of the Acropolis and up through the Lion Gate of Mycenae and all about the medieval city of Rhodes (Rhodes is simply the Earthly

Paradise). It was as if she were divinely supported. She came back in a *nunc dimittis* frame of mind, having realized, beyond hope, her greatest, lifelong, this-worldly desire. There was a heavy price to pay in increased lameness and leg-pains: not that her exertions had or could have any effect on the course of the cancer, but that the muscles etc., had been overtaxed. Since then there has been a recrudescence of the original growth in the right breast which started the whole trouble. It had to be removed last Friday – or, as she characteristically put it, she was "made an Amazon". This operation went through, thank God, with greater ease than we had dared to hope. . . .

'I had some ado to prevent Joy (and myself) from relapsing into Paganism in Attica! At Daphni it was hard not to pray to Apollo the Healer. But somehow one didn't feel it would have been very wrong – would have only been addressing Christ *sub specie Apollinis*. We witnessed a beautiful Christian village ceremony in Rhodes and hardly felt a discrepancy. Greek priests impress one very favourably at sight – much more so than most Protestant or R.C. clergy. And the peasants all *refuse* tips.'

Joy's decline was slow and peaceful, and both she and Lewis carried on their lives as if her death were likely to be years rather than months away. Lewis was in excellent spirits at a gathering at the 'Bird and Baby' on 25 April, and was still writing *After Ten Years* when Green stayed with him at Magdalene on 3 May.

But on 15 July he wrote to his American friend Mrs Gebbert: 'Alas, you will never send anything along "for the three of us" again, for my dear Joy is dead. Until within ten days of the end we hoped, although noticing her increasing weakness, that she was going to hold her own, but it was not to be. Last week she had been complaining of muscular pains in her shoulders, but by Monday 11th seemed much better, and on Tuesday, though keeping her bed, said she felt a great improvement; on that day she was in good spirits, did her crossword puzzle with me, and in the evening played a game of Scrabble. At quarter past six on Wednesday [13 July 1960] morning my brother, who slept over her, was wakened by her screaming and ran down to her. I got the doctor who fortunately was at home, and he arrived before seven and gave her a heavy shot. At half past one I took her into hospital in an ambulance. She was conscious for the short remainder of her life, and in very little pain, thanks to drugs; and died peacefully in my company about 10.15 the same night.'

'Two of the last things she said were "You have made me happy" and "I am at peace with God",' he told Chad Walsh – and the second is recorded on the last page of *A Grief Observed*, where also he recalled 'How long, how tranquilly, how nourishingly, we talked together that last night.'

With whatever thoughts Lewis had entered into marriage with Joy Davidman, her loss, however much expected, when it came was shattering. The whole experience is told with almost unbearable poignancy in *A Grief Observed*, a collection of almost daily thoughts and attempts at self-analysis jotted down during the first few months after her death, and published over the pseudonym of N. W. Clerk in 1961. The possibility of its publication was mentioned under pledge of secrecy to Green, who stayed at the Kilns for several days at the beginning of September 1960; but when it came out, Lewis does not seem to have sent copies to friends, and never alluded to it.

Any idea that Lewis could take up his bachelor life again where he left off is totally annihilated by the confessions in this book. He had indeed been surprised by Joy – surprised into an absolute love and a complete marriage, the overwhelming fulfilment of an intense nature long unsatisfied, a tremendous capacity for love long channelled into strong friendship and immense literary creativeness.

'For those few years H. [Joy's first name was Helen] and I feasted on love; every mode of it – solemn and merry, romantic and realistic, sometimes as dramatic as a thunderstorm, sometimes as comfortable and unemphatic as putting on your soft slippers. Her mind was lithe and quick and muscular as a leopard. Passion, tenderness and pain were all equally unable to disarm it. It scented the first whiff of cant or slush; then sprang and knocked you over before you knew what was happening. How many bubbles of mine she has pricked! . . . The most precious gift that marriage gave me was this constant impact of something very close and intimate yet all the time unmistakably other, resilient – in a word, real . . . No cranny of heart or body remained unsatisfied.'

XII. 'THE TERM IS OVER'

In following Lewis from his first meeting with Joy Davidman to their marriage, the bright brief summer of supreme and unexpected happiness that followed it, and her death in 1960, we have departed from strict chronology and omitted much of importance that was happening to him in his more public and academic life.

The usual round of tutorials, lectures and faculty meetings continued at Oxford: in an attenuated state during the war, and for several years after it in a state of suspended animation as ex-servicemen returned to finish their pre-war courses, and veterans in their late twenties rubbed shoulders with schoolboys ten years their juniors.

When the 'bulge' grew slimmer Oxford began to consider what changes the unique conditions of the last dozen years had brought about or made essential. The type of undergraduate was altering more speedily and more noticeably than anything else as Government-financed education threw open the universities to all, and the changing background turned 'the young gentlemen' into 'the students' – and these demanded more and more to be supplied with a training rather than an education, to leave armed with certificates rather than culture.

The older dons found it hard to adapt to the new conditions – and sometimes hard to accept the new and often revolutionary outlook of the young dons who were fast outnumbering them as the swelling numbers of students demanded an unprecedented number of new appointments to, or on the fringes of, the Senior Common Rooms and the Combination Rooms.

Lewis, who was over fifty when the great change began to be evident, found it hard to accept much of what was happening;

hard to see the Oxford which he had known and loved changing and passing away; hardest to feel that the old values with which he felt secure were being scrapped for new ones in which he could feel little confidence.

Outside Oxford he was still a best-selling author of world-wide reputation, the accepted 'Apostle to the Skeptics' of Chad Walsh's apt description, the famous Christian apologist and author of *The Screwtape Letters*. And if the next decade was to witness some lessening of this fame, it was to see it replaced and even surpassed by the unexpected achievement of the seven *Chronicles of Narnia*.

But outside fame has often been known to breed inside mistrust at Oxford. Although still the most popular lecturer, Lewis was regarded with some suspicion or even antipathy by many Senior Members. In 1945 Tolkien had been elected to the Merton Professorship of English Language and Literature in succession to H. C. K. Wyld; in 1947 Lewis was passed over for the Merton Chair of English Literature on David Nichol Smith's retirement, and F. P. Wilson was brought back to Oxford to fill it. In 1951 in an election open to all Senior Members, whether in residence or not, Lewis was defeated by nineteen votes for the Professorship of Poetry, which went to Cecil Day-Lewis – the third candidate, Edmund Blunden, standing down rather than risk letting C. S. Lewis get the Chair.

Not long after this certain alterations were made to the syllabus of the English School which, Lewis felt, were the thin end of the wedge that would split off medieval and Renaissance studies into a mere shaving on the solid core of 'modern literature' for the inclusion of which the younger generation was beginning to campaign with ruthless vigour. Green remembers meeting him later in the day after the meeting at which the first steps had been taken in this direction, and how upset he was by what had happened and was, he felt sure, bound to follow. 'Even Tolkien didn't understand what it means!' he exclaimed. 'He at least should have supported me!'

Disillusioned and disappointed with the English faculty at

Oxford, Lewis felt that there would no longer be any disloyalty in leaving the university which had been the centre of his life for so long. And apparently others realized this too and – since a prophet is not without honour save in his own country – acted upon it and took steps to do for one of her greatest sons what Oxford had failed to do.

On 6 June 1954 Lewis wrote to Dr Banner: 'I'm on the eve of a great adventure, having accepted the new Chair of Medieval and Renaissance English at Cambridge. I'm already half frightened of what I have done; but twenty-nine years of pupils' essays is enough, bless 'em. There have been many nice people: even nice essays. . . .' And on 30 July he amplified this to Sister Penelope at Wantage: 'Yes, I've been made Professor of Medieval and Renaissance English at Cambridge. The scope of the Chair (a new one) suits me exactly. But it won't be as big a change as you might think. I shall still live in Oxford in the Vac. and on weekends in the term. My address will be Magdalene, so I remain under the same patroness. This is nice because it saves "Admin." re-adjustments in Heaven; also I can't help feeling that the dear lady understands my constitution better than a stranger would. . . .'

'I have exchanged the impenitent for the penitent Magdalen,' was how Lewis described the change to Nevill Coghill. Realizing what they had lost, penitent Oxford tried to get him back in 1957 when F. P. Wilson retired from the Merton Professorship, but Lewis remained faithful to his new university – and had indeed made one of the happiest decisions of his career when agreeing to go to 'the other place' in 1954.

The change was happy both as far as university and college were concerned. The Chair had been founded with Lewis in view as its first occupant, and all difficulties were smoothed out before him to make his acceptance wholehearted – particularly, he could continue to live at the Kilns during vacation and return there for most weekends during term. The status of professor freed him from any further tutorial duties, and the scope of his Chair allowed him to lecture on all those branches of literature nearest to his heart. Cambridge received the final versions of the 'Prolegomena to Medieval and Renaissance Literature' before their ultimate transference to *The Discarded Image* in 1963; lectures on Spenser which he did not live to make into a book, though Dr Alastair Fowler has since done so very cleverly from the original lecture notes, as *Spenser's Images of Life* (1967); and a new series of lectures which formed the basis for his *Studies in Words* (1960) which was to have been followed by a second volume of which only three chapters or lectures were written, now incorporated in the second edition (1967) of the original work.

These books and the stimulating *Experiment in Criticism* (1961), the full flowering of the thought which had been seeded in the talk on 'The Kappa Element in Romance' and budded as 'On Stories', represent Lewis's more academic publications during the Cambridge years. But he had left Oxford with a memorial of his years there, which was also a bridge to his new university: Volume III of *The Oxford History of English Literature – English Literature in the Sixteenth Century, Excluding Drama*, published in 1954, which was based on his Clark Lectures at Trinity College, Cambridge, in 1944.

During the ten years or more during which Lewis was preparing and writing this his most onerous academic labour, it had inevitably become rather more of a chore than a pleasure as the work drew to a close. It was overlapping the Narnian books, and keeping him from other schemes that by now were seeming more worthwhile, and he confided to Green that he was longing for the day when he would be able to turn away from 'this critical nonsense and write something really worthwhile – theology and fantasy'.

The main body of the book was well out of the way by 1952, but in July 1953 he was writing to Green about another proposed trip to North Wales in search of castles. 'Look: I think I must abandon the idea of an expedition on my way back from Ireland, for *this* year. It is becoming clear that I shan't finish the proofs and horrible bibliography of my OHEL volume before we sail on Aug. 11th. That being so, every day between our return and the beginning of Michaelmas Term becomes precious as gold: for if the job once drags on into another term, I don't know what will become of me.'

Whether or not there was any cause and effect, the book did not meet with anything like as much approval as *The Allegory of Love* or even *Preface to 'Paradise Lost'*. 'The merits of this book are very great indeed', Helen Gardner summed up in her British Academy obituary pamphlet. 'It is, to begin with, a genuine literary history. It is perfectly apparent which poets and which poems Lewis thinks "the best", and the book exemplifies again and again his gift for summing up the peculiar virtues of a work, and his genius for the brief, pregnant quotation that gives the quiddity of a writer. But he respected the nature of his commission and attempted to provide a continuous narrative history of literature in the century. The volume satisfies his own criterion of a good literary history: it tells us what works exist and puts them in their setting. The book is also brilliantly written, compulsively readable, and constantly illuminated by sentences that are as true as they are witty. Who else could have written a literary history that continually arouses delighted laughter! There is hardly a page that does not stimulate and provoke thought.'

However, Dame Helen goes on: 'But the book is marred throughout by an insistent polemical purpose, expressed in the title of its first chapter "New Learning and New Ignorance". This extraordinary chapter, in which eight pages are devoted to "magic" and only two to "education", is devoted to proving by skilfully selected quotation and a complete refusal of imaginative sympathy that Humanism was inhumane and that the Humanists, grudgingly thanked for their labours in the recovery and editing of ancient texts, otherwise did immense harm', which with other peccadilloes less monstrous, show 'how out of touch Lewis was with contemporary scholarship in his own field.'

Nonetheless, as W. W. Robson in a study of Lewis in the *Cambridge Quarterly* (Summer 1966) which can hardly be described as eulogistic picks out this very chapter as an example of Lewis at his best, Dame Helen's criticism may be no more than a

personal reaction dictated by a difference of opinion rather than
the detection of error.

But Lewis was an adept at 'throwing out powerful assertions
that challenged discussion', as Nevill Coghill pointed out (in
Light on C. S. Lewis), going on to illustrate this with an anecdote
which may contain the germ of this very chapter:

'I remember, on one occasion, as I went round Addison's
Walk, I saw him coming slowly towards me, his round, rubicund
face beaming with pleasure to itself. When we came within speaking distance, I said "Hullo, Jack! You look very pleased with
yourself; what is it?"

' "I believe," he answered, with a modest smile of triumph, "I
believe I have proved that the Renaissance never happened in
England. *Alternatively*" – he held up his hand to prevent my
astonished exclamation – "that if it did, *it had no importance!*" '

Lewis, like Mr Dick, was occasionally troubled by a 'King
Charles's head' that he could not keep out of the Memorial. For a
long time it was the 'Inner Ring' which was being given undue
prominence when he delivered his lecture on 'Kipling's World' to
the English Association on 24 November 1944, but was finally
exorcised in *That Hideous Strength* the following year. The regrettable effect of humanism on English literature and thought from
the sixteenth century onwards found its fullest catharsis in the
introductory chapter to the O.H.E.L. volume, but was really a
part of Lewis's dislike for 'chronological snobbery' – the growing
insistence that what was new and modern was *ipso facto* better
than what had gone before. Lewis was largely responsible for
breaking down the artificial barrier that had been erected by
scholars and historians between the Middle Ages and the Renaissance. The very title of his Cambridge Chair went to prove the
extent of his success, and in his first pronouncement from it, the
inaugural lecture, *'De Descriptione Temporum'*, delivered on 29
November 1954 (his 56th birthday), he put forward the further
proposition that the only really definite and indisputable change
in recorded history (with particular reference to literature, the

arts and learning generally) had come within the last hundred years – indeed almost within his own lifetime.

'I have said that the vast change which separates you from Old Western has been gradual and is not even now complete,' Lewis concluded the lecture. 'I myself belong far more to that Old Western order than to yours. I am going to claim that this, which in one way is a disqualification for my task, is yet in another a qualification. . . . It is my settled conviction that in order to read Old Western literature aright you must suspend most of the responses and unlearn most of the habits you have acquired in reading modern literature. And because this is the judgement of a native, I claim that, even if the defence of my conviction is weak, the fact of my conviction is a historical *datum* to which you should give full weight. That way, where I fail as a critic, I may yet be useful as a specimen. I would even dare to go further. Speaking not only for myself but for all other Old Western men whom you may meet, I would say, use your specimens while you can. There are not going to be many more dinosaurs.'

The delivery of the lecture was an overwhelming success. Dr G. M. Trevelyan the historian, Master of Trinity, introduced Lewis by saying that in all his long experience of elections to university posts Lewis's was the only one in which he had found a complete unanimity of votes on the part of the committee. The hall was packed to capacity, as his successor Professor J. A. W. Bennett was to record in his own inaugural lecture a year after Lewis's death: 'The regard he inspired in his pupils was happily illustrated on the night he inaugurated this professorship; when a platoon of them who had made the journey from Oxford could find no place to sit save on the dais, on which they ranged themselves like a *sceldtruma* or shield-wall resolved to defend their liege-lord. In fact, of course, he found here friends rather than adversaries, and friends who added happiness and solace to his last years. No man was ever more indifferent to "status". But no man could have relished more the friendliness and the freedom that Cambridge accorded him. And assuredly he was not distressed to find here that the dinosaurian culture which he described so memorably in his opening lecture was not quite so moribund as he had suggested.'

Perhaps exaggerating a little for effect, Lewis declared to several of his Oxford friends that he had gone to Cambridge expecting the worst – and at Magdalene found himself back in a college more like those he had known as a young man than any in the slapdash cafeteria atmosphere of so many at Oxford since the Second War. 'It's like Magdalen or Merton as we knew them before the war,' he said, when inviting a friend to stay at Magdalene for the first time; and, after a string of eulogies ended with a sudden impressive pause, and concluded with his superb timing: 'But I must warn you of one thing . . . we only get one glass of port after dinner!'

And to an American pen-friend Mrs Allen he wrote (26 November 1955): 'Cambridge is charming. No Lord Nuffield (drat the man!) has come to turn it into a huge industrial city, and one can still feel the county-town under the academic surface. In that way it is more like what Oxford was in my young days.'

Lewis's two appointments overlapped by a term. He was still teaching in Oxford late in 1954, giving his last tutorial on 3 December, and he spent his first night in his new rooms at Magdalene on 7 January 1955. It took him a little time to fit comfortably into his new place at Magdalene: the other Fellows found him at first a trifle over-assertive; 'it was not that he out-shone all in conversation, but that he felt that brilliance was expected,' and was rather on the defensive.

But he was soon very much at home and his new colleagues were fast becoming friends and companions. 'Lewis was frequently jovial,' recalls Richard Ladborough, with whom he was soon on friendly Christian-name terms, 'and not only delighted in hearing funny stories, but also was an expert in telling them. No one was less like the puritanical, tight-lipped moralist which some people thought he was after reading the *Screwtape Letters*. Some of his own stories were certainly not prudish, though never obscene. They were meant for men only, and indeed in certain respects

Lewis was what is known as "a man's man". He liked, for instance, to talk about his experiences in the Army during the First World War, and to hear those of others. His rooms in College, which with their panelling and antique appearance, could have been made attractive with little cost and even with little thought, were, it seemed to me, merely a laboratory for his work and his writings. Here he would sit with pen and ink, in a hard chair before an ugly table, and write for hours on end. Indeed, he seemed to be oblivious to his immediate surroundings, although I suppose that the beauty of them in both his universities must have had an effect upon him. It is always a matter of astonishment to me that during the whole of his period at Magdalene he should only once have visited the Pepys Library, and that for only twenty minutes when incited to do so by two eminent Oxford visitors. And yet he read the whole of Pepys's Diary with insight and, of course, intelligence, and made one of the best speeches on Pepys I have ever heard. This was in Hall at the annual dinner held to celebrate Pepys's birthday. [This was on 23 February 1959.] Pepys in fact was a late acquaintance of his, and he took it for granted, with his usual modesty, that his hearers knew the text as well as *he* did. The same was true for most other authors. It is now common knowledge that his memory was prodigious and that he seemed to have read everything. The authors and books I liked hearing him talk about most were, I think, some of his own favourites: Dr Johnson (with whom he had many affinities), Jane Austen, Stevenson's *The Wrong Box*, and – curiously perhaps – that pearl of schoolboy stories, Anstey's *Vice Versa*: I never tired of hearing him recite from memory the German lesson of the superbly humourless Herr Stohwasser. The one author he was usually silent about was himself. Little did we know, or even guess when he dined with us in Hall of an evening, that he had been engaged in penning during the day one of his *magna opera*. He was silent even when occupied in translating the Psalms into the new version. As is known, he had illustrious colleagues in this task, including, for example, T. S. Eliot. But he was unforthcoming about the whole enterprise. Again, I think this was partly due to his modesty and to his reticence. No man was less given to name-dropping, and no one was ever less of a snob.'

Lewis's work on the psalms was done mainly between 1959 and 1962, and consisted not in making a new translation but in revising the old one as it appears in the Book of Common Prayer. This was undertaken by a committee of seven, and a selection of their work appeared in 1961, the whole in 1963 as *The Revised Psalter*; Lewis was also asked to advise on several prayers in the proposed revision of the Prayer Book; and he had also been consulted on the translation of the New Testament for the New English Bible, which came out early in 1961. The work that he and T. S. Eliot did on these translations of the Scriptures bore a strange resemblance – as he was quick to hail with delight when it was pointed out to him – to Kipling's late story 'Proofs of Holy Writ', in which Ben Jonson finds Shakespeare engaged on precisely the same task in revising the language of the translation of Isaiah for the Authorized Version during his retirement at Stratford. How much Lewis contributed to the modern translations we shall probably never know: as Dr Ladborough says, he was remarkably reticent about this particular work.

According to Dr Ladborough, Lewis 'was essentially a College rather than a University man. He rarely seemed to be interested in the affairs of the University as a whole, or even (and this was a fault) in those of his own faculty. He never attempted to master regulations. He hardly ever read the *Reporter*, the University's official journal, and it was some time before he discovered its existence. But, as time went on, he became more and more interested in College affairs, in some, of course, more than others. He was ignorant of anything to do with finance, and during debates on figures his eyes closed and he was even known to snore. But it might surprise some people to know that, when genuinely interested, administration did not entirely pass him by. I suspect that few would guess that one passage in the *Reporter* on a particularly intricate subject dealing with the relationship between the University and the Colleges was penned largely by the hand of C. S. Lewis.'

He certainly knew his own limitations. In October 1956 Professor Basil Willey wrote to him suggesting that he might consider being chairman of the Faculty Board of English. Lewis replied firmly: 'No. It would never do. People so often deny their own capacity for business either through mock-modesty or through laziness that when the denial happens to be true, it is difficult to make it convincing. But I have been tried at this kind of job; and none of those who experienced me in office ever wanted to repeat the experience. I am both muddlesome and forgetful. Quite objectively, I'd be a disaster. But thank you for your suggestion.'

Lewis went on to suggest Dr Leavis for the position: 'I know it's risky: but "malcontents" have before now been tamed by office.' With their diametrically opposed opinions on literature and criticism, Lewis and Leavis have often been set up as deadly enemies ready to spring metaphorically at each other's throats at the first opportunity. Aware of this, Lewis, who was the last person to bear any ill-will on account of a purely literary disagreement, was inclined to treat the supposed hostility as a joke – with the aid of an amusing nightmare about being introduced as 'Dr Leavis' to give some important lectures. When he became Leavis's colleague on the English Faculty Board at Cambridge, he described his surprise at meeting him in actual fact. 'I expected to be pounced upon and shaken!' he said. 'But instead I found a quiet, charming and kindly man who welcomed me to Cambridge. Usually he sits and says nothing at Faculty Meetings – but if he does start to speak, Heaven help us! No one can stop him!'

Besides living at the Kilns during vacation and at most weekends, Lewis kept up fairly close ties with Oxford itself. Shortly after vacating his fellowship he was elected an Honorary Fellow of Magdalen, and would often take a friend to lunch in the Senior Common Room there. He had also been elected to the same honour at Univ., and had in fact had dining rights there and kept up his connection at least until 1947 when he gave up tutoring the relatively few undergraduates reading English there. After the war the numbers increased to such an extent that Magdalen took up all his time, and Hugo Dyson, English tutor at Merton, took over his Univ. pupils until one of Lewis's last ones, Peter Bayley, was elected as first full-time tutor there.

He also continued to have some say in the English faculty at Oxford, since on 12 January 1959 he was attending an Electors' meeting in the Delegates' room at the University Registry on choosing a successor to Tolkien in the Merton Chair of English Language and Literature.

As soon as Cambridge became a second home, Lewis thoroughly enjoyed his double life. 'Oddly enough the week-end journeys (to and from Cambridge) are no trouble at all,' he wrote to a friend in December 1955. 'I find myself perfectly content in a slow train that crawls through green fields stopping at every station. Just because the service is so slow and therefore in most people's eyes *bad*, these trains are almost always empty. I get through a lot of reading and sometimes say my prayers. A solitary railway journey I find quite excellent for this purpose.'

That journey on the 'Cantab Crawler' soon became a new joy to those closer friends who, after the weekly meeting at the 'Bird and Baby' (changed from Tuesday to Monday) and a snack lunch, often at the Trout at Godstow, would accompany Lewis to Cambridge for dinner, a long evening of talk, a comfortable night in the guest room across the court from his rooms above the Old Library, and a leisurely breakfast ending in time for Lewis's lecture at 10.00 a.m. and his guest's departure.

The years at Cambridge were mellow years and – in spite of Joy's death in 1960 – happy years for Lewis. The junior Fellow at Magdalene enjoyed being a 'new boy' whose duty was to wait on the senior Fellows in the Combination Room and pour out the port for them. He took a genuine pleasure in welcoming Oxford friends to his new university and showing them triumphantly what virtues, lost to Oxford, the 'Other Place' had revealed to him.

Anxious to take as much part in the life of so friendly a college, so welcoming a university, he began even to attend undergraduate theatricals – and found delight not only in the Greek plays, still done in the original, which the Greek Play Committee put on every third year, but in the French Society's performance of Racine, Corneille and Molière, and even in English Restoration comedies. To the latter he was still not converted; but a production in English of *Tartuffe* excited him so much that he hastened home to read the French text, and had soon added the complete works of Molière to his literary estate.

The wideness of Lewis's reading must come as a constant surprise to those critics who accuse him of a narrow conservatism and a lamentable 'squareness'. (When accused of being the latter he used to quote, with a merry twinkle in his eyes, the title page of one of his favourite books in the field of minor literature: *Flatland – by 'A Square'*.) Seldom indeed did he condemn a writing unread: when he dismissed a writer such as Joyce or Lawrence to a friend of similar tastes as 'good, I'm sure – but not for us,' he had read *Ulysses* or *Sons and Lovers* from cover to cover, and formed his opinion from actual experience. In Combination Room or Senior Common Room he would often make a point of sitting next to the youngest person present and pump him for information on his personal, professional or secular outlook with almost the relentless curiosity and interest of Kipling himself.

With more leisure than he had enjoyed for years at Oxford, Lewis fell back happily into the ideal day which derived basically from Bookham. 'His normal existence followed an extremely orderly pattern,' writes Dr Ladborough. 'Early rising, chapel, Communion at least once a week, early breakfast, and then attendance to his huge correspondence which came from all over the world. In Cambridge he had no secretary and answered most of his letters in his own hand. If time allowed he would also write his lectures or books, or else read till lunch time. Then the afternoon walk and tea, and then more work both before and after dinner. That was, I suppose, his ideal programme, but, like most great men, he never seemed to be in a hurry and always had time to see people who wanted to consult him. There were many of these, and often strangers, but they were hardly ever turned away.

'Until his health declined, Lewis would go for an afternoon walk. He was good with a map, and soon he tracked down most of the foot paths in and around Cambridge. He preferred to go for his walks alone, but just occasionally he would allow himself to be conveyed to some special spot by car, for he did not himself drive, and was hopeless with any form of machine. Those of us who were privileged to accompany him on his walks in the country-side were impressed by his intense enjoyment of scenery. I think that he had more feeling for Nature than for man-made objects. He would, for instance, rhapsodize about the "sky-scapes", as he called them, of East Anglia. And at the end of a walk or drive in the country, he liked to drop into a tea-place. Tea was as much a part of his routine as port or beer.'

'You can't get a cup of tea large enough or a book long enough to suit me,' Lewis remarked to Walter Hooper, and the zest for both remained with him to the end. In a more human moment he expressed a wish that when he reached the Next World he might find that Spenser had written another six books of *The Faerie Queene* for him to read and Rider Haggard the trilogy of romances about the Wandering Jew which he did not live long enough to write.

His enjoyment of getting into a new world and living there for as long as possible gave him easy access to Proust and the Russian novelists: *War and Peace* he considered the greatest novel ever written. But his personal preference was for romance, either in verse or prose, and to this he remained faithful. Ariosto re-read near the end of his life he found less enjoyable than his recollections of former readings had led him to expect, but the Arthurian romances and Malory in particular were read again and again with no diminution of delight. Nor had he any inhibitions about new versions of old legends. Although he disliked *The Sword in the Stone* and its sequels – considering *Mistress Masham's Repose* to be T. H. White's one really successful and outstanding fantasy – he was enthusiastic about versions as various as *The Misfortunes of Elphin*, *Taliessin through Logres*, and even Green's retelling of *King Arthur* which he admired particularly for its overall construction. For although he was never put off by the intertwined or picaresque methods of Ariosto or Cervantes, he rejoiced in a good, complex plot worked out as a whole from start to finish. This he found satisfyingly present in the best of Rider Haggard and in E. R. Eddison's *The Worm Ouroboros* (though he didn't care for *Mistress of Mistresses* and the other sequels), and in as divergent works of fantasy as Morris's *The Well at the World's End* and Anstey's *In Brief Authority*. On the other hand he took little interest in detective stories, apart from Sherlock Holmes whom he could quote as readily as the best Baker Street Irregular.

But the delight in the heroic and in the more imaginative type of fantasy found glorious vindication in Tolkien's *The Lord of the Rings* when it finally appeared after its long years of gestation. 'The *Lord* is the book we have all been waiting for,' he wrote to a friend in 1956. 'And it shows too, which cheers, that there are thousands "left in Israel" who have not bowed the knee to Leavis.'

Another delight, which found gratification in *The Lord of the Rings*, and was perhaps partly responsible for his liking for *The Worm Ouroboros*, was in the accumulation of high-sounding names, used with such gloriously sonorous effect by Milton: 'I love 'em,' he wrote. 'Launcelot and Pelleas and Pellinore, Aragon and Owlswick, Arbol and Tormance, the more the merrier.'

Besides high-sounding names, Lewis never lost his delight in multiple epithets and heroic language. He would not have it that Eddison or Haggard ever approached 'Wardour Street English' or what Stevenson called 'Tushery', and was on surer ground defending the archaism in Morris's prose romances and Butcher and Lang's translation of the *Odyssey* and Gilbert Murray's versions of Euripides.

On the subject of translations of the classics, Lewis gave one of his most provocative lectures to the Annual Conference of the Classical Association at Cambridge on 7 August 1958. 'In spite of the unlikely hour (immediately after breakfast) the hilarity of Professor C. S. Lewis, in his most mischievous mood, proved irresistible this morning when he delivered to the conference of classical teachers here a withering attack on modern translations of the classics,' wrote *The Times* Special Correspondent. 'They apparently sprang, he declared, from "a very real hatred" of what most poetry, other than that of relatively recent times, has been.' Lewis went on to express little sympathy with the new idea that a translation should try to be 'what the author would have written if he had lived in our own day'. What reason had we to suppose that Virgil, for instance, would have written anything at all, or got it published if he had? 'Our age with implacable hostility would have known how to deal with him.' He found much of the answer to the modern theories of translation in 'the fact that the two cardinal sins today are archaisms and poetic diction. I have seen strong young men almost turn pale at the use of an archaism.' Lewis went on to deny staunchly that 'poetical language' was only fit for 'toffs and cissies', and pointed out how we still kept archaism and ritual elsewhere in life 'because there could not be a more obvious way of heightening the effect'. Lewis further did not subscribe either to 'the theory that translations should try to recreate the impression the originals gave to their contemporaries. In this case we were not dealing with a snark or a boojum, but how could we know what any poem sounded like to its contemporaries? The only safe way was to seek as closely as possible the effect it would give a reader if he was really a tiptop, modern classical scholar' – which was why he approved of translations by first-class scholars who were also poets, such as Lang and Murray.

'The lecture on translation was great fun,' he wrote to Green on 29 August, 'though I felt a bit shamefaced on unexpectedly meeting Rieu[1] a few days later; all the more so when the dear old man behaved like an angel.' Unfortunately when Green stayed with him a month later Lewis had lost the script of the lecture, and it has never turned up since.

Modern *interpretations* of the classical world were, however, welcome, and Lewis was an enthusiastic reader of Mary Renault's *The King Must Die* and *The Bull from the Sea*, and was even more impressed by the former after visiting Knossos in 1960; and

[1] Well known for his translations of the *Odyssey* and the *Iliad* in Penguin classics.

Naomi Mitchison's stories such as *The Conquered* were also favourites.

The years 1958 and 1959, when Joy's cancer healed miraculously, and they were able to live a more or less normal married life, saw Lewis at his happiest and most relaxed. In 1959 he even considered seriously a visit to the United States, but had decided against it by the middle of the year, before Joy's relapse began. At this time she would occasionally come over to Cambridge, and Lewis would give luncheon or dinner parties in college at which she was able to act as hostess. 'I think that he enjoyed these parties as much as we did,' Dr Ladborough recalls. 'He even enjoyed dining out.'

After Joy's death in July 1960 Lewis sought solace in work. He was unable to write much more of *After Ten Years*; but while compiling *A Grief Observed*, he also began *An Experiment in Criticism*, which came out the following year and was much more successful than he expected. 'My *Experiment* has elicited fanmail from a few Cambridge undergraduates,' he wrote to Kathleen Raine in October, 'can it be that the tide *is* turning at last?'

By this time, however, he was rather seriously ill. In September 1961 he wrote to Green: 'I am awaiting an operation on my prostate; but as this trouble upset my kidneys and my heart, these have to be set right before the surgeon can get to work. Meanwhile I am on a no-protein diet, wear a cathatin, sleep in a chair, and have to stay on the ground floor.' Visiting him later in the month Green found him 'looking very ill, and he got tired soon'; and in October he was spending short spells in a nursing home, for blood transfusions. 'I've just had a blood-transfusion and am feeling very drowsy,' he concluded the letter to Kathleen Raine quoted above. 'Dracula must have led a horrid life.'

Lewis seemed much better in November, but had another relapse and only rallied slowly. He was better in January 1962 and wrote that 'I seem to have turned a bio-chemical corner and shall soon be ready for the surgical one. But on the whole I haven't had a bad time. I knew I was in danger but was not depressed. I've read pretty well everything – *War and Peace*, *Odyssey*, *Modern*

Painters, Prelude, Orlando Furioso and what not.' At the end of March, 'Locomotion as well as protein is one of the things I must cut down to a minimum'; and to T. S. Eliot on 18 May, 'Apparently I shall always be an invalid – but I have no pain and feel tolerably well.'

Even in August he was hoping that the operation would still be possible, to deliver him from 'the low-protein diet'. But he realized that even if it were satisfactorily performed he would still be an invalid – 'I shall have to be careful about my heart – no more bathing or real walks, and as few stairs as possible. A very mild fate: especially since nature seems to remove the desire for exercise when the power declines.'

In spite of his illness Lewis returned to Cambridge for many weeks during 1962, often accompanied by an Oxford friend on the Monday, via the 'Cantab Crawler', for dinner, enthralling talk, a night in the guest room at Magdalene, breakfast – and then a parting of the ways. Lewis was also writing, most of his time being taken up with turning his old Prolegomena lectures into *The Discarded Image*, which was ready for the dilatory Cambridge University Press by the beginning of 1963. He was also collecting his miscellaneous lectures, sermons and essays into volumes: *They Asked for a Paper* came out in 1962, and he was putting together another volume, which was to be called *A Slip of the Tongue, and Other Pieces*, which did not appear until two years after his death, shorn of his Preface and of two essays – 'Historicism' and 'The Vision of John Bunyan' – and renamed *Screwtape Proposes a Toast, and Other Pieces*.

But so far as imaginative work was concerned, his inspiration had dried up. He no longer 'saw pictures', or not such as would grow together into a book, and he could not even continue with *After Ten Years*. Anxious, nonetheless, to write more fiction, he proposed a collaboration with Green in a story to be based on Green's still unpublished *Wood that Time Forgot* which Lewis had always considered his best imaginative effort. At the end of March 1962 he was eagerly engaged in working out a new way of telling the story – 'the defect of the book as I see it is that it is not a children's story and masquerades as one. The two alternatives that float before my mind are these: A. Re-write as a straight romance about people living no one knows where or when and cut out the children altogether. B. Re-write as a *novel* told in the first person . . . Can I (I mean have I got the guts) to do it?'

But this too came to nothing, and he turned to the final revision of *The Discarded Image*. But Lewis was still able to write one more book, which he had been trying to compose for many years. As early as 1954 he was writing to Sister Penelope: 'I had to abandon the book on prayer. It is clearly not for me,' and from time to time there was mention of this as something he wanted to write. During the second half of 1962 the form suddenly came to him, and he began the *Letters to Malcolm: Chiefly on Prayer* which was to be his last book. These letters (to a purely imaginary correspondent) occupied such time as he was able to spend profitably upon writing – and how much more time on still more profitable thought – for the next year, being finished just before his almost fatal illness in July 1963. It was very much of a swan-song, a 'thanks before going', and, as the reviewer in the *Church Times* (27 January 1964) pointed out, 'It is the grasp of the reality of God, the determination to put truth before passing fashion, the apprehension of the mystery and the glory of grace which help to make this book pure treasure.'

Lewis rallied and was able to carry on more or less normally at Cambridge for the Hilary and Trinity terms of 1963, and to meet friends and entertain guests as usual. There was one small change at this time: the Eagle and Child had to be given up regretfully as the setting of the Monday meetings which had been going on since the Inklings' high noon during the war. 'Note that our *causeries de lundi* are now permanently transferred to the "Lamb and Flag",' he wrote. 'We were sorry to break with tradition, but the "B. and B." had become intolerably cold, dark, noisy and child-pestered.'

When Green met him there and accompanied him to Cambridge on 11 March he seemed 'almost completely well again', and there was no apparent falling off in Lewis's mental vivacity either on this occasion or on the next in June when, since term was over, the Kilns was substituted for Magdalene.

This had happened once or twice before – and such visits were always pleasant and comfortable. Lewis's younger stepson, Douglas Gresham, was now living at home and attending Magdalen School as a day-boy; when in, he was excellent company and Lewis found him a great comfort. And he was supremely fortunate in his domestic arrangements: Mr and Mrs Miller who looked after him (with some help from Paxford, whose real domain was the garden) were devoted to 'Mr Jack' and 'The Major', and tended Lewis with the love and care of the true friends which they had become.

Dinner was always preceded by a short Grace; and only fish was served on a Friday – 'but I'm afraid it's no penance: I *like* fish!' Lewis would exclaim. After the meal Lewis and his guest would retire to the sitting-room – the 'Common Room' as it was called – or occasionally to Lewis's study, the new 'little end room'; if at home, Douglas would sit with them for half an hour or so, and then depart. Warren Lewis would have gone off to his own study immediately, but he would return at about 10 o'clock with the traditional pot of tea and remain for half an hour or so, after which Lewis and his guest would go on talking until midnight, rounding off the evening with a glass of whisky.

Early in 1963 Lewis made a new friend, who was destined to become part of the household for several months later that year. This was Walter Hooper, who had been a correspondent for some years, but had come over to England that year to write a critical study of Lewis for an American series on English authors.

'Certainly I shall be happy to see you when you visit England,' wrote Lewis to his young American admirer in July 1962. 'But I feel very strongly that a man is ill advised to write a book on any living author. There is bound to be at least one person, and there are probably several, who inevitably know more about the subject than ordinary research will discover. Far better write about the unanswering dead.'

Walter Hooper persevered, however, and was in Oxford early in

1963 when he went to call on Lewis at the Kilns for what he expected to be his only visit. He knocked nervously at the door, and was welcomed by Lewis – 'so bright, loud and jovial that I quickly forgot my fright. We went into his sitting-room and were soon talking about – well, what seemed like everything under the sun.'

After two hours' talk, Lewis saw him to his bus back into Oxford, stopping for a drink at his favourite local, the Ampleforth Arms, on the way. When Hooper began thanking Lewis for giving up so much of his time to him, he 'looked surprised and said: "But won't I see you again? You're not getting away. Meet me at the 'Lamb and Flag' on Monday as I want to talk with you some more." '

The meeting at the Lamb and Flag was a success; Lewis asked Hooper out to the Kilns again the following Thursday, and suggested that they should go to Communion together that Sunday at Holy Trinity, Headington, the church where Lewis normally worshipped when at home. Lewis had lent Hooper the manuscript of *Letters to Malcolm* at the end of their Thursday meeting, and after the service they returned to the Kilns for breakfast to discuss it. Lewis always cooked breakfast himself, the menu seldom altering from eggs and bacon, sausages and toast or scones.

After this they settled into a more-or-less regular routine of thrice-weekly meetings: Mondays at the Lamb and Flag, Thursdays at the Kilns, and Sundays when they went to church together. Hooper found that, 'true to his definition stated in *The Four Loves*, Lewis liked his friends to know and like one another, and I think it gave him as much pleasure as it did me to introduce me to Colin Hardie, Gervase Mathew, R. B. McCallum, Roger Lancelyn Green, Humphrey Havard and Cecil Harwood. I had already met Austin and Kay Farrer on my own account, so we had these friends in common as well.' On most Mondays Humphrey Havard would drive Lewis, Hooper and any friend who was to accompany Lewis to Cambridge that afternoon to some less-crowded place for lunch: the Trout at Godstow was a favourite haunt in summertime.

Lewis survived the Trinity Term in a reasonable state of health. His Cambridge friends noticed little more than that his diet had become stricter. 'In food and drink he had, on the whole, simple tastes, but he enjoyed well-cooked food and vintage wines,' records Dr Ladborough. 'It was all the more remarkable that at the end of his life, when almost no alcohol was allowed, and he was on a horribly strict diet, he should make no complaint and draw no attention to the fact'; and he comments on the reticence as to private troubles that Lewis showed, notably when Joy was dying, and 'about the illness which caused his retirement from Cambridge and which eventually killed him. He accepted it with a sort of saintly patience. Right to the end he was his usual gay and humorous self.'

Since his illness began, Lewis had travelled less and less frequently by the 'Cantab Crawler' and would be driven to and from Cambridge by Clifford Morris, whose taxi he had been accustomed to hire for the previous ten years or so whenever he needed transport. During these longer drives they became quite intimate friends, and Mr Morris writes, 'I shall always consider myself fortunate to have been included in his circle of friendship. It has meant a great deal to me, more than I can put into words. Jack Lewis was the greatest man I have ever known. He was never an intellectual snob, and he was willing to talk to anyone on any subject, having the ability to "put the other person or persons at their ease". I have been with him in the company of Oxford and Cambridge professors, and I have overheard some of their conversation – conversation that I was totally unable to understand or share; and I have also been with him, sitting in the middle of a crowd of lorry drivers in a transport cafe, while he enthralled them with his wit and his conversational powers. After one of these occasions one of the men came to me and said, "Hey, mate, who's the guv'nor?" And when I told him, he expressed surprise, and then said, "Blimey, he's a toff, he is! A real nice bloke!" When I told Jack about this, he took it as a compliment, and I was glad, because I think it was the greatest compliment I ever heard paid him. I very much enjoyed our drives to and from

Cambridge. If it was in winter-time we generally found a snug little inn, somewhere on the way, and had a meal there. If it was in summer-time, we generally took sandwiches and picnicked where we fancied.'

When Lewis came back from Cambridge in mid-June 1963 he had no idea that it was for the last time. He still seemed very much his usual boisterous self when Green met him at the Lamb and Flag on the 17th, and accompanied him back to the Kilns. Lewis now rested during the afternoon; and the usual evening of animated talk ended at 10.30; but otherwise there was no difference.

At the beginning of July he was describing himself as 'pretty well an invalid now, and professional lectures are all I can manage,' when declining an invitation to preach. But by the 13th of the month he was writing, 'I am now suffering a relapse and at present waiting to be admitted to hospital as soon as there is a vacancy. I am but a *fossil* dinosaur now.'

On the next day, Sunday 14th, Walter Hooper came out to the Kilns early in the morning to accompany Lewis to Communion as usual, and found Lewis still in his dressing-gown and looking exceedingly ill. He could hardly sit up, and asked for some tea. When Hooper made and brought this, he found that Lewis could not hold the cup and that the cigarette kept dropping from his fingers. 'He told me that he'd be going into the Acland next day for a blood transfusion, and asked me if I'd stop in England and act as his private secretary, beginning immediately. Though terrified for him, I was enormously gratified by his offer and, of course, accepted it. He told me he'd pay me the same amount I had been earning at the University of Kentucky.'

Lewis went into the Acland Nursing Home as arranged on Monday 15th, and at 5.00 p.m. had a heart attack. On the Tuesday morning Austin and Kay Farrer came to tell Hooper that Lewis was dying – that he was already in a coma and was not expected to live out the day. Fr Michael Watts, the curate of St Mary Magdalen's, was in attendance, and as Lewis was unconscious gave him Extreme Unction – the service of anointing a dying man who, being unconscious, was not able to receive the Sacrament. This was at 2.00 p.m. – and to the amazement of doctors and nurses Lewis suddenly woke from his coma and asked for his tea. Austin Farrer and Walter Hooper hurried round to the Acland as soon as the news was received by the Farrers at Keble, and found Lewis 'looking as though he'd woken from a twenty-year sleep. Noticing our worried looks, he said "Why do you look so anxious? Is there anything wrong?" "You have been asleep for quite a while, we were concerned about you," said Austin. "I do not think," said Jack vigorously, "that it could be urged that I am a very *well* man!" '

Next day Austin Farrer returned to give Lewis the Sacrament, after which Lewis sent Hooper out to buy writing paper and set him down to answer his correspondence. Lewis remained in the nursing home for three more weeks as, to begin with, the poison from his infected kidney ran through his blood stream and for a few days affected his brain. One morning when Hooper came to the hospital as usual 'his nurse looked distraught and asked me to hurry to his room. He was dressed in pyjama trousers and a sports jacket and wished to be taken to the Bodleian, completely unaware of what he was doing. At other times this confusion came out in dictating letters which, though they made good sense, had no basis in fact.'

But by the end of the second week Lewis was normal again, and early in August he returned to the Kilns, but with a male nurse, Alec Ross, to be on call at night in case of need. A bedroom was made for Lewis on the ground floor so that he would not have to go up any stairs, and he settled down to a life of quiet retirement, well and without pain, but increasingly conscious that the end was drawing near.

'The period that followed was one of the most pleasant I've ever known,' Walter Hooper recollects. 'Though Jack did not appear to be in any immediate danger, he believed it only fair to Cambridge to resign his Chair and Fellowship. He dictated his resignation letter to me and I think it left him sad as he seriously doubted if he would ever be able to visit Cambridge again.

Accordingly he wrote to a number of dons over there saying how much he'd like to be visited.'

He was eager to see his friends and, for example, dictated a letter to Green on 11 August. 'I can't blame you for not knowing I had been so ill, seeing how I didn't know myself until it was all over – I am now unofficially an extinct volcano, i.e. I have resigned the Chair and the Fellowship. I hope very much you can come and dine and sleep here on 26 September. If Jeronimo is mad again by then (I was for a bit) someone will warn you in time.'

For the next six weeks or so Lewis's health seemed steadily to be improving. He lived as restful a life as possible: a cup of early morning tea in bed at 7.00 a.m. after which he dozed on for an hour or so and then got up to make his breakfast. Most of the morning was spent over correspondence, Walter Hooper doing as much of it as he could. After lunch he read or dozed in his chair until tea-time at 4.00 p.m. when he fulfilled any business appointments that were necessary and was free by 6.00 p.m., when Hooper was sent into the kitchen to fetch Mrs Miller to join them in a drink. Dinner at 7.00 p.m., served by Mrs Miller or Paxford. After dinner, and some help with the washing-up, Lewis read or talked with Hooper until 10.00 p.m. when they had their final cup of tea.

On one occasion when Austin and Kay Farrer came to tea, Kay said to Lewis, when Hooper was out of the room: 'Jack, Austin and I always thought you guarded very jealously your private life. Is it uncomfortable having Walter Hooper living in your house?' Lewis answered at once, 'But Walter is *part* of my private life!'

'Looking back, I find it hard to understand why Jack was so very kind to me,' writes Hooper. 'He was so vastly superior to me in every way that this fact – being known to *both* of us – may have made it easy to see me as a friend, perhaps, as he once said to Mrs Miller, "the son I should have had". Then, there is the fact that I came along when he was ill and needed someone near him.' (Neither David nor Douglas Gresham was there any longer, and his brother had been in Ireland all that summer and was himself ill, and unable to return until late in September.) 'The big change in our relationship came when I moved into "The Kilns": he had always seemed to be "talking for victory" before, but in his own home he was very comfortable and easy to be with.'

Late in September Walter Hooper had to return to America to wind up his affairs there before returning to resume his place as Lewis's private secretary. Lewis was so much his old self by this time that there seemed no danger of a relapse. 'Jack was *very* well, to my delight, in spite of his near death last month (sic) – and we had a marvellous evening of talk,' wrote Green in his diary on 26 September.

'My last fear has been taken from me,' said Lewis on this occasion. 'I had always been terrified at the thought of going mad: but I was completely mad for a week and never realized it. Indeed I was happy all the time. And death would have been so easy: I was nearly there – and almost regret having been brought back!' As he had written to Sister Penelope the previous week, 'it would have been a luxuriously easy passage and one almost regrets having the door shut in one's face. Ought one to honour Lazarus rather than Stephen as the protomartyr? To be brought back and have all one's dying to do again was rather hard. When you die, and if "prison visiting" is allowed, come down and look me up in Purgatory. It *is* all rather fun – solemn fun – isn't it?'

But the flame of the candle was only burning up brightly before sinking for the last time. Lewis had these few extra months in which to put all his affairs in order, arrange for trustees and guardians to look after his brother's and his stepsons' affairs after he was gone, and tidy up the loose ends of his literary work. *The Discarded Image* should have been out that autumn, but there had been some mistake over the printing of it and over its index, and final revised proofs only arrived in October; *Letters to Malcolm*, though written later, was already in the press.

He was also well enough to write his last article: 'I'd like to have a try at that article', he wrote to the editor of the New York *Saturday Evening Post* on 17 October, 'but must warn you that I may fail. . . . It would be impossible to discuss "the right to happiness" without discussing a formula that is rather sacred to Americans about "life, liberty and the pursuit of happiness". I'd do so with respect. But I'd have to point out that it can only mean "A right to pursue happiness by legitimate means", i.e. "people have a right to do whatever they have a right to do". Would your public like this?'

The article was written with the usual clarity and depth of thought, and despatched to New York, where it appeared at the end of December.

But the brief St Martin's summer was already drawing to a close even as he wrote. 'Early in October it became apparent to both of us that Jack was facing the onset of death,' wrote Warren Lewis, who by now was back at the Kilns and tending his brother with touching care. 'Yet those last weeks were not unhappy ones. Joy had left us, and once more as in bygone days we had no one but each other to turn to for comfort. The wheel had come full circle. Again we were together in a new "little end room", shutting out from our talk the ever present knowledge that the holidays were ending, and a new term fraught with unknown possibilities awaited us both.

'Jack faced the prospect bravely and calmly. "I have done all I wanted to do, and I'm ready to go," he said to me one evening. Only once did he show any regret or reluctance: this was when I told him that the morning's mail included an invitation to deliver the Romanes lecture. An expression of sadness passed over his face and for a moment there was silence – then, "Send them a very polite refusal," he said. It was obvious that he would have wished to end his long academic career by being able to fulfil that engagement worthily.'

Lewis had refused all honours, such as the C.B.E., at the disposal of any government of whatever political persuasion; but the Honorary Fellow of University and Magdalen Colleges, Oxford, and of Magdalene College, Cambridge, the Hon. D.D. of St Andrews and Hon. D.Litt. of Manchester, Fellow of the British Academy and of the Royal Society of Literature, and holder of the Gollancz Memorial Prize for Literature and the Carnegie

Medal for the best children's book of 1956, would indeed have rounded off his career worthily as Romanes lecturer.

Even if he himself knew that death was drawing near, Lewis kept the knowledge from his friends, though he did his best to see as many of them as possible, almost as if to say goodbye to each.

'I am finding retirement full of compensation,' he wrote to Professor Willey on 22 October. 'It is lovely to reflect that I am under no obligation to read Rowse on the Sonnets. I have re-read the *Iliad* instead . . . I delight to be visited – the sooner, and oftener, the better.'

'Only about a fortnight before his death I received a card from him from Oxford,' writes Dr Ladborough: ' "Have been reading *Les Liaisons Dangereuses*. Wow what a book! Come to lunch on Friday (fish) and tell me about it." I'm glad to say that I went, and of course it was Jack who told *me* about it; and not the other way round. But C. S. Lewis reading *Les Liaisons Dangereuses* when on the point of death! All in all, I don't think it uncharacteristic. I somehow felt it was the last time we should meet, and when he escorted me, with his usual courtesy, to the door, I think he felt so too. Never was a man better prepared.'

One of Lewis's typical cards clinching an invitation was sent to Green on 1 November: 'Good. Dinner-bem-breakfast it is. Fri–Sat. 15–16 Nov., and most welcome you will be. J.'

Green reached the Kilns in time for dinner on 15 November. Lewis had just been correcting the proofs of his last article, 'We Have No "Right to Happiness" ', and was furious that the final paragraph had been altered. He had a call put through to New York, and insisted that it should either be put back as he had written it, or the whole article cancelled.

After dinner they sat and talked as usual. But he was obviously ill, and kept falling asleep – and for alarming intervals apparently ceasing to breathe at all. For the first time ever the talk flagged; and when Warren Lewis brought in the tea about 10 o'clock he seemed worried, and suggested that Lewis should go to bed. 'But I don't want to go to bed!' expostulated Jack, waking up suddenly.

'I want to go on talking with Roger – but I suppose I'd better.'

Next morning he was up late, but in time to see his last guest off. As he passed the window Green turned to wave goodbye to Lewis who was sitting at his desk just inside. There was something in that last look both of affection and of farewell that told Green he knew it was 'goodbye' indeed – and he groped his way down Kiln Lane blinded with tears.

The following Monday Lewis was better again, and was driven down to the Lamb and Flag for the last time. It so happened that only Colin Hardie was there: but the talk was as animated as it had ever been: 'Perhaps the best of all such Mondays.'

His last visitor was Kaye Webb, editor of Puffin Books in which *The Chronicles of Narnia* were appearing. 'We had a nice talk on Wednesday,' she wrote to Green, who had arranged the meeting. 'What a very great and dear man. How I wish I'd had a chance to know him well, but how grateful I am that you "introduced" us to each other. He promised to re-edit the books (connect the things that didn't tie up) and he asked me to come again . . . It must be nice to know that you helped him to have that lovely holiday in Greece. He talked about it with such warmth.'

'Friday 22 November began no differently from any other day for some weeks past,' wrote Warren Lewis. 'I looked in on Jack soon after six, got a cheerful "I'm all right" and then went about my domestic tasks. He got up at eight and as usual breakfasted in the kitchen in his dressing-gown, after which he took a preliminary survey of his cross-word puzzle. By the time he was dressed I had his mail ready for him and he sat down in his workroom where he answered four letters with his own hand. For some time past he had been finding great difficulty in keeping awake, and finding him asleep in his chair after lunch, I suggested that he would be more comfortable in bed. He agreed, and went there. At four o'clock I took him in his tea and had a few words with him, finding him thick in his speech, very drowsy, but calm and cheerful. It was the last time we ever spoke to each other. At five-thirty I heard a crash in his bedroom, and running in, I found him lying unconscious at the foot of his bed. He ceased to breathe some three or four minutes later. The following Friday would have been his sixty-fifth birthday.'

'Then Aslan turned to them and said: ". . . you are – as you used to call it in the Shadowlands – dead. The term is over: the holidays have begun. The dream is ended: this is the morning . . ."

'And for us this is the end of all the stories, and we can most truly say that they all lived happily ever after. But for them it was only the beginning of the real story. All their life in this world and all their adventures in Narnia had only been the cover and the title page: now at last they were beginning Chapter One of the Great Story which no one on earth has read: which goes on for ever: in which every chapter is better than the one before.'

INDEX

Abbott, Edwin Abbott (1838-1926): *Flatland*, 291

Abercrombie, Lascelles (1881-1938): 88, 140, 160

Acts of the Apostles, The: 64

Aeschylus (525-456 BC): *Prometheus Bound*, 44

Aesop (6th cent. BC?): 252

Aldiss, Brian Wilson (1925-): 124-5

Aldwinckle, Elia Estelle, 'Stella' (1907-): 214, 215, 216, 217

Alexander, Samuel (1859-1938): *Space, Time and Deity*, 101

Alfred, King (849-901): 72

Allen, Arthur C.: 29, 30, 33

Allen, Belle (1885-): 286

Amis, Kingsley (1922-): 124

Anderson, Edward (1898-): 34

Anscombe, Gertrude Elizabeth Margaret (1919-): 'Reply to Mr C. S. Lewis', 227; men., 217, 228

Anstey, F. (pseudonym of Thomas Anstey Guthrie: 1856-1934): *In Brief Authority*, 293; *Vice Versa*, 26, 287; men., 145

Apollonius Rhodius (3rd cent. BC): *Argonautica*, 45

Apuleius (b. c. 114): 179, 261, 263

Apuleius, Pseudo- : *Asclepius*, 162

Arbuthnot, John (1667-1735): 155

Ariosto, Ludovico (1474-1533): *Orlando Furioso*, 163, 179, 296; men., 147, 292

Aristotle (384-322 BC): 44, 90, 126, 154

Armour, Margaret: 31

Arnold, Edwin Lester Linden (1857-1935): *Lepidus*, 176

Arnold, Matthew (1822-88): *Sohrab and Rustum*, 29; men., 74, 96

Arthur, King: 44, 176, 252, 253

Ascham, Roger (1515-68): 179

Askins, John Hawkins, 'the Doc.' (1877-1923): 77

Askins, Very Rev. William James (1879-1955): 197

Athanasius, St (c. 296-373): *Incarnation of the Word of God*, 115

Auden, Wystan Hugh (1907-73): 89, 153, 158

Augustine, St (345-430): 108, 209

Austen, Jane (1775-1817): 152, 287

Bailey, Cyril (1871-1957): 61

Baker, Leo Kingsley (1898-): 69, 80

Banner, Delmar Harmood (1896-): 281

Barfield, Arthur Owen (1898-): 10, 47, 69-71, 78, 84, 92, 102, 106, 108, 109, 111-12, 121, 123, 127-8, 129, 134, 153, 155, 200, 213-14, 220, 224, 233, 268

Barnes, Rt. Rev. Ernest William (1874-1953): *Rise of Christianity*, 227

Barrie, Sir James Matthew (1860-1937): *Mary Rose*, 263; *Peter Pan*, 28

Barth, Karl (1886-1968): 211

Baudelaire, Charles (1821-67): 48

Baum, Vicki (1896-1960): *Grand Hotel*, 186

Baxter, Richard (1615-91): 211

Bayley, Peter Charles (1921-): 290

Baynes, Pauline Diana (1922-): 243, 246

Becker, Wilhelm (1796-1846): *Charicles*, 31

Beethoven, Ludwig van (1770-1827): 185

Belloc, Joseph Hilaire Pierre (1870-1953): 59, 74

Benecke, Paul Victor Mendelssohn (1868-1944): 148, 149

Bennett, Jack Arthur Walter (1911-): 'Humane Medievalist', 285

Benson, Sir Francis Robert, 'Frank' (1858-1939): 33

Beowulf: 45, 124